Seeing the Whole Through

SOCIAL STUDIES

TARRY LINDQUIST

SECOND EDITION

SEEING
THE WHOLE
THROUGH
SOCIAL STUDIES

SECOND EDITION

Thompson

SEEING THE WHOLE THROUGH SOCIAL STUDIES

SECOND EDITION

Tarry Lindquist

HEINEMANN
PORTSMOUTH, NH

Heinemann
A division of Reed Elsevier Inc.
361 Hanover Street
Portsmouth, NH 03801–3912
www.heinemann.com

Offices and agents throughout the world

The author and publisher wish to thank those who have generously given permission to reprint borrowed material:

The Mouse Moral reprinted by permission of Philomel Books from SEVEN BLIND MICE by Ed Young, copyright 1992 by Ed Young.

Introduction: National Council for the Social Studies, Martharose Laffey, Executive Director. "A Vision of Powerful Teaching and Learning in the Social Studies: Building Social Understanding and Civic Efficacy," *Social Education*, September 1993.

Chapter 1: Linda McCrae-Campbell for her descriptions of children's learning strengths and preferences based on Dr. Howard Gardner's theory of multiple intelligences. From a workshop she conducted in February, 1989 for Mercer Island Public Schools, Washington.

Credit lines continued on page 285

Library of Congress Cataloging-in-Publication Data
Lindquist, Tarry.
   Seeing the whole through social studies / Tarry Lindquist.—2nd ed.
     p. cm.
   Includes bibliographical references.
   ISBN 0-325-00448-X
   1. Social sciences—Study and teaching. I. Title.
H62 .L4844 2002
372.83′044—dc21   2002003003

Editor: Danny Miller
Production coordinator: Elizabeth Valway
Cover design: Linda Knowles
Cover art: Michelle Chan
Interior photos: Judith Slepyan
Typesetter: House of Equations, Inc.
Manufacturing: Steve Bernier

Printed in the United States of America on acid-free paper
07 08 09 RRD 10 9 8 7 6

To our granddaughters,
Taylor, Taryn, and Harriet,
The world is a better place
because of you!

THE MOUSE MORAL

KNOWING IN PART MAY MAKE A FINE TALE,
BUT WISDOM COMES FROM SEEING THE WHOLE.

—Ed Young, *Seven Blind Mice*

CONTENTS

FOREWORD

When Emily Dickinson wrote, "I dwell in possibilities. . . . not wishing to miss the dawn, I open every door," she could have been describing Tarry Lindquist. Tarry dwells in possibilities and her book opens an intimate door into her classroom. Tarry is a teacher's teacher who communicates her love of children and enthusiasm for teaching on each page of this book.

You will travel through the school year as Tarry shares the journey she has taken to reconstruct her teaching day and to develop an integrated curriculum. As you read this book, you will feel as though you are watching a day in Tarry's classroom unfold—a classroom where good things happen for children. The story of Tarry's classroom is one of valuing each child, respecting ideas, and being concerned for the common good. Tarry shares her insights in practical terms, thus providing a helpful model for others.

Tarry begins with the children in her classroom and their needs, weaving them and their aspirations into a rich tapestry of teaching and learning experiences. Classroom ideas for integrating the curriculum abound, but this is much more than a book of teaching ideas. Tarry offers a structure and purpose for integrating, and grounding decisions about it in sound learning theory and best practice.

This book is a must for the teacher just beginning the process of integrating the curriculum. It provides inspiration and a realistic assessment of what's possible on the journey toward holistic learning experiences. If you are a teacher already in the midst of integrating the curriculum, you'll find a soul mate who freely shares her successes and her challenges.

Seeing the Whole Through Social Studies is the story of one teacher who has opened the door to a multitude of possibilities. Walking with Tarry through that door on the journey to holistic learning is an inspiration.

Margit McGuire
Professor and Chair
Teacher Education
Seattle University
Past President,
National Council for the Social Studies

ACKNOWLEDGMENTS

Where to begin, that's the question.

I wish to honor the memory of my mother and father.

Special thanks to the Class of 2001, their parents, and the wonderful people I work with every day at Lakeridge Elementary.

Thanks to all the kids who've taken the time to teach me and to those kids who have given me permission to share their products and pictures. Thanks to parents for trusting me to teach their kids.

Thanks to my principal, John Cameron, and school secretary, Peggy Chapman, for providing support and friendship. Thanks to the Lakeridge lunch bunch, who offer so much wisdom and laughter. Thanks to Nancy Kezner and Carole Muth, both of whom laugh and cry with me as we live, learn, and teach. Thanks to Paula Fraser, who responded to the draft with an intuitive and intellectual eye, to Barbara Inman, who added wisdom, to Jan Alleman who asked key questions, and to Katie Roberts McLean who inspired me to become a teacher. Special thanks to my teaching colleague, Paula Christoulis, who balanced my random style with her sequential order.

Some people have profoundly affected my teaching and me. Over the years, they have invited me to learn at their institutions, sharing of themselves and helping me to grow as a person and as a teacher. Those people include Gary Howard of the REACH (Respecting Ethnic and Cultural Heritage) Center, Mary Bernson of the East Asia Resource Center, Alita Letwin of the Center for Civic Education, Julie Van Camp from CRADLE (Center for Research and Development for Law-Related Education), Margaret Armancas-Fisher and Julia Gold of

University of Puget Sound Citizen Education in the Law, Harvey Segal of the Community College of Micronesia, Ann Sweeney from the Office for the Administrator of the Courts, Jane Brem and Margit McGuire of Seattle University, Gary Phillips from the School Improvement Project, Larry Strickland of the Washington State Office of the Superintendent of Public Instruction, and Frank Koontz of the Bureau of Education and Research.

Thanks to my colleagues on the National Council for the Social Studies (NCSS) Board of Directors, the Advanced Certification for Teachers of Social Studies Committee, the Middle Childhood/Generalist Committee of the National Board for Professional Teaching Standards, and the NCSS/CBC Notable Books National Selection Committee, who have helped me verbalize what I believe about teaching and learning and who have encouraged me to continue my quest for an integrated, holistic curriculum.

Thanks to Judi Slepyan, who tirelessly gives of her time and talent to photograph the children of Lakeridge as they are exploring, learning, and caring. I am so pleased to share her photos, the result of a very special combination of head, hands, and heart.

Thanks to my husband's family, especially the twenty-two who are teachers.

Heartfelt thanks to Marj Montgomery, Marte Peet, Oralee Kramer, and Rick Moulden, who read and reread this manuscript, listened to me talk it through, and still say they want a copy of the book.

Thanks to Carolyn Coman, who was willing to give me a chance to publish a book that wasn't stapled, would stand up on a shelf, and would have an ISBN. Thanks to Alan Huisman, who edited the original manuscript and to Bill Varner for instigating the second edition. Special thanks to Danny Miller for the incredibly positive support and helpful advice he provided even though he inherited me midrevision of this new edition. And thanks to Elizabeth Valway for making this revision true to the vision of first edition. Special kudos to Michelle Chan for creating a memory quilt that Linda Knowles incorporated so effectively into the cover design. Thanks to Marilyn Rash, a wonderful copy editor.

Finally, warm thanks to my husband, Malcolm, a true partner in life as well as in the writing of this book.

SEEING
THE WHOLE
THROUGH
SOCIAL STUDIES

SECOND EDITION

INTRODUCTION
Reflections from a Classroom Teacher

I teach. And in my heart of hearts, every time I teach social studies, I believe that maybe, just maybe, this lesson is the one that will provide the skills, knowledge, and values that will make it possible for my students to change the world. *This* lesson will really make a difference! So in our self-contained classroom, we "do" social studies all day long. After all, changing the world takes time.

But it's not open-the-text, read-the-chapter, answer-the-questions-at-the-end social studies. It is integrated, active, meaningful social studies. And it is fun. Social studies is the core of our day, providing powerful learning in the humanities, social sciences, and civics for the purpose of helping children learn to be good problem solvers and wise decision makers.

I have reorganized my year with intermediate-grade children to reflect an integration of knowledge, skills, and processes. Social studies content is the thematic base around which I wrap other disciplines, the day is unified by purposes and goals. All the components—content, instructional approaches, learning activities, and evaluation methods—are selected because they help students acquire important capabilities and dispositions. It is through the language arts that my students most often reveal their knowledge and apply their skills. Reading, writing, listening, and speaking are integral to all learning. Without language arts, the construction of meaning in specific topics is impossible. I use the natural integrative nature of language arts to promote powerful social studies learning and teaching.

REORGANIZING THE CURRICULUM

Now, nearly every part of the year is integrated in my classroom. But I didn't start that way. My initial attempts at connecting the chunks of content that I was supposed to teach were clumsy, often lopsided. The revision took time, and I now know that integration is never finished. It starts slowly and builds over time. I've been at this for twenty-plus years and recognize it is an evolutionary process, calling for continual refinement as I incorporate new resources, respond to students' interests and needs, and encourage them to investigate current issues and concerns. Reorganizing the curriculum is *intensely personal and fluid*. This kind of integration will never be put in a box or plastic bag and sold off the shelf. This kind of teaching trusts the teacher to be a good problem solver and wise decider because the teacher has a vision. This kind of teacher not only knows the likely prior knowledge and experiences of her students, but also has a good idea of what will happen next in their intellectual, social, physical, moral, and emotional development. Such a teacher capitalizes on areas of strength and bolsters areas of weakness.

I began integrating in the early 1980s. Recently returned from several years of teaching in the South Pacific, I was frustrated and dismayed by the fragmentation of the school day. More demands were placed on me all the time: global studies, economic education, sex education, higher-order thinking skills, personal safety, and cooperative learning. However, no class time was added, no content was deleted. I felt like a juggler keeping a dozen or more glass balls in the air, and I knew I had already dropped a couple. Their shards lay at my feet, and there were corresponding squares in the plan book with a big X hastily drawn over them. It was also obvious that there would be new balls for me to juggle every year. Some of these balls were legislatively mandated— AIDS education and environmental awareness, for example. Others reflected concerns, such as multicultural education and technology, within my community. Still others were of my own choosing: a new passion for Southwestern archeology and a personal commitment to raising salmon in the classroom.

In spite of the overwhelming demands, some days seemed to flow. The day would be over and the students and I would look at each other astonished that we didn't have more time together. Those days were accidents of planning that integrated knowledge, skills, and processes. Over time, I realized that flow happened on those days when I hadn't taken out the teacher's manual and followed what it said to do page by page, when I had ignored the sequential school-mandated, district-sanctioned, state-enforced learning timetable—math for fifty minutes daily, social studies and science for forty minutes three times a week, spelling fifteen minutes right after lunch.

WHERE ARE WE GOING?

Using social studies as the framework, I began to explore ways to network knowledge, skills, and teaching strategies across the curriculum. But first I needed to know where I was going. Basically, I had twelve goals (Mercer Island Public Schools 1988), so that I could provide students the opportunity to:

1. Learn about the past to better understand the present in order to anticipate and prepare for the future.
2. Develop an understanding of and an appreciation for our American heritage.
3. Understand the relationship between human societies and their physical world.
4. Understand how the economy and a changing workplace affect their lives now and in the future.
5. Accept the integrity and importance of the individual in the context of his or her culture and appreciate the multicultural nature of the United States and the world.
6. Understand the interdependence of their own community and the world.
7. Recognize change as a natural part of life and deal with it effectively.
8. Increase their understanding of and appreciation for systems of law.
9. Appreciate self and demonstrate respect for every human being.
10. Develop critical thinking skills.
11. Improve their individual and group communication skills.
12. Demonstrate responsible citizenship through active participation.

With these overall goals in mind, I could begin to plot a conceptual map, analyzing and reorganizing my curriculum to reach them. Years ago there wasn't a lot of help. I floundered around doing the best I could.

POWERFUL TEACHING AND LEARNING

The National Council for the Social Studies (NCSS) issued a position statement titled "A Vision of Powerful Teaching and Learning in the Social Studies: Building Social Understanding and Civic Efficacy." Published in 1993, this document still has tremendous implications for classrooms because it identifies five features for ideal, or powerful, teaching and learning in the social studies. When it is *integrative, meaningful, value-based, active*, and *challenging*, social studies teaching and learning is powerful.

These features have enduring applicability across grade levels and content. After analyzing my own teaching, I find that the five features are the essential ingredients for my classroom program, which is centered on the social studies—the purpose of which is to help students develop social understanding and civic efficacy. *Social understanding* is defined as "the integrated knowledge of social aspects of the human condition: how they evolved over time, the variations that occur in various physical environments and cultural settings, and the emerging trends that appear likely to shape the future." *Civic efficacy* is "the readiness and willingness to assume citizenship responsibilities," including social studies knowledge and skills; related values, such as concern for the common good; and dispositions, such as an orientation toward confident participation in civic affairs (NCSS 1993, 213).

Standards

In 1994, the National Council for the Social Studies published ten thematically based curriculum standards, accompanied by corresponding sets of performance expectations in their book, *Expectations of Excellence: Curriculum Standards for Social Studies*. These curriculum standards provide a guide for content and purpose within the classroom. The performance expectations identify the knowledge, skills, perspectives, and commitments to the democratic ideals that we strive to meet or exceed with our students. Many states and school districts across the country have adopted all or some of these thematic standards as their own statements of what they feel is important for students to know and to be able to do. The following are the ten themes that provide classroom teachers, as well as administrators at the local, state, and national levels, a way to organize social studies learning for all students:

    I. Culture
   II. Time, Continuity, and Change
 III. People, Places, and Environments
 IV. Individual Development and Identity
  V. Individuals, Groups, and Institutions
 VI. Power, Authority, and Governance
VII. Production, Distribution, and Society

VIII. Science, Technology, and Society
  IX. Global Connections
  X. Civic Ideals and Practices

These curriculum standards are interrelated. There is no hierarchy. A student doesn't study each as a stand-alone topic nor do they start with Culture and work down to Civic Ideals and Practices. How would one study cultures without learning about the relationships between people, places, and environments as well as time, continuity, and change? Not only are the standards interrelated but the social science disciplines from which they are drawn are integrated. History, geography, economics, and civics, in addition to other fields, provide core knowledge and ways of thinking. Other social sciences need to be tapped to extend and enrich core content.

Teachers find the social studies standards helpful in several ways. The first is to use them to provide outcome goals for units and courses, thereby aligning classroom learning with outcomes that have been identified as important in a larger arena such as the district, county, or state. A second way is to use standards to evaluate current practices. A third is to use them as a resource for instruction and assessment ideas. Standards help classroom teachers decide what is important and how well kids at various developmental ages should know it. A social studies text no longer drives the curriculum. Now, standards are available to provide an alternative path to student acquisition of content and skills. (See pages 84–88 for books that feature these ten themes.)

Hands-On, Heads-On, Hearts-On

Powerful social studies teaching requires reflective thinking and decision making as the lesson takes place. Beginning with John Dewey, curriculum advocates have called for hands-on learning. In the seventies, the notion of heads-on learning came to the fore as we examined higher-order thinking. I believe these early years of a new century will add a third dimension critical to learning; "hearts-on."

For years many educators skirted the affective and sought refuge in the observable. Remember, not so long ago, learning didn't count if it couldn't be seen, touched, tasted, smelled, or heard a replicable number of times. Understanding, knowing, feeling, appreciating, caring, and loving were depreciated as attributes of learning. Yet teachers always knew the affective was not only a vital outcome, but also an important part of the process.

5

Genuine Questions

Teachers need to encourage students to ask genuine questions throughout the day; and teachers need to take that risk themselves. In a readers workshop session at Regis University's Literacy Institute, Patricia Hagerty, author of "Readers' Workshop: Real Reading" (1992), stated that genuine questions are those questions we don't know the answer to. We need to gain the confidence to move away from the teacher's manuals, workbooks, and answer keys, not because they are bad, but because they raise nongenuine questions.

Teachers, at last, are no longer expected to be the font of all knowledge. Instead, we are becoming facilitators, guides, managers, mentors, and fellow learners. We share in the discourse of the classroom, enjoy the hunt for knowledge, and celebrate as our efforts culminate into a personal "whole" for each learner.

INTEGRATED LEARNING

Deliberately and specifically using language arts as the foundation for acquiring knowledge, skills, and values in social studies moves teachers and students to integrated learning. I believe the demands of the intermediate-grade classroom push us to finding networks of knowledge and content connections beyond those found in language alone. Think of language arts skills, processes, and knowledge as the warp of learning, with each specific skill or understanding symbolized by a thread running vertically through the loom. Then picture another discipline, such as social studies, as the horizontal threads providing the pattern and individual design of the fabric that eventually will be woven by each learner. Integrated learning is a way of balancing content and instructional strategies to nurture and nudge students away from self-centeredness toward self-realization and self-actualization.

Putting It All Together

The key to integrated learning is putting it all together. Integration is a concept that has been promoted by many a good educator but is illusive when one tries to pin it down. I suspect that's because integration happens in the classroom at varying levels. If one were to draw a continuum and label one end "I have a totally integrated classroom" and label the other end "I never integrate," few teachers would identify themselves as being on either end of the continuum. Integration in the classroom can be an accidental correlation, like learning about measuring to scale in math in the morning and estimating distance on a map in the social studies text in the afternoon. It can also be as pervasive as a yearlong theme with units deliberately tied together to emphasize and elucidate that theme.

When I listen to colleagues talk about integration, I am reminded of Ed Young's wonderful book, *Seven Blind Mice* (1992), based on the fable of the blind men and the elephant. There is "Something" in the garden. Each of seven blind mice venture out to examine "the Something" and each mouse comes back with a different idea. The first mouse examines only a leg and determines the Something is a pillar. The second mouse examines the trunk and is sure the Something is a snake. The third mouse runs up and down a tusk and decides he's found a spear. Standing on the Something's head, the fourth blind mouse decides he's discovered a great cliff. The fifth mouse, perched on an ear, exclaims he's found a fan. The sixth mouse, finding the tail, concludes he's holding a rope. From each individual perspective, each mouse is right. But the seventh mouse examines the whole and discovers the Something is an elephant. The moral to the story? As Ed Young writes, "Knowing in part may make a fine tale, but wisdom comes from seeing the whole" (36). Isn't that true of teaching and learning? Over the years we've woven some fine tales for our students. We've created worthwhile and engaging units of study. What we've done hasn't been bad, but I believe there's more that we can do. We can bring wisdom to our classrooms as well.

Our Something in education is integration. And all my colleagues are right. Integration is what each individual perceives at a particular time and place. A dictionary definition of *integration* reveals this part-to-whole nature: "1. To make into a whole by bringing all parts together; unify. 2. To join with something else; unite" (Morris et al. 1982). Integration occurs when one thing is joined with another or when all the parts of something are unified into a whole.

Two Kinds of Integration

My experience tells me that there is not one but two specific kinds of integration that occur in the classroom. The first, and most obvious, is *integrating the curriculum*—what we teach. Several different approaches to curriculum integration can be used successfully (Shoemaker 1991, 793):

◆ Looking for places where skills from one curriculum can be infused into another (i.e., transferring thinking skills across the curriculum).
◆ Identifying themes and selecting subject matter appropriate to the organizing topic (i.e., pioneers, immigration).

- ◆ Choosing concepts (i.e., interdependence, change) around which to organize a school year. This approach is often selected when a whole school decides to begin integrating across grade levels and across curriculum.
- ◆ Taking advantage of natural subject linkages (i.e., language arts and social studies).
- ◆ Establishing an integrated language arts program (connecting writing, reading, listening, and speaking).

Many teachers combine several of these approaches, customizing integration to fit the curriculum goals and the resources available.

The second, more subtle, kind of integration focuses on the needs and strengths of the whole child. This occurs when we specifically consider and plan for the continued development of the *cognitive, physical, affective, and moral dimensions of each child* (Shoemaker 1991, 793), carefully devising learning strategies to deepen and extend his or her arena of competence, confidence, creativity, and cooperation. It is here that knowing our students, being aware of their learning orientation and prior experiences, begins to fuse with curriculum. The way we emphasize content, how it is presented, and how it is developed through activities is incredibly important. It is this fusion of the child, the curriculum, and our teaching that results in integrated learning. Only then can wisdom enter our classroom.

Analogical Thinking

Integration calls on the teacher, initially, and later the students, to identify the connections or overlaps between content areas, between similar processes or applications of skills, and then to build on those connections. Don Bragaw (1986), former NCSS president, identifies this ability as "analogical thinking." He calls it the ultimate form of critical thinking—"that moment when a student responds in class by saying, 'Hey, that's like when so and so did whatzis back in the Civil War' (or the Renaissance, or in economics class, or in third grade, or in a book they just read, or in a classroom discussion held just yesterday)." Integration encourages the learner to draw on observations and resources from both academics and the arts. When learning is rooted firmly in the social studies, meaningfulness is enhanced. Children develop the skills and attitudes, as well as the knowledge, to be able to participate in the decision making that is basic to a democratic system.

8

As one's comfort with integration grows, the connections become larger than a topic; more global than a theme; and, in the intermediate grades, last longer than a day. Centered on the child, connected by the curriculum, driven by learning goals, and encompassing the amount of time the teacher and the students spend together, the threads of content continue to interweave with the skills of communication, the patterns of problem solving, and the synthesis of decision making over an entire school year.

After a few years of focusing on connections, teachers who seek to integrate will find more and more ways to put it all together until they discover, as I did, that their day is overstuffed with connections. It's not a disaster. It's like winning the lottery. Now there are options; students can choose how they want to approach a question, explore a topic, or develop a plan. Enough material and approaches have been collected and connected to encourage individualization within integrated learning.

LEVELS OF INTEGRATION

Many of us start integrating by deliberately making connections across the curriculum; that is how I started out. This kind of approach is often referred to as interdisciplinary. I took traditional subjects—social studies, language arts (including reading), science, and art—and found those places where content could intersect, where skills could be applied across the curriculum. Although social studies was the core for me, other teachers have used science, math, and/or some other subject as the core organizer. Looking back, I can trace four levels of integration in my teaching.

Level 1
Connections were few, rather formal, and carefully planned the first year. The question I repeatedly asked myself was: "How can I connect this reading content, that writing skill, and an art perspective to my existing social studies curriculum?" Because I was new to the grade level, new to the curriculum, and new to integrating, I had to seek out every connection. I didn't have many connections that first year (see Figure I–1). Picking content I had a personal interest in and knowledge about helped because I didn't have to start from scratch. It helps to know something about what you're trying to connect!

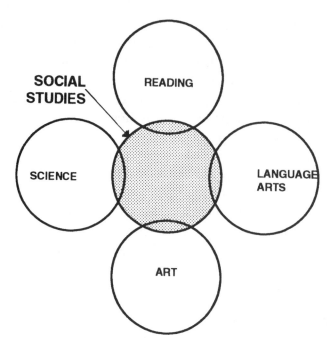

Figure I–1:   Level 1: New to grade level, new to curriculum, or first effort at integration. Two or more subjects can be connected.

Level 2

A couple of years later, my planning became less formal but broader in scope, blending skills and content through the disciplines. The question I asked myself was: "How can I blend this social studies concept with those skills, with these learning strategies of reading, writing, science, and art?" I began to use the connections to weave the disciplines together, to connect subjects in a new way (see Figure I–2). I believe this shift occurred because I was more familiar with the curriculum and could identify a larger number of resources to support it. I was getting smarter about the central content (social studies) and the ways to teach it. I was also getting better at knowing what my students would probably know and not know. I could anticipate and plan for their understanding and misunderstanding.

Level 3

I call this level highly accomplished. Planning in an inclusive, integrative manner became not only natural, but essential—I no longer viewed learning as a mixture

10

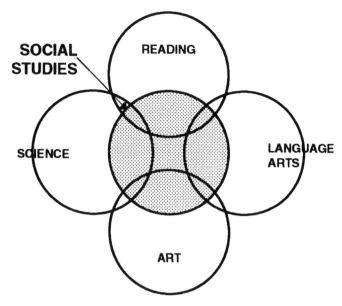

Figure I–2:   Level 2: Greater familiarization with curriculum, student's development, resources, and activities that work weave multiple connections.

of separate subjects. I knew the curriculum intimately and was well aware of resources within the school and throughout the community. I knew where the class and I were going, and I had created or adapted teaching strategies to get there. Subjects began to fuse as the new patterns of teaching and learning became established. Discipline identity was no longer the focus (see Figure I–3).

Level 4

Recently, I have noticed a fourth level in my personal evolution of integration. In the past, the focus, or center, of my integrating was always the topic, the theme, or the concept. But I've realized that teaching a series of disconnected units, no matter how integrated each unit is, does not tap the potential power of integration in the classroom. My organizational center has shifted. The child, not the subject, is now at the center of my planning (See Figure I–4).

I've also observed that I function on several different levels of integration within a school year. Let me give you an example. I know a great deal about Northwest Coastal Native Americans. I have studied the culture for years and continue to expand my knowledge. When we focus on Northwest Coastal Native Americans in my classroom, I easily and effectively make connections

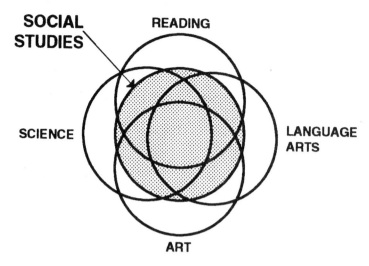

Figure I–3:   Level 3: Highly accomplished. Almost all learning intersects as subject distinctions begin to blur. Concepts and skills cross disciplines.

with everything else we do during the day. Finding appropriate materials, devising substantial projects, and facilitating the students' individual investigations is stress-free—I know the content; I know the kids. I have collected a wide variety of strategies and resources to enhance learning.

But *integration is not linear.* Just because I have this facility with Northwest Coastal Native Americans does not mean that all the work and planning for the rest of the year is equally accomplished. I would categorize my ability to promote integration during our Civil War studies as being at Level 2. Content—my knowledge of the issues and events—is not as substantial as it could be. My classroom resources aren't as rich and diverse as I'd like. Similarly, the level of integration reached during our study of explorers is at Level 1 because only recently have accurate and engaging resources, which present data from different points of view in easily accessible formats for intermediate-age students, started to appear. Resources, knowledge of the content, and an array of teaching strategies are essential elements on which to build higher levels of integration.

ABOUT THIS BOOK

When the NCSS published "A Vision of Powerful Teaching and Learning in the Social Studies," I analyzed my teaching and my students' learning by compar-

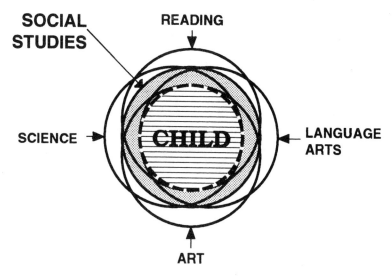

Figure I–4: Level 4: Subjects no longer drive learning. Instead, learning is a meaningful, child-centered, holistic experience that helps children become good problem solvers and wise decision makers.

ing the "Vision" to my classroom. This book grew out of that analysis and of my own journey toward a classroom in which learning is integrated for the benefit of the whole child. Frequently, the strategies I employ and the learning going on in my classroom match the "Vision." Sometimes they don't.

This book chronicles a twelve-year period of my life. First published in 1995, it has found its way into countless teachers' hands, shaping their instructional decisions, affirming what they have been doing, and influencing the decisions districts are making about the teaching of social studies.

This new edition takes a reflective look at that twelve-year period, keeps what is still relevant, revamps what was dated, includes what was left out, and introduces what is new. Looking back at my years of teaching has deepened my commitment to integrated learning. With all the emphasis on literacy, social studies often gets short shrift, but that need not be so. Certainly, in the light of events in late 2001, citizenship and how decisions are made for the public good is more important than at any other time in our history. Those of us who use social studies content to teach reading skills such as fluency, mental imaging, predicting, comprehension, and prior knowledge are capitalizing on latest brain research, which tells us that the brain loves connections. We continually encourage our students to network "what I know" with "what I am learning" and "what I want to know." Social studies, however, remains the core. The things we do in March and in January relate to and build on knowledge, skills, and ideas we explored in September. Substantive underlying concepts and, often, yearlong themes bridge my teaching, day by day, throughout the year.

Moving the child to the center of the curriculum has added a deeper layer of understanding for me and for my students. Whether learning is highly integrated or barely connected, today's student must interact with worthwhile content in a meaningful way so that they "develop the ability to make informed and reasoned decisions for the public good as citizens of a culturally diverse, democratic society in an interdependent world" (NCSS 1993, 213).

I use a fifth-grade classroom in this book to show what a social studies integrated curriculum looks like over a year's time. But I don't, and please reread this next statement, I don't *do all of this* in one year. For the flow of the book, it looks like I do but, in fact, some of the strategies shared here have only happened in my classroom two or three times in twenty years. Others, however, have been repeated annually or are practiced multiple times over the course of one school year.

Learning is connected. For too long we have tried to keep our classrooms mentally tidy, setting up schedules that parse the day into bits of disciplines, expecting students to be satisfied with the outcome. How content is presented and how it is developed through activities is as important as what is presented. I'm constantly seeking to balance the message and the medium. Too much process and an activity becomes "cute." Intermediate-age children need substance. Too little process and learning becomes a drudge. Intermediate-age children need to be engaged in learning to excel. We need to choose strategies that create an active, child-centered classroom where students can expose and explore critical content.

Children need to deepen their reservoirs of knowledge. And they need the opportunity to dip into that knowledge, blend it with the ability to solve problems, and make good decisions in developmentally appropriate ways. This book is about reorganizing curriculum and choosing instructional strategies to make learning integrative, meaningful, value-based, active, and challenging for both the students and the teacher. It is also about one teacher's quest for the balance that brings a completeness to learning, for her students and for herself.

The chapters that follow illustrate how social studies concepts, issues, and themes can become the core of intermediate-grade students' day. Language arts, art, science, and math can be interwoven to integrate learning in any class-room. Teachers can intentionally capitalize on the connections between subjects and among processes to strengthen their teaching and increase learning. Detailed plans for many of the strategies are included in the Appendix, with the intent that readers will take them, shape them, and integrate them into their classrooms. Although I don't use all these strategies in any one year, they are all useful and versatile, and my students find them appealing. These same strategies have been successfully used by elementary and middle school teachers in a variety of subjects to teach a number of topics, themes, and concepts.

Throughout the book, I also share *read-alouds*, those picture books and chapter books that I read to my students to expand or to affirm their universe of knowing, as well as *read-alones*, those books that I either recommend or require my students to read as a part of our integrated approach to learning. Additionally, my students do *read-togethers*, those books that they read with a buddy or in a small group such as a literature circle, guided reading, or a book club.

In this revised edition, new sections are added to each chapter. They include Tarry's Teaching Tips—a special section dealing with organizational decisions to foster the building of a democratic classroom community and to provide core knowledge about learning that some teachers are unaware of or don't think to include in their plans. Seasoned classroom veterans may find this section a gentle reminder of some best practices that they used to do but have somehow lost during the last few years. Literacy connections are emphasized in each chapter. In the Teacher's Notebook, specific reading and writing skills that I have taught using social studies resources and content are described. Sometimes the struggling reader is the focus; at other times, it's the kids in the middle and those high-end achievers who are ready to "fly." Occasionally, the reader will find a special section—How It Worked for Me—interspersed within the chapters. These are brief accounts from teachers around the country who have used ideas and information from *Seeing the Whole Through Social Studies,* or from my seminars, in their own classrooms with success. They represent diverse regions of the nation, different class sizes, varied socioeconomic status, and various high-stakes testing requirements. In their own words, teachers share how they have shaped some strategy or adapted some project presented in this book so that it fits a unique situation. Best practices and recent brain research are applied throughout the book. Additionally, the references have been expanded and updated.

Finally, sketches of how to create kinesthetic organizers are placed throughout the book. The value of graphic (two dimensional) organizers has been recognized for the last decade. I am of the opinion that kinesthetic (three dimensional) organizers are equally valuable. A kinesthetic organizer requires students to manipulate paper as they construct records of their learning. Storing knowledge in two forms—the kinesthetic (or imagery form) and the linguistic—supports powerful learning. This often means that brain activity is stimulated and increased. It also means that students begin to think "outside the box." I think moving away from the standard rectangular piece of notebook paper encourages divergent, higher-level thinking. Called by some psychologists the "dual-coding" theory of information storage, there is research to support my observation that since using kinesthetic organizers my students are better able to think about and to recall knowledge. Research shows that teachers who use kinesthetic, as well as linguistic forms of learning find positive effects on student achievement (Marzano et al. 2001, 73).

I once heard that in any given classroom, 60 percent of the students are kinesthetic learners, yet it is the least-addressed learning style in classrooms. Long before inclusion, I started using kinesthetic organizers when I decided to keep special education kids in my integrated classroom all day. Over time, I noticed the talented and the middle kids were equally enriched as they used kinesthetic organizers to manage information, to explore new ideas, and to record their comprehension of knowledge. I wish I could say I created each of the organizers included here, but I didn't. I learned them from other teachers, watching what my own kids brought home, and tinkering with possibilities. I hope readers will try the kinesthetic organizers in their classrooms, change or create new ones, discover their versatility, and enjoy the success of all their students.

Chapter 1, Making Connections

This chapter offers a historical perspective of my own journey toward seeing the whole. Sometimes knowing the path someone else has taken can save time and energy or affirm that we are, in fact, on a path that leads to "Something."

Chapter 2, Setting Up for Success

Starting off positively and productively affects learning dynamics for a whole year. Some procedures and strategies seem to promote a more successful year in our classroom than others do. This chapter presents underpinnings that will help enhance and encourage student learning and participation.

Chapter 3, Implementing Integration
What does integration in the intermediate-grade classroom look like when social studies is the center? This chapter provides classroom vignettes and specific teaching strategies you can use in your classroom tomorrow.

Chapter 4, Making It Meaningful
This chapter reaches to the heart of teaching. At the intermediate level, students not only have to learn how to learn, they also have to learn something. Determining issues worth spending time on, and devising activities of substance, while at the same time developing lifelong learners is all a part of making learning full of meaning.

Chapter 5, Exploring Values and Points of View
Helping students gain an understanding of and an appreciation for multiple perspectives is critical. Being aware of how our own values affect selection of materials and the amount of time we choose to spend on a topic helps us provide a balanced program for students. This chapter clearly illustrates strategies and activities for making multiple perspectives real.

Chapter 6, Activating Learning
Moving students beyond the classroom walls, both literally and figuratively, brings learning to life. Authentic learning in the form of thinking, feeling, and doing energizes the learner and the learning. By actively constructing meaning, students are able to apply it to their lives. This chapter focuses on how to make learning active without losing substance or skills.

Chapter 7, Making Teaching and Learning Challenging
Developing a learning community in which each member of the class is challenged to meet a high level of understanding and a depth of purpose takes time, and the teacher needs to offer a model. This chapter shows how thoughtful discussion and the practice of thinking skills, both critical and creative, contribute to seeing the whole.

Chapter 8, Assessing Student Achievement

Grades, student-created criteria, peer critiques, and projects of excellence are all part of my quest to authenticate assessment. This final chapter offers some ideas and strategies for looking at assessment in an integrated classroom. A brief discussion of standards, high-stakes testing, and what teachers can do to improve test scores, and still teach, is included.

Chapter One

MAKING CONNECTIONS

THERE ARE MANY CONNECTIONS BETWEEN
WORTHWHILE CONTENT AND EFFECTIVE PROCESS.
—NCSS's "Vision"

THE BEGINNING

It all began quite intentionally. My colleague Jan Hoem and I were convinced that if we started putting things together in our classrooms, the world could become a better place. We were given a minigrant from our school district to do just that. The grant didn't specifically state that we were to change the world, of course, but it underwrote planning time in which to reorganize our fifth-grade curriculum to increase student learning. We read somewhere that Native American children tend to learn better in a holistic classroom. We weren't sure what this meant, but it sounded better than the fragmented curriculum we were juggling each day—kibbles of content, bits of skills, pieces of predetermined information taught in a sequence ordered by someone who had never seen our classroom, never met our students, never asked what we thought. Because a Native American child was to be in my classroom in the fall, and because Jan and I team planned, we were given Title IV funds to support our efforts.

Jan taught fifth grade next door to me. One of those "born" teachers; always curious, ever alert, incredibly sensitive, Jan gave of herself in ways that inspired me to be a better person. A poet, a pragmatist, and a good friend, she was frustrated by too little time and too much content. I agreed and added my pet peeves of too much rote and too little active learning. We talked many times about finding ways to challenge the able kids and ways to enable the challenged kids. Teaching in those days was presented as series of sequential student objectives that limited learning to a single, narrow focus. We weren't happy with boring workbooks, "pretend" writing, or dull textbooks. We searched for ways to take the isolation out of our basal readers. Learning was fragmented, generalizations rare, motivation sporadic. We were determined to do something about it. Both of us knew learning could be fun because we had fun learning. We got excited about solving problems. Why didn't our students? So, on a hot August day, we agreed that we were going to try to reorganize our curriculum in a way that would bring cohesiveness to the school day and meet children's needs as best we could anticipate.

SOCIAL STUDIES AS THE CORE CURRICULUM

We wanted to make thinking fundamental in our classroom studies, to reach beyond the standard text and workbook format for more creative ways to teach and learn. And, because both of us loved social studies more than any other subject, we wanted to use it as the center of our curriculum. An analysis of social studies convinced us that social studies was a solid core for organizing our learning.

Integrates Naturally
Social studies is about life. It is a naturally integrative subject. Look at all the pieces that are frequently included in a K through 12 social studies strand: anthropology, archeology, civics, economics, geography, government, history, political science, psychology, religion, sociology, ethnic studies, global studies, law-related issues. It has a richness to draw from that promotes multilevel thinking. Children need not start from recall or memory in social studies. They can move directly to analysis, synthesis, and problem solving, depending on whether the task is to form a group, develop an argument for one side of an engaging issue, or create a plan of action.

Accommodates Learning Styles
Social studies is so diverse that it invites the learner to explore content through many different avenues. For example, a historical document like the Bill of Rights can be studied through singing, dancing, writing, drawing, debating, deliberating. A few years after we began our first attempts at integration, Dr. Howard Gardner published *Frames of Mind* (1985) in which he identified multiple intelligences. Jan and I knew children could show what they know in many ways but hadn't ever deliberately planned to tap into multiple intelli-

gences. Dr. Gardner's work has become a useful intellectual tool for planning and talking about integration.

So often research comes to the classroom in this way. We do things because we know they are good for kids, but we haven't articulated why. Researchers like Dr. Gardner help us understand why the things we do work. I make a deliberate effort to plan learning activities that provide opportunities for all children to deepen and extend the ways in which they learn. I often use Dr. Gardner's multiple intelligences as a way to guide my choices of teaching strategies and learning activities. Multiple intelligences can be described in this way (Campbell 1989):

LINGUISTICALLY ORIENTED STUDENTS

Love language: speaking it, hearing it, reading it, writing it
Often have well-developed vocabularies
Demonstrate rich expression, elaboration, fluency
Do not avoid difficult reading material
Like to work with books, records, and tapes

INTERPERSONALLY ORIENTED LEARNERS

Enjoy learning by interaction
Like cooperating with others
Are eager to participate in group work
Respond to discussions
Are interested in how peers feel about class work
Get involved in clubs, community service
Desire to know social relevancy of learning activities
Enjoy all kinds of social activities

INTRAPERSONALLY ORIENTED LEARNERS

Are self-directed
Are independent
Enjoy quiet times
Like private places to work and reflect
Need opportunities to fantasize, dream, imagine
Are concerned about the meaning of life
Look for personal relevance and purpose
Benefit from processing feelings
Need to solve problems

VISUALLY/SPATIALLY ORIENTED LEARNERS

Love learning with images, pictures, charts, graphs, diagrams, and art
Enjoy films, slides, videos, maps, models
Arrive at unique solutions often
Are willing to experiment
Do not rely on traditional approaches

KINESTHETICALLY ORIENTED LEARNERS

Learn best by moving, touching, doing
Need short movement breaks
Enjoy all kinds of hands-on activities
Find multisensory experiences appealing
Are often not attentive to visual or auditory instruction
Remember best what they have done physically

LOGICALLY/MATHEMATICALLY ORIENTED STUDENTS

Enjoy forming concepts
Like looking for patterns and relationships
Are comfortable doing step-by-step activities
Like proceeding in a sequential manner
Need time to complete all the steps
Enjoy experimenting with new materials
Ask questions frequently
Desire logical explanations
Think games, kits, and puzzles are fun

MUSICALLY ORIENTED LEARNERS

Enjoy rhythm and melody
Learn easily when information is sung, tapped, or clapped
Like to listen to music as they work
Enjoy using instruments
Like attending musical performances
Seek out opportunities to create music

NATURALISTICALLY ORIENTED LEARNERS

Discriminate among living things
Are sensitive to features of the natural world—clouds, rock formations,
the shape of leaves, and so on

Are familiar with issues regarding nature

Recognize patterns in the natural world

Classify living things

Develop appreciation for nature and understand its operations

Attend to nature's continuance

When I started using the multiple intelligences theory intentionally in my planning, I painstakingly made sure that I fashioned activities for my students highlighting each of the eight intelligences. Thinking back now, I twitch with embarrassment at how mechanical and contrived some of these activities were. They did not move the students to a greater understanding or appreciation for the topic. They did not foster finding connections. And you know, I don't think this is unusual for teachers who are beginning to assimilate new information into their practice. But over time, I came to visualize multiple intelligence as eight pigments on a painter's palate, distinct and boldly colored. Rarely does a painter use isolated pigments to create a masterpiece. Instead, the artist blends the colors on her palate to create hues of widely varied combinations, creating a unique landscape; and that's what multiple intelligences have become for me, a landscape for learning, a blend of knowing and doing, a synthesis of skills and content acquisition. What is important is giving students multiple entry points to knowledge and providing them with multiple ways in which to share or to represent what they know (Gardner 1999, 186–187).

Fosters Multicultural and Global Education

Social studies engages the learner personally in recognizing and valuing differences and similarities. It is inclusive, putting what is familiar to students into historical, geographical, and cultural perspectives. It enlarges the narrow vision students frequently have of their immediate society, one they may take for granted without much awareness or appreciation. Teaching students about diverse points of view and fostering appreciation for cultural differences is easier when the whole day revolves around social studies concepts and themes. The very process of the democratic classroom, where all members are valued and respected and there is an absence of threat, is the foundation of multicultural global education (see Figure 1–1).

Promotes Flow

Using social studies as the core for the day promotes flow. Flow occurs in the classroom when the day's activities are a cohesive and productive whole.

Figure 1–1: During our hobby fair, Katie introduces us to her love of faraway places.

Practicing skills from language arts such as writing a friendly letter or a newspaper article fits authentically within a social studies framework. Why should children have to generate a make-believe topic for a newspaper article when they can create a newspaper as a culminating activity for their study of the Civil War? Why should they struggle over a friendly letter to a nonexistent person when they can be Pocahontas writing to her father from England? Knowledge, skills, beliefs, and values are all revealed in assignments like these—they fit like giant puzzle pieces. Students are given time to assemble analogies, to find the "Hey, Mrs. L., isn't that just like . . .?" They are given time to mix knowledge and process into a workable whole for themselves. At the end of the day, there is a sense of accomplishment and closure. It is the kind of satisfied feeling that makes everyone want to rub their hands together, place them on their hips, and survey the well-done job. Over the years, I have discovered that flow can be planned. It can be predicted and directed as significant content, skills, and perspectives are consciously connected from a variety of disciplines to create essential learning experiences. Learning for the whole child, every child, is not only possible, but powerful.

Values Time

Although we didn't realize it when we first started connecting skills, knowledge, and processes across the curriculum, I have since learned that when children read a historical novel, such as *The Starving Time: Elizabeth's Diary, Part Two—Jamestown, Virginia, 1609* (Hermes 2001), write about it, and compare it to other data—for example, what's given in the social studies textbook—they become aware that learning is a process. They recognize the deliberate layering of learning, and students begin to see assignments' validity. No longer do assignments seem arbitrary and capricious. No longer are they rushed from one small segment of study to another. No longer does the teacher hear a chorus of, "Do we have to?" Time is allowed for initial study, knowledge application, and reflection, by both the children and the teacher.

Time is a key factor in today's classroom. Finding the time to track the important ideas of social studies *after* reading, writing, listening, and speaking is usually a scramble for minutes instead of the time needed for in-depth study. By reorganizing the curriculum and devising teaching strategies so that social studies content becomes the center of language arts practice and enjoyment, intermediate-grade teachers can find the precious time needed to teach their students not only what they need to know but new ways of knowing it. Students are able to become more engaged in learning; they aren't just covering a subject. Instead, they are excavating, exploring, and examining it. Time is used most effectively and efficiently when content is linked with skills practice. For example, when the teacher doesn't need to create a whole new setup for a friendly letter but can suggest that the students recall from their reading of Elizabeth's experiences in Jamestown. When students don't need to take ten minutes to decide whom to write to, time can be spent on the quality of the letter and the depth of comprehension. Practicing voice, word choice, and sentence fluency contribute to the writer's portrayal of Elizabeth's feelings.

As time went on, we began to create strategies to strengthen the links across the curriculum. From the beginning, we used language arts skills to showcase social studies knowledge. We found that we seldom needed to have a formal language arts period because those skills were applied during the integrated block. Practice, models, and critiques helped firm up language arts skills within the social studies context.

Combines Breadth and Depth

We wanted the curriculum we created to be more authentic and more productive. Our planning strategy was to reorganize after first identifying where current content touched. We knew we couldn't do it all in one year, but we could begin.

We identified the broad topics that we wanted the students to learn about: first peoples, exploration, colonization, Native Americans with a Northwest Coastal emphasis, the Revolution and documents of democracy, the westward movement, the Civil War, immigration, and industrialization. We wanted to study these topics broadly and deeply. In-depth studies provide the time and intensity needed for students to construct a thorough understanding of important concepts, acquire skills and knowledge, and explore values. We felt that each of these topics was significantly important to developing a historical understanding of our country. We also felt they were broad enough to encourage generalizations across content. These topics allowed us to choose from a variety of organizing themes—conflict and cooperation, continuity and change, community, power, unity and diversity, justice, civic virtue, or liberty.

We saw we could spend about a month on each topic, maybe five weeks here, six weeks there. Or we could hurry up with some topics and really dive into another for an extended period. It is the balance between breadth and depth that requires good teaching judgment. It felt good to contemplate the number of days we would have in the social studies, not minutes or hours (see Figure 1–2).

TARRY'S TEACHING TIPS: ADVANTAGES OF BEING A SOCIAL STUDIES PROFESSIONAL

Twenty-two years ago my husband and I had just returned to the Northwest after teaching in Micronesia for eight years. Teaching in a Seattle suburb was a long way away from our expatriot lifestyle. I think it was Einstein who said something like, "The human brain, once stretched, never returns to its original shape." I think the same is true of those who travel. Once someone has lived overseas, there seems to be an itch to travel again that never quite subsides. Attending a World Affairs Council Education Conference, we found a home for our desire to continue to learn about ourselves and others. That home was with a group of social studies teachers who belonged to the Washington State Council for the Social Studies.

I want to encourage you right here and now to become a social studies professional. The rewards are enormous! How do you do this? First you join your state or regional Council for the Social Studies, and you join the National Council for the Social Studies (NCSS). You will begin receiving magazines and newsletters that will inform you of upcoming events, such as conventions and conferences, as well as travel and study opportunities. New books will be reviewed. Lesson ideas will be shared. Research will be revealed. You will be invited to join local, regional, and national social studies committees. Most of all, you will have an opportunity to meet and talk with others like yourself—people who care about their profession, their students, and the impact they have for the common good.

As a direct result of my involvement, both at the state and national level, I have been able to travel and study in China for a whole summer, traveled in Japan for almost two weeks, attended law-related education courses at law schools on both coasts, worked on national committees for assessment and teacher education, presented at national conventions, been awarded national honors, and traveled all over the United States—all expenses paid! A little secret: elementary and middle school teachers are highly valued by the professional education organizations, whether the National Science Teachers Association (NSTA—*www.nsta.org*), the National Council for Teachers of Mathematics (NSTM—*www.nctm.org*), or the National Council for Teachers of English (NCTE—*www.ncte.org*). So many of us K through 8 folks don't belong that those who do are welcomed with open arms.

To tell the truth, if I hadn't been an active member of my state and then the national social studies organizations, I never would have written this book or been asked to participate in a professional speakers' bureau. I never would have had the opportunity to hear about diverse approaches to teaching, learn about new resources, discuss scholarly investigations, or grow personally in the profession. I've learned so much. I was not born with a history gene; few, if any, of us are. Although I was a history minor, I've had a long way to go to understand and appreciate the many facets that make up social studies education. And I'm still learning. The fellowship and opportunities to deepen one's personal knowledge as well as professional expertise is priceless. Get online right now and go to *www.ncss.org* (National Council for the Social Studies). You'll never be sorry you did.

	Reading	Social Studies	Science	Language Arts	Art/Other
Sept.	Read Across America: Legends, folktales, myths and environmental literature	U.S. Geography: regions, landmarks, products, similarities and differences	Introduction to managed forests	Posters, student-created books, and storyboard; Story elements; Beginning research skills	Second-grade buddies; Juggler visit; Art part
Oct.	Nonfiction research and biographies of famous Americans	U.S. Geography continued: Does environment shape culture?	Forest field experience; Lifecycle and habitat of salmon	Biography billboards; One-page plays	Salmon speaker; World Hunger Days; Historically accurate dress; Halloween
Nov./Dec.	Biographies continued and U.S. historical fiction; How to read history	American Revolutionary War: events, people, decisions, and results	Elements of powered flight; aerospace	Ledgerbooks—student autobiographies; Rewrite Constitution for space colonies	Salmon hatchery field trip; Space bubble; Trade fair; Art elements
Jan.	Reading to learn: skills and strategies; Science fiction; Nonfiction research	1790–1850—Turning the Pages: Pre–Civil War, slavery	Space; Raise salmon	Independent research and presentations; Space journals based on *The Green Book*	Mission to Mars—simulation at Museum of Flight; Watercolors
Feb.	Biographies, primary documents and historical novels of Civil War era	Causes, connections, and issues of Civil War	Raise salmon (continued); Watersheds; Experimental survey design projects	Art elements; Cooperative biographies; Little bigger book of salmon facts	Fifth-grade operetta
Mar.	Stories, novels, and histories about immigrants and immigration	Study of immigration to America	Mock Senate hearings; Old growth forests	Poems for two Voices; Student-made books: Journals, Through the Eyes of . . .	Group portfolios
Apr.	Stories of westward expansion, including primary documents and maps	History of westward expansion	Drug and alcohol education unit:	ABC Vocabulary Charts; Story ladders; Structural poetry	Salmon Summit; Release salmon
May	Stories to do with self-concept, decision-making, problem-solving, and nonfiction information	Study of multicultural America	The human body—study all the systems but two	Book of Knowledge or Create Your Own Comic Book; Graphic art	International district field trips; Open House
June	Research for independent project of excellence (Health)	History of health: class book	Health Fair—an interactive, independent, integrated project	Organization and graphic presentation of project	Nordic heritage; Locks field trip; All-school musical; Fifth-Grade Event

Figure 1–2: Integrating Instruction Through Reorganization.

Meets the Standards

National standards, state learning requirements, and district objectives based on strategic plans loom large in our lives as teachers, especially when accompanied by high-stakes assessment. Like deer caught in the headlights, many teachers seem to freeze when overwhelmed by increasingly stringent goals and heavy repercussions. They lose interest and/or confidence in their ability to deliver a program that is best for kids and still meets everyone's demands. Their reaction, often, is to shrink the demands to something manageable . . . and, generally, mechanical. Their response, frequently, is "Tell me what to teach and I'll do it." They give up their classroom autonomy and spend their days doing what someone else has predetermined they should do. The excitement generated by their own creativity dims and teaching becomes a job.

I think it is in times like these that we need to become more creative, more assertive, and more ready to defend our efforts to make the school day more connected for kids. We know the brain-compatible classroom is a place where children learn more, better, longer. Standards are not only met but exceeded in classrooms that integrate content, skills, and brain research.

What I've noticed is that often what gets tested is what gets taught. Literacy and math hit the standards circuit first, hence they are where most schools are spending their time and their dollars. Science, social studies, the arts, and health and physical education are often treated as leftovers. What time remains is parceled out among these leftover disciplines.

It doesn't have to be this way. By integrating content from a discipline like social studies with literacy or math skills, our students' knowledge will be enhanced, their competencies as contributing members of the community will increase, and their behaviors as lifelong learners will be supported.

Here's an example. The NCTE and the International Reading Association recently published their *Standards for the English Language Arts* (International Reading Association 2000). Their first standard reads as follows:

> Students read a wide range of print and nonprint texts to build an understanding of texts, of themselves, and of the cultures of the United States and the world; to acquire new information; to respond to the needs and demands of society and the workplace; and for personal fulfillment. Among these texts are fiction and nonfiction, classic and contemporary works.

Is there anything that would stop a teacher from using social studies-related texts to meet this standard? In fact, it sounds like it could be a social studies standard, doesn't it? Could students read about Harriet Tubman or Abraham Lincoln as partial fulfillment of this standard? Could they study human rights around the world as well as in the United States, perhaps focusing on slavery, internment or racial profiling? Could they survey their peers to see if foreign students should have to respond to stricter controls on their visas? Could they read about ordinary and extraordinary people who inspire and intrigue them? Of course they could. And would they be doing social studies or language arts? They would be doing both. That's what I mean when I press for integration. How much richer a book becomes when it is surrounded by additional data and experience. How much more likely a student is "to get it" when immersed in the time, the place, and the people of an event.

Let's look at another example. The data analysis and probability standard listed by the NCTM includes the following skills: formulate questions that can be addressed with data and collect, organize, and display relevant data to answer them; select and use appropriate statistical methods to analyze data; develop and evaluate inferences and predictions that are based on data; and understand and apply basic concepts of probability. Not once do the mathematicians suggest what the content of these constructs should be. Could the kids collect information about worldwide food distribution or analyze who uses most of the world's resources? Could they create and display graphs indicating the increasing disappearance of the rainforest in South America or the numbers of immigrants to this country from 1800 to 2000? Rather than develop a math unit built around an illusionary issue that the kids have little prior knowledge of or current interest in, why not create a social studies unit that incorporates the practice of skills identified by NCTM?

The NSTA includes one specific standard, "The History and Nature of Science," which states that students should have opportunities to learn science in personal and social perspectives and to learn about the history and nature of science, as well as to learn subject matter, in the school science program. Whether studying flight and space, rainforests, or the environment, the civics of each is as critical to learning as the science is.

Finally, the standards posted on the Web by the National Council for the Social Studies, the National Council of Teachers of English, the International Reading Association (IRA), the National Council of Teachers of Mathematics, and the National Science Teachers Association have a common caveat. Each group stresses that their own standards are interrelated, that no standard takes precedence over another, that they are integrative in nature. Each of these professional associations acknowledges a linkage among their separate disciplines but do not indicate much of a connection among each other. I guess it is up to us, the classroom teacher, to make that leap, creating a vibrant, deliberate, truly integrated study for our students by using the standards as guideposts as well as justification for the choices we make.

ESTABLISHING READING CONNECTIONS

The easiest link for us to develop was between social studies and reading. First, we decided the textbook would be another resource, not the whole curriculum. We observed that when the textbook is used as the sole source for social studies education, students are often turned off by its stale, static, impersonal, and, often, unreachable presentation. And no wonder! Allington (2001) notes in his book that readability studies show that the preponderance of social studies texts are written at a level of difficulty two years above their intended grade level. Second, we knew that intermediate-age students needed to add a new and important skill to their reading repertoire—the skill of reading to learn through frequent practice in reading factual material. They needed to summarize, analyze, synthesize, and realize their own potential as self-directed learners.

We also knew that reading to learn needed to be balanced with reading literature. Basals, combined with the teacher reading aloud after recess, were the state of the art in reading instruction. Pounds of paper were used for worksheets. Even though many teachers read aloud to their classes after lunch or before recess, it wasn't considered a valued part of reading. Literature was something that happened in high school. Because the order of stories in basals have no significance whatsoever, we looked through all the old fourth-, fifth-, and sixth-grade reading series books to find stories that enriched, extended, or enhanced the concepts we were studying in social studies. Then we added novels. We encouraged students to try many different kinds of printed material.

That first year, we chose stories from the basal readers that, in some way, connected to our topics. Where there were none, we found literature to read aloud and shared magazine and newspaper articles. Sometimes the students created their own textbooks. Later, we developed lists of books, which examined, extended, or enriched our specific social studies topics, students could read independently. By saving coupons from various book clubs and by pooling coupons with other teachers, we acquired sets of books to share.

Today, I use a reading workshop–plus approach. What I mean is for one hour and a half each day, we do reading and related activities. This often includes various styles of organization. I remind myself that the human brain loves novelty; therefore, we don't do the same thing all year long. Journals and journaling are wonderful, but not day after day, week after week, month after month. Variety is the spice of the intermediate learners' life!

The first fifteen minutes of my reader's workshop is when we discuss yesterday's reading or I read aloud. This is frequently followed by a teacher-led minilesson or a presentation by students for another fifteen minutes. The second half hour often includes the following: book club discussions, written responses to prompts, small-group rehearsals for dramatic reenactments, individual work on visual representations of the reader's response to a reading, guided reading groups, literature circles, and other strategies that foster reading-skills acquisition and practice. The final half hour is usually spent in silent reading.

In this way, kids who read slowly or who are struggling aren't punished, pushed, or singled out in class because they aren't capable readers yet. They can take the book home and read it as homework, use the library, or read at recess time in a pinch. Inclusion kids get the support they need because an aide or a parent can work with them one-on-one during the silent reading time without the pressure of finishing within a specific time limit. By placing the class or group discussion a day later, they don't miss part of the "action." I've also noticed that all my kids' comments are more thoughtful, deeper, and full of insight. I think having the conversation about the reading the next day promotes this kind of dialog. Additionally, more kids take an active role in discussion when they have had time to process their reading.

The public library system is also an excellent resource. Ours is a countywide system, with many libraries networked together. By placing an "all call" for a specific title, fifteen to twenty copies of a single title, or a collection of related books, are often available within a week. Grant money can also bring books into the classroom. My most successful grant came when I explained how I was integrating my curriculum around social studies themes and concepts and why I needed literature to support that effort. The result? About 200 social studies–related literature books for our classroom library! Over the years, the basal has been replaced by historical fiction, biographies, picture books, and factual material. It has taken ten years to build a personal library that supports fifth-grade teaching and learning. Each year my library grows, as new books are published connecting content and teaching goals and as resources are found to buy them.

Finding worthwhile books is time-consuming. Fortunately, there are resources available to assist the busy teacher. One of the best is the Notable Social

Studies Trade Books for Young People. This annotated book list is evaluated and selected by a Book Review Committee appointed by the National Council for the Social Studies and assembled by The Children's Book Council. The Committee, made up of NCSS members who are classroom teachers, college professors, curriculum supervisors, and educational consultants, choose about 150 of the most notable social studies-related books out of approximately 700 that are submitted by publishers. The selection criteria include representation of diverse groups, sensitivity to a broad range of cultural experiences, presentation of an original theme or new slant on a traditional topic, readability, and high literary quality. The list is published every spring by the NCSS and is available online at (*www.socialstudies.org*). A similar list of outstanding science trade books is also available—go to *www.nsta.org* to see what the NSTA is recommending.

I've found a resource that is quite wonderful for teachers who want to accumulate more sets of books, whether for the whole class or a small group; call 1-800-Scholastic and ask for their catalog division (Canadian teachers, call 1-800-268-3848). When you reach someone, ask that a Catalog of Supplementary Materials be mailed to you free of charge. I am amazed at the hundreds of marked-down paperbacks that are available, just begging to be integrated into a social studies curriculum! Many of these books are "golden oldies" or classics whose content connects kids to the past as well today as they did years ago when first written.

ALIGNING LITERACY CONNECTIONS

After identifying stories to read, we connected literacy skills by linking them through strategies that require reading, writing, listening, and speaking. We looked at the school district's list of skills and objectives for the language arts. We thought about our students' skills, abilities, and interests. It was not difficult to weave together language arts skills and social studies content—letters, news articles, speeches, poetry, outlines, and other forms of written and spoken communication are all wonderful tools. In fact, we wondered why we hadn't intentionally done this before. We both recognized that successful past projects were a blend of language arts and social studies, but it had been accidental!

In addition to the district goals, we had some personal ones. For instance, we wanted our students to do more expository writing. We felt they needed to move from writing narratives to organizing facts in an informational or persuasive way. Students at this age have a highly developed sense of justice. We decided that studying issues, whether current or historical, would capture their interest. Various points of view can be recognized as students begin to wrestle with the reality that there is seldom a single side to any issue. We decided to teach the students how to make hypotheses and to find proof. We wanted to give them practice in choosing the best alternative and supporting that choice with facts. We provided opportunities for them to "try on" past and current decisions and to evaluate actual or potential consequences.

Listening with a critical ear is a skill preadolescents need, given that they are plugged in, glued to, and centered on music, radio, videogames, and television. Learning to discriminate fallacious arguments, weak substance, and shaky premises increases their street smarts as well as helps them acquire intellectual skills. The persistent dilemmas and issues of social studies provides excellent forums for practicing critical listening.

This age group teeters on the brink of public-speaking phobia. Increasingly more concerned about their public image, many of them find speaking before a group an ordeal. Yet public speaking is becoming an ordinary way to share information or to persuade. Talk shows abound on radio and television. Public meetings for airing grievances, identifying problems, and discussing alternative solutions vie for spots on the community calendar. With frequent practice in a variety of settings, intermediate-age students can gain competence and confidence in their ability to contribute orally in any context. Conducting mock trials, simulating public meetings, or creating persuasive ads to sway public opinion about a historical event are just a few of standard social studies strategies we decided to use.

SEEKING SCIENCE CONNECTIONS

After carefully connecting reading and language arts to our social studies curriculum, we looked at our science curriculum. We were expected to teach the moon, classification of plants and animals, earth science, flight, and movement of air. We decided to connect the moon with explorers, since it seemed to us that if we were exploring the earth, then we could look at the sky as well. We didn't intentionally integrate. We simply placed the moon activities and content adjacent to our primary study of explorers.

Flight and movement of air fit together naturally. We decided to place it at the end of immigration. Using Laurence Yep's *Dragonwings* (1975), we segued from Chinese American life to airplanes and extended it with an independent study of inventions. Earth science fit nicely with Inuit studies. Classification of plants and animals felt right with Native Americans.

Most science topics have related civic issues: Should dams be demolished to restore natural migration patterns for salmon? Can we take the U.S. Constitution into space? Is clean air worth banning private transportation in cities? Integrating civics along with science has proven very successful in my classroom. Sometimes after a science unit, kids would ask, "So what?" Not any more. My students have discovered that we not only study scientific systems and phenomena for its own worth, but also to be able to make rational decisions regarding their use or value to the community (see Figures 1–3 and 1–4).

Figure 1–3:   A favorite classroom activity: Watching our salmon grow.

Figure 1–4: Patrick, Matt, and Peter create plants for the understory of our classroom rainforest.

MAKING MATH CONNECTIONS

Jan and I decided that first year that we wouldn't attempt to integrate math. We thought that finding ways to productively connect social studies, science, language arts, reading, and art would be enough. After trying to make up story problems that had a cultural motif, we decided it took more time than it was worth.

Even today, I do not fully integrate the math curriculum into the rest of the day. Our district math curriculum is quite demanding and very specific. I start the day with math, and then the rest of day spins together in a web of content, concepts, and skills. Sometimes science or health is at the center, oftentimes, social studies. One could use math as a core integrator. We find we often use math processes, skills, and ways of thinking during other times of the day. Problem solving in the classroom is often linear, sequential, and systematic. However, the initial teaching happens outside the context of the integrated curriculum. My students *apply* mathematical content, concepts, and skills naturally in the context of what they are doing. They practice math in realistic settings based on need, whether it's using a ruler to set up a quilt square; figuring the mean, mode, and median to analyze data collected in a class survey; determining how many pages they've read on the average; or wondering about the probability of history repeating itself. But I don't turn myself or my math program upside down just to integrate. Early on, I was uncomfortable with math, doubting my ability to reorganize and not foul up the learning. So I did the easy thing, I shut math out. Not any more. While seldom the focus, math is a valued tool for thinking, organizing, and problem solving. (See Marte's Million on page 147.)

ATTACHING ART CONNECTIONS

Next we connected the arts to our curriculum reorganization. Jan and I wanted to add music, movement, voice, acting, and visual arts. Giving the music teacher a copy of our yearlong plan accomplished more than we imagined. She began to connect the music of America with our study of American history. She introduced the students to popular songs of the periods we were studying. She had the students dance the minuet and the reel. American composers and uniquely American music, like jazz, were listened to and talked about.

In our classrooms, we taught Chinese shadow-puppet theater and studied calligraphy with the help of a local artisan as we discussed Asian immigration. We borrowed artifacts from museums and individuals. Native craftspeople came into our classroom to demonstrate their expertise. Art history and art appreciation added new dimensions to classroom learning. With the help of some parents, we developed six art-appreciation classes, using a chronological exploration of American artists. Since we were teaching about intellectual perspectives, it seemed reasonable to teach visual perspective from an artist's point of view.

Providing models of art projects really helps children, especially if you don't feel particularly gifted in art. I've also learned that having students analyze the form as well as talk about what is effective, what gets in the way, what intrigues them, and what puzzles them helps create a finer product. Mostly, quality artwork of any kind by children takes time. If it truly is worth doing, then providing the time for it is essential. The integrated approach makes finding that time possible.

Students don't like junk. How many times have we seen papers handed back only to be tossed in the garbage or dropped on the ground on the way home? Some pieces, precious pieces, are carefully safeguarded and proudly displayed. One dramatic aspect of integrating art around social studies is that students have a context for their art. They aren't expected to turn on an artistic self at a specified time each week for a limited number of minutes. Instead, the art they do is an intellectual and graphic extension of their knowledge. It is another way of knowing.

MAKING REAL-WORLD CONNECTIONS

Finally, we scheduled field trips and guest speakers. We were determined to have some civic action projects in the year, still based on our social studies content. Field trips to local museums to view Northwest Coastal Native American artifacts and speakers from other countries to enhance our immigration studies were pretty predictable. But having our students work with the PTA to get a street adjacent to the school declared a dead end by the city council so that our school children would be safe grew out of a real need perceived by the students and their parents.

The social studies–integrated classroom provides many opportunities for students to formulate, define, and investigate problems that are important to them and their communities. They learn to value an informed approach and reasoned decisions based on what is important to their lives. By placing concepts and generalizations in past, present, and future contexts, students learn to analyze, interpret, and use information. They have the opportunity to examine recurring issues and dilemmas. They actively practice citizenship at developmentally appropriate levels through this kind of classroom. It might be choosing to sponsor a clothing drive for flood victims. It could be writing letters to a congresswoman about why the government should require double-hulled oil tankers. It might be spending lunch hours trying to solve the problem of inappropriate language on the playground. For learning to be realized, it has to be real.

NO SINGLE RIGHT WAY

The longer I live, the more I am convinced that there is no single right way to integrate. Like the mice in Ed Young's fable, each of us "sees" the whole based on our own experience and knowledge. The first-year teacher at any grade

HOW IT WORKED FOR ME—JESSICA,* FIRST-YEAR TEACHER

Stats and Facts: Fourth- and fifth-grade split, 8 ESL students, 4 special education students, 7 LAP students. More than half of the class speaks a different language at home: Ukrainian, Russian, Spanish, Tagalog, Vietnamese, Korean, and Chinese.

As the teacher of a split-grade classroom, I wanted my students to have new and fun experiences—ones that the fifth graders hadn't already had in fourth grade and ones that the fourth graders wouldn't be repeating when they became fifth graders. I wanted us to study about another culture, since were such a diverse group. I also needed something that would engage all the students and would help us work on communication skills. I decided to try the "Three Precious Pearls," a Chinese shadow puppet play that Tarry wrote a script for. Tarry calls it a play of hope and wisdom, revealing values from the Chinese culture. It also really helps the kids develop reading fluency. The play lends itself well to my classroom, it is easy to understand, and the parts are not intimidating—even for my ESL students.

The kids loved decorating and putting together the puppets, and became very excited about the play the first time they saw the shadows their puppets created. The creativity of my students was sparked, and they worked hard trying to figure out how to change scenes, backgrounds, and make the play flow well. Everybody mastered their lines and cues, and we decorated the room with Chinese art we designed.

On the day of our three performances, there was electricity in the air. The lights went out, the shadows came up, and the play began. There was complete silence from the audiences during the performances, only smiles when they recognized the voice of a fellow student. After the performance, the actors came out and introduced themselves, then went on to discuss the meaning and morals of the play—and help the audience make comparisons with other legends and fairy tales.

The "Three Precious Pearls" project increased my students' individual and group communication skills and gave them problem-solving experience, and an appreciation for the stories and art of other cultures. We had SO much fun; many students later said it was their favorite classroom experience. I felt proud that I had managed to find a way to successfully integrate all of my students—regardless of their ability level. This is a project that I will definitely be doing again!

* Jessica did her student teaching in my classroom where we did Chinese shadow puppets at the beginning of the year. For a complete description of this strategy, see Lindquist, *Ways That Work* (1997).

---

level will make connections much different from the teacher who has been teaching the same grade, in the same district, for several years. Goals and standards can guide the novice teacher as well as the seasoned professional, providing an initial target and a final evaluation. Knowledge of and comfort with the curriculum, as well as familiarity with the developmental level of the students, supported by collections of resources definitely impact the number and substance of connections. Probably more significant, the ways of knowing demonstrated by the kinds of activities the students have to choose from will be much richer if the teacher has had the opportunity to develop a "history" in that grade level.

There is certainly no single right way to connect content and skills across the curriculum. I'm not sure it can be mandated, but districts can have their instructional staff develop a disposition toward integration by identifying it as a worthwhile and desirable process. Districts can encourage inservice education and support by providing both time and money. But districts must remember that, overall, each teacher's teaching style, passions, and values affect the connections that will be identified and fostered in individual classrooms. Integration has to make some kind of sense to the teacher. If the connection, no matter how tenuous, does make sense, then ways will be found to reveal that integration to students, or, as I continue to discover, the students will bring it to my attention—"Hey, Mrs. L., isn't that just like . . . ?"

BEST PRACTICES IN LITERACY

When we teach social studies, we also teach literacy—reading, writing, listening, and speaking. These are the hows of learning. Social studies content provides the what of learning: what to research or learn about, what to think about, and what to do something about. Reading, writing, listening, and speaking are the tools we use for that exploration, thinking, and doing. In their 1998 book, *Best Practices: New Standards for Teaching and Learning in America's Schools, Second Edition*, Zemelman, Daniels, and Hyde list practices in reading, writing, and social studies they have observed that tend to be more successful for most kids. Notice how their research supports the integration of content into a literacy program. There isn't one of these best practices that can't be done using social studies content. Their lists guide my current practice, reminding me what works best.

Best Practices in Reading
Increase the following (Zemelman et al. 1998, 54):

Use of reading in the content fields

Reading aloud to students

Time for independent reading

Children's choice of their own reading materials

Teacher modeling and discussion of his or her own reading processes

Teaching reading as a process:

    Use strategies that activate prior knowledge

    Help students make and test predictions

    Structure help during reading

    Provide after-reading applications

Social, collaborative activities with much discussion and interaction

Grouping by interests or book choices

Silent reading followed by discussion

Teaching skills in the context of whole and meaningful literature

Writing before and after reading

Measuring success of reading program by students' reading habits, attitudes, and comprehension

Evaluation that focuses on holistic, higher-order thinking processes

Whether a student is writing a summary, working on a biography, expressing a point of view in a letter to an editor, trying a new structure for a poem, or responding personally in a journal, writing, too, can be centered on social studies content. Look over these identified practices and note how they do not conflict with using content from social studies as the foundation or the impetus to write.

Best Practices in Writing

Increase the following (Zemelman et al. 1998, 82):

Student ownership and responsibility by:

    Helping students choose their own topics and goals for improvement

    Using brief student-teacher conferences

    Teaching students to review their own progress

Class time spent on writing whole, original pieces through:

    Establishing real purposes for writing and students' involvement in the task

    Instruction in and support for all stages of the writing process

Teacher modeling writing—drafting, revising, sharing—as a fellow author and as a demonstration of the processes

Learning of grammar and mechanics in context, at the editing stage, and as items are needed

Writing for real audiences, publishing for the class and for wider communities

Making the classroom a supportive setting for shared learning, using:

Active exchange and valuing of students' ideas

Collaborative small-group work

Conferences and peer critiquing that give responsibility for improvement to authors

Writing across the curriculum as a tool for learning

Constructive and efficient evaluation that involves:

Brief, informal oral responses as students work

Thorough grading of just a few student-selected, polished pieces

Focusing on a few errors at a time

Cumulative view of growth and self-evaluation

Encouragement of risk-taking and honest expression

Consider how these best practices in literacy can be introduced, practiced, and perfected using social studies content. Practical? Absolutely! Possible? You bet! Preferable? Why not? I've yet to see any research that points to kids learning less through the deliberate integration of content and skills. I have seen research that emphasizes how the brain loves patterns, seeks connections, looks for networks, and makes meaning across the curriculum (Jensen 1998; Caine and Caine 1994).

Let's close this discussion with a look at best practices in social studies. Keep in mind while reading this book that best practices form the backbone of integrated teaching and holistic learning. Put a sticky note or a bookmark right here to be able to thumb back easily and check how the strategies suggested throughout this book do model best practices.

Best Practices in Social Studies

Increase the following (Zemelman et al. 1998, 139–55):

Richer content in the elementary grades, building on the prior knowledge children bring to social studies topics

Integration of social studies with other areas of the curriculum

Emphasis on activities that engage students in inquiry and problem solving about significant human issues

Participation in interactive and cooperative classroom study processes that bring together students of all ability levels

Regular opportunities to investigate topics in depth

Opportunities for students to exercise choice and responsibility by choosing their own topics for inquiry

Involve students in both independent learning and cooperative learning

Involve students in reading, writing, observing, discussing, and debating

Explore a full variety of the cultures found in America

Use of evaluation that involves further learning and that promotes responsible citizenship and open expression of ideas

REFLECTIONS

That was our first year. That was the first level of integration, some of the time. We connected our curriculum, sort of. It didn't go perfectly. Our focus was more on content than it was on the child. We worried more about what we were going to teach than whom we were teaching. We didn't always stick to the time lines we had set up. We didn't provide the time we had promised we would for art projects. Science integration was minimal.

But, teaching felt good. All the children learned. Gone were the bits of skills and kibbles of concepts. There was a hopefulness and positiveness that permeated our relationships with others in the class. It seemed like discipline was easier.

Every year since, integration in my classroom has become more together, stronger, and more exciting. Now I know that integration can never be complete. For me, it is an ever-evolving, intensely personal balancing act. It is balancing content with process, the group with the individual, personal growth with academics, curriculum with community demands, and teacher fulfillment with state standards. Integration makes my classroom more challenging and more fun every year as I try to bring learning to life through curriculum connected to each child.

Over the years, the intermediate curriculum has changed. We've embraced technology and participate in worldwide computer networks. Video cameras have opened up new ways of research, new ways to approach drama. Math has become easier to connect naturally as we've moved from a computation-based program to a conceptual orientation. All in all, centering the day on social studies themes, concepts, and knowledge has weathered well. It is still the core of the day—the essential integrator. I'm still excited about teaching and being with children as they learn, grow, and explore. I'm learning to trust myself more and to leave the teacher's manuals on the shelf; they have become resources rather than daily lesson planners.

Jan moved to another part of the state after our first couple of years and I still miss her. Our team planning and collegial relationship helped us both grow. We talked about what worked and what didn't. We brainstormed, often piggybacking on each other's ideas to create better ways to get where we wanted to go. I think what we shared was special, and I know I wouldn't be this far along in my quest for integrated learning without her. I really like what has happened to my students and to me. They come to school each day eager and ready to learn—and so do I. They don't whine or complain about the work we do—and neither do I. They ask questions, treat each other kindly, and care about the world—I do too!

Chapter Two

SETTING UP FOR SUCCESS

TEACHER–STUDENT INTERACTION IS THE HEART
OF EDUCATION,

—NCSS's "Vision"

PROMOTING COMMON GOOD

I am more convinced than ever that social studies is what schooling is truly about. While knowing facts and figures, being able to spell, read, write, and do arithmetic are incredibly important, there are greater goals for education. One is the ability to work well with others. Another is to make thoughtful, reasoned decisions. A third is to be a good neighbor. Yet another is to be a good listener, to be able to identify bias and discern more than one point of view. When community members meet today to identify the learner outcomes they want for the children in their communities, they use words and phrases like *capable, a good communicator, productive,* and *citizen in a global community.* The concept that the "common good" is the responsibility of each student often underlies these descriptions.

This emphasis on the outcome of education is reinforced by the definition of social studies, as stated by the National Council for the Social Studies (1993, 213):

> Social studies is the integrated study of the social sciences and the humanities to promote civic competence. Within the school program, social studies provides coordinated, systematic study drawing upon such disciplines as anthropology, archaeology, geography, history, law, philosophy, political science, psychology, religion, and sociology, as well as appropriate content from the humanities, mathematics, and natural sciences. The primary purpose of social studies is to help

45

young people develop the ability to make informed and reasoned decisions for the public good as citizens of a culturally diverse, democratic society in an interdependent world

LEARNING SOCIAL STUDIES ALL DAY LONG

I am equally convinced that social studies happens all day long. It begins with the morning greetings and continues through the remainder of the day, however it's structured. Issues of governance are crucial to the school day. I suspect more is learned about the real meaning of democracy, freedom, and justice in the first three days of school, before the social studies textbook is even opened, than is taught the rest of the year.

The ways in which the teacher and the class organize the room, set up protocols, and manage the classroom are vital pieces of learning that many teachers overlook. Human organization is crucial to developing civic competence. One teacher may arrange the desks in straight rows and put a name on each desk before the first day of school. Another may follow the suggestion made by Priscilla Lynch (1992):

> Leave all the supplies, materials, and books stacked in the room. Don't hang up one piece of commercial poster or border. In fact, don't hang anything. When the kids come in and look like they've obviously come to the wrong room, welcome them by saying, "Hi, I'm glad you're here. We've got some decisions to make!"

Most of us fall somewhere in between these two approaches. I let my students choose where they want to sit. Of course, the early birds get the choice seats and the latecomers are stuck with what's left. I assure my kids that we will change seats often. Sometimes we'll be changing because the work we will be doing lends itself to a different configuration. Sometimes we'll change because behavior needs some shaping up.

Naming the Classroom

Several years ago our school enrollment was so high that one class had to be moved from the building into a portable. No one was eager to leave the building, but we generally agreed an older class would be more appropriate because there would be no lavatory, no sink, no water. The portable classroom was placed in a corner of the play field, surrounded by a sea of unattractive blacktop. Guess who ended up there? It was pretty dismal at first, but the move became a lesson in making lemonade when you get lemons! We painted the door bright golden yellow and instead of being known as P-1, we named our classroom Paradise Island! It became a place where fantastic and wonderful things could happen, where the students would love learning, and they would all succeed beyond their dreams. Ever since that year, my classrooms have had a name, rather than a number. A decade later, I realize we set up a self-filling prophecy—naming our room created an overarching goal we tried to meet throughout the year.

Planning Ahead

One of the things that makes teaching challenging and rewarding is the problem solving we do daily to make sure the class runs smoothly. Envision each day before it begins and anticipate where problems might occur. Most often, management issues arise when kids are at the beginning of a period or project or at the end. At the beginning of a project, make sure materials are immediately available, directions are clear, models are provided, and appropriate behavior is agreed on. At the end of a project, make sure those who finish early have something worthwhile and engaging to do, such as creating a cover, finding graphics or photos on the Internet, or constructing a class bulletin board. This is a perfect time to remind the class about their independent reading requirements.

Determining Classroom Rules

Organizational decisions are deeply rooted social studies activities. We've moved past that time when all the rules were in the teacher's head and students had to guess what they were through trial and error. Since the behaviorist movement, we've learned to clearly state and post rules for expected behavior in the classroom. Now we are moving on to letting students determine their own rules.

I often start out in September by asking the class to brainstorm all the things we could do to make our classroom a terrible place, a place where no one would want to come, a place where we could guarantee no learning would occur. As we list the surefire ways to destroy a classroom, each suggestion more outrageous than the last, we begin to build a community. Examples of some of the suggestions my kids have made include: Throw things. Pinch people. Don't do any work. Give wedgies. Say mean things. Don't listen.

Eventually, when we have exhausted our efforts, most sincere and many hilarious, I ask the class to picture a room like the one we've just described. I

Figure 2–1:   Jon and Aaron find working and sharing together promotes peace and enriches learning.

ask them, "What would you know if you stayed in a classroom like that one all year? What would you be able to do? How would you feel?" After that discussion, it doesn't take long to reverse the list, identifying what needs to happen to make our classroom a place of joy where all students want to be and where all students can learn (see Figure 2–1).

Planning for Peace

The students and I create an action plan for producing a peaceful classroom. This usually occurs the second week of school. This plan becomes our reference for classroom behavior, our "protocol." We have a discussion. We refer back to the day when we listed all the things we could do to hinder learning. I read a picture book to the kids; two I particularly like are Katherine Scholes' *Peace Begins with You* (1989) and Anais Vaugelade's *The War* (2001). We talk about how some people like to work in a classroom that is noisy or has music playing and others need a quiet place. Discussion continues. It's not a quick process, but a vital one. The energy and time expended reaps all kinds of benefits later in the year in terms of classroom management. When we complete the action plan, each child signs it and so do I. I send a copy home because

I want parents to understand what we value in our classroom. When misbehavior does occur, I then have a place to begin discussing my concern: "You recall the action plan for peace the class created in September? I'm very concerned about Nancy because she doesn't seem to be able to help the class reach this goal. Specific things about Nancy's behavior that have prompted my concern are . . . ."

To turn these kinds of decisions over to students requires confidence and trust on the part of the teacher. I heard Horace Smith, formerly with the Seattle Public Schools, talk about this one day in a teacher-training session in Renton, Washington. He pointed out how teachers with low self-esteem develop their classroom organization differently from teachers who have high self-esteem. I found his insights to be very helpful as a quick check of my own behavior.

Smith says teachers with low self-esteem are likely to be more critical of students. They complain more frequently about disciplinary problems and lack of student motivation. You'll hear them using terms such as *obedience, laying down the law*, and *demanding respect*. They are the ones who often campaign for tougher school policies and more stringent punishments. They find it difficult to form friendly relationships with students for fear their authority will be undermined. These teachers tend to focus on student limitations rather than potential.

On the other hand, teachers with high self-esteem treat every child with unconditional regard. They encourage students to test their abilities and to set personal goals for themselves. They accept their students. These teachers help students develop problem-solving strategies. They build a sense of trust in their students by first modeling trust. Teachers with high self-esteem help students develop an internal locus of control, basing classroom control on understanding, joint cooperation, and working problems through.

Distinguishing between these two kinds of teachers significantly altered my teaching behavior. I always perceived myself as a teacher with high self-esteem. Yet, as I analyzed my behavior, I discovered that I did not treat all children with unconditional regard. Sometimes I blamed children for my lack of success. I occasionally thought: "What's wrong with that kid? Why doesn't she try harder? Why doesn't he work more carefully? Why don't they act more pleasantly and do what I want them to do?" I was trying to make students fit my convenience. I was not accepting them as they were. It seems so self-centered now, and it was.

Reflecting on these observations snapped me from a no-win position. The simple words "unconditional regard for every child" freed me from the bondage of perceiving children as I wished them to be rather than as they are. I no longer get angry or aggravated with my students. My patience has increased tenfold. I enjoy every single day. I can laugh at my mistakes and help my students laugh at theirs. My classroom is no longer a contest of wills, it is a collaboration of willingness.

Connecting Literacy and Civics

How is it that kids get all the way to third, fourth, fifth grade and beyond and still don't know how to work in a group? This is not new stuff. Cooperative groups have been around for a long time. Right? While the process may have been around, certain kids just don't get it. They miss the cues. I don't know why they do—getting along in a group is a basic civics skill. I have started directly teaching my whole class how to be good group members. One of the skills I teach is Active Listening; another is Encouragement. Both of these contribute to a more positive classroom community. Using Bellanca and Fogarty's format, I elicit from the kids what these behaviors sound like and look like (1991, 48):

ACTIVE LISTENING

Sounds like: Uh huh, I see, clarifying questions, silence, paraphrasing.

Looks like: Eyes alert and focused on talker, leaning forward or toward the speaker, head nods at right time, taking notes.

ENCOURAGEMENT

Sounds like: Keep at it. Atta girl. Atta boy. Way to go. Nice try. Great idea. Keep trying.

Looks like: thumbs up, pat on back, high five, smile, head nodding, applause.

Using the goldfish-bowl technique (a small group rehearses and then role-plays or demonstrates to the rest of the class members who are sitting around the demonstrators, as if they were watching fish swim in a goldfish bowl), I have the class list the behaviors they observed and then have them practice with a partner or in a threesome. We don't do both behaviors on one day, sometimes not even in one week. From this exercise, we move to the peaceful classroom unit where the kids use the five senses to move the abstract concept of peace to something more literal: "What does peace sound like? What does it feel like? What does it look like? What does peace smell like? What does it taste like?" Each of these questions generates a wide range of responses from kids. After listing the responses on chart paper, I pass out standard copy paper and have the kids make their first of many books in my classroom. I call this kinesthetic organizer the step book (see Figure 2–2).

Each step becomes one of the five senses. Each starts with the same stem: peace looks like . . . , peace sounds like . . . , and so on. The kids fill in the stem and then draw a picture of their sentence inside each step. What they end up with is something like poetry—Peace looks like a field of flowers. Peace smells like peanut butter cookies. Peace tastes like chocolate. Peace feels like warm sunshine. Peace sounds like a beautiful waterfall. What they also end up with is a book of similes, a literary device often introduced to young readers. This book becomes a student-made reference for the rest of the year. Intermediate and middle school students need to include similes and metaphors in their writing. During revision or prior to writing, I often say, "Please remember to include at least one metaphor or simile in your writing." When a kid looks quizzically at me and murmurs, "Huh?" I am able to provide a meaningful cue: "Remember when you wrote your peace book at the beginning of the year? What did you say peace smelled like? What did it taste like? Do you remember what that structure was called? Yes, a simile. Now, can you create a simile that reveals how you feel about slavery?" (see page 268 in the Appendix, The Peaceful Classroom Unit).

SHARING WISDOM AND HOPE

I read stories to the children. "Stories of wisdom and hope," my friend Barbara Inman calls them. These are stories that highlight universal truths like honesty, caring, and sharing, that reinforce common bonds, ones that promote prosocial behavior or resolve persistent dilemmas in positive ways. These stories make us dream, affirming our creativity and reminding us how worthwhile pursuing the impossible is. Examples include Chinese myths, Native American legends, African tales, Japanese folklore, familiar fairy tales with a feminist twist, or biographies of the famous and the not-so-famous—all of which have to do with valuing, maintaining perspective, and making choices. Using traditional cultural stories, especially those retold by authors indigenous to the culture, keeps me from reinforcing old stereotypes or inventing new ones as the students and I look for universal connections. Understanding and respecting different points of view is a valued social studies skill.

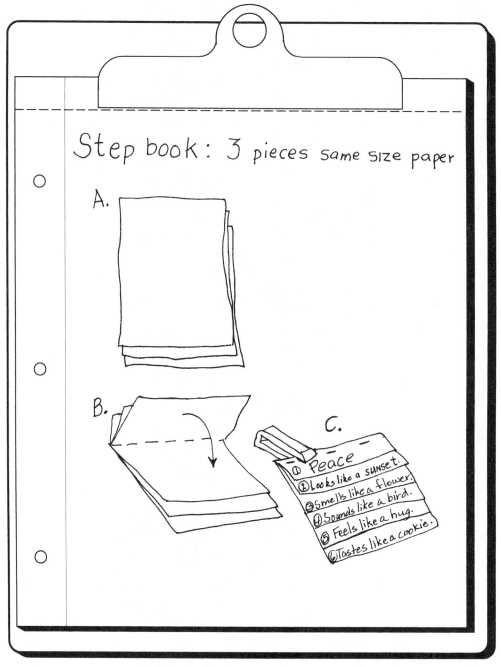

Step book: 3 pieces same size paper

A.

B.

C.

① Peace
② Looks like a sunset.
③ Smells like a flower.
④ Smells like a bird.
⑤ Sounds like a bird.
④ Feels like a hug.
⑥ Tastes like a cookie.

Figure 2–2:   How to Make a Step book © 2002 by Tarry Lindquist from *Seeing the Whole Through Social Studies, Second Edition*. Portsmouth, NH: Heinemann.

Sometimes we discuss the story, sometimes we don't. When we do, it is to share feelings and to discover what we would have done in that situation. When we don't, it's because of something I learned from a Native American story-teller. Northwest Coastal storytellers never analyze their stories with their listeners. They feel that every person who hears the story will take away with them what he or she was ready to hear. Sounds pretty obvious, doesn't it? I, however, talk everything to death. But maybe, just maybe, people hear what they hear because of where they are at the time. Maybe when they hear the story again, they'll hear something different; and maybe what they hear is exactly right for them at that time.

KEEP PLANNING AHEAD

When making unit plans for a multiday topic, try starting with where you want to end up. What is it you want the students to know, do, and feel? Imagine the last day of the unit. What is the big "ta-da"? How do the kids know they are "done"? Will you have a performance, a presentation, or a personal piece of writing? What do the kids have to know, do, and feel to reach this goal? By working backward on a daily basis, you can plan where you need to instruct or the kids need to work. You can anticipate when certain materials need to be available or when related experiences need to occur.

When you finish your backward planning, think about the first day of the unit and come up with the "big idea" that the kids will experience. What will you do that will engage the students' attention? How will you "hook" them? Find a book, read a poem, share a personal experience, show a piece of artwork, turn on music, take a walk, invite in a guest, go on a field trip, ask a question, bring in a prop, use a map, or perform an experiment. Big ideas are often difficult for new teachers to identify. Here are some I've used over the years:

Exploration	Change	Choices	Patterns	Diversity
Civilization	Contact	Justice	Connections	Common good
Leadership	Liberty	Governance	Power	Truth

Some teachers like to use phrases or titles for their big ideas:

My Country, Right or Wrong
Custodians of the Earth
Spaceship Earth

Other teachers like to frame their big idea as a question:

> How does citizenship vary among cultures?
> Is history written by the winners?
> Does environment shape culture?

Some teachers feel a way to test for a big idea is to determine whether the kids intuitively understand it. If so, then the big idea immediately becomes a useful organizer that promotes integration. Remember, the brain loves patterns and seeks known networks. Other teachers feel a powerful big idea is the one the kids end up with at the completion of a unit or when the year is drawing to a close. Either way, the big idea does act as an organizer for us, the teachers. It helps us decide which activities and resources will move us toward the conceptual underpinnings of the unit and which ones just leave us treading water or gasping for air. Some teachers choose one big idea that shapes the whole year. Others think it is more effective to give students experience with more than one.

Whether new to teaching or new to a grade level, I think it is unrealistic to expect to integrate everything that first year. Integration takes years. Start with a goal of putting together one integrated unit a year. Maybe it'll be a social studies unit. Perhaps a science or math or health focus. But one a year is a reasonable goal.

When the unit plan is complete, turn to the district, state, or national standards—whichever your school uses—and plug in those standards that your planning meets. You'll be surprised at how many of the standards your plan will meet or exceed. If you feel driven, tweak a couple of the days by altering the project so that you can meet the standards that you have yet to attain. This backward planning has always worked for me.

MEDIATING IN THE CLASSROOM

One thing for sure in fifth grade, there will be differences of opinion. We use mediation when the difference can't be easily addressed. In my classroom, early the first week of school we begin identifying problems that might need mediation. I ask the students to think back to problems they had that bothered them at school the year before. After we've listed four or five of these on the board, the students get into groups to role-play the STAKE steps our school adopted three years ago to help students solve their own problems (see Figure 2–3). The STAKE steps are the result of six months of meetings with fourth

Figure 2–3: Lakeridge students create a GEM (goodwill, equity, mediation) of a little book to teach mediation skills.

and fifth graders to devise a mediation strategy for all the children in our school. The steps are: stop, talk softly, ask key questions, keep an open mind, and examine alternatives.

I begin by putting four or five students together and giving them a scenario of a typical playground problem, like arguing over a kick-ball call or cutting someone out during a game. One student is identified as the mediator. A couple of students adopt one point of view, and the others take opposing perspectives. In front of the whole class, we begin the role-play. I coach. As the problem unfolds, the mediator steps in. The conversation goes something like this:

Mediator: Hi, is there a problem?

Group: Yes.

Mediator: Would you like me to help you solve it?

Group: Sure.

Mediator: My name is Jerry. What's yours? *(Introductions all around if the students don't know each other.)* Let's start with John. John, what do you think the problem is? *(Each child shares his or her point of view.)* Let's see if we can brainstorm some solutions. Who has an idea about how we might solve this? *(The involved students offer suggestions.)* Which one can you all accept? *(The group reaches a consensus.)*

My quiet coaching from the side seems to help the students prepare for successful problem solving. Working on the principle that those involved in the problem need to generate a solution removes authority (teacher, principal, whoever is bigger or tougher) from the matrix. Students need to solve problems in a peaceful way themselves.

We also spend a lot of time talking about this quotation: "Mediation begins with Me." We explore its meaning and whose responsibility it is to solve problems. We make posters of children solving problems and create more role-plays to remind ourselves when problems arise.

When the mediation process is firmly set for each student, I remove myself from playground squabbles, tattling, and issues of fairness. When I need to, I simply say, "Would you like me to get you a mediator?" Mediation makes classroom management easier.

In our school, the upper-grade students teach the lower grades the STAKE steps. Mediation is the option of choice for problem solving. The process of mediation is accessible to all the students in our K through 5 school because we believe all students, not just a chosen few, need to master mediation skills. Therefore, fourth and fifth graders become trainers for the primary grades. Once a year they go into every classroom in the school and present a program that includes role-playing, a panel discussion, and questions from the class. Two times a month primary children are invited to have lunch with their intermediate-grade partners to discuss playground problems and mediation strategies and to play games that teach cooperation and compromise.

TURNING DOWN THE HEAT

One of the best pieces of advice I ever got was in the form of a classroom management metaphor: "When the cookies in the oven are burning, turn down the heat." This concept, simple to understand but surprisingly easy to ignore, has made my classroom a more peaceful place. Every time I notice that I feel like yelling at the kids, or wringing my hands and pleading with them, I find I've inadvertently turned up the heat. I have (1) required too much (2) in too little time and/or (3) given too few or too many directions (4) with too little background or (5) insufficient resources. Obviously, I need to "turn down the heat" by changing or reshaping the activity.

Students misbehave when they feel threatened or powerless. Deciding on due dates and deadlines as a class reduces threat. Asking the kids if they need more time or a plan for additional study periods turns down the heat. Constructing a classroom where the kids are self-actualized empowers students. I don't think kids should have to ask me if they can go to the restroom, use art supplies, turn on the computer, or talk quietly to a neighbor. Our classroom structure, created as a community early in the year, should set these and other protocols for learning.

Don't blame the whole class for the misbehavior of the few. Making the whole class put their heads down or miss a recess may backfire. Instead, I've learned to talk privately and independently with the student or students who lose control. I enlist their aid to rein in behavior that interferes with learning. Without threats, we create a plan that includes a signal when a student is losing control, using gradual steps and increasing the severity of consequences if needed. Work at keeping responses to misbehavior more professional than personal. When I find myself saying the same kid's name ten or more times a day, I stop to analyze what is going on. Which of my buttons is this cookie pushing? Am I turning up the heat?

DECIDING ON JOBS

On one of the first days of school, we brainstorm the jobs that will need to be done each week. These usually include lunch monitors, attendance taker, messenger, and classroom librarian. We choose the jobs by a lottery system: all the students' names are placed on cards and put in an old pencil box. Every Monday morning, we draw out cards until all the classroom jobs are filled. I note on each card what jobs each student has done so no one repeats a job until everyone has had a turn. This lottery system works well in my classroom for all kinds of choosing. The children think it's fair.

Acting Appropriately

During the first week of school, the principal, the school counselor, and other people come to our classroom to explain their roles and how they want to assist the students during the year. I think these visits set the tone for how students behave when speakers come into the classroom or when we go to assemblies, so I teach the kids the four A's right away. I learned these from Julie Gustafson, a children's drama teacher. They are:

Attend	Listen to the presenter. Give your complete attention.
Allow	Let the presenter share information.
Appreciate	Acknowledge the talent, skill, information, risk, or time that the presenter is giving to you. It takes time to prepare. It's a risk to stand up in front of people to share anything.
Applaud	Express your appreciation through applause.

Over the past few years, I've noticed that many of my students have forgotten how to clap. They hoot, whistle, stamp their feet, and wave their fists or they do nothing. The four A's reintroduces applause as an acceptable way to express appreciation.

The four A's are also a guide to proper behavior when peers are presenting in the classroom, which happens often. Valuing and supporting a peer's efforts is important in building everyone's confidence. This, too, is a social studies activity. Helping students become self-disciplined and sensitive to others is important in becoming a good neighbor and a good citizen.

INTRODUCING ME

We also make a book the first week of school. Called *All About Me*, it is based on a form adapted from a Seattle Public Schools multicultural curriculum kit (see Figure 2–4). The students fill in the blanks in pencil the first day of school. When they finish, they bring their work to me. While the student reads her responses out loud, I am reading along silently. As we come to misspelled words or other errors, I stop the child. We fix the errors together, erasing the incorrect response and penciling in the correct one. The child returns to her seat with a corrected copy, which she will now go over in a black fine felt-tip pen. This is not the writing process—this is quick publishing. If I had the kids write a new copy, I can guarantee you that they would make new mistakes! Not only do I immediately have something to talk personally about with every child, but shoulder-to-shoulder editing guarantees the activity will be successful for everyone. I begin collecting information about prior experiences from their writings, and I find out how the students present themselves on paper.

By Friday of the first week, I have collated the children's papers and we celebrate the publishing of our first book. Out comes the lottery box. The student who "wins" gets to take the book home for the weekend. On Monday afternoon, we'll have a second drawing. That student gets *All About Me* for that night. Tuesday, we draw again. On it goes, until every child in the class has had the book at least one night. Every family has had an opportunity to see who else is in their children's classroom. This strategy helps build a sense of community, both within the classroom and in the homes of the students. (See page 218 in the Appendix for a blank prototype of the form.)

IDENTIFYING YEARLONG THEMES

My overarching theme for the year is usually some variation of unity and diversity. This broadly stated theme is particularly appropriate because fifth graders and the fifth-grade curriculum are so diverse. Building a community of learners with a unity of purpose is paramount to having a successful year. Getting ready for middle school means fostering greater appreciation for differences and developing greater competence in working with others. Our fifth-grade social studies curriculum exemplifies unity and diversity through the study of U.S. history.

M E

NAME: _Peter_

HOME ADDRESS: _4836 84th Ave SE_

BIRTHDATE/AGE: _Oct 11 1982   10 yrs of age_

HOBBIES: _Stamps   Sports cards_

FAVORITE SPORT: _Football_

FAVORITE TV PROGRAM: _Rescue 911_

FAVORITE FOODS: _Mac + cheese_

FAVORITE BEVERAGE: _Coke   Dr Pepper_

FAVORITE COLORS: _Orange_

FAVORITE SUBJECT: _Math_

FAVORITE SAYING: _What goes around comes around_

FAVORITE BOOK: _Hatchet by Gary Paulsen_

FAVORITE PLACE TO VISIT: _Library_

SOMETHING I'M PROUD I'VE DONE: _Finish 5th in the midlakes division for the 50 breaststroke_

FUTURE OCCUPATION: _Doctor_

Figure 2–4: *All About Me* is one of the first activities we do to build a classroom community.

I like yearlong themes. They act as a central organizer for the choices I make. However, it is not a particularly overt theme for me. There is no major bulletin board dedicated to it, nor do I follow it rigidly. Instead, it is an "internal organizer." I share the theme with the class but I don't belabor it.

Picture books are especially helpful in setting up an awareness of and an appreciation for diversity. We become "biphrasal" rather than bilingual, as students bring in greetings from other languages. We write each greeting on a large card and display it in the room. We use the phrases as we greet each other during the day. We learn a variety of sign language techniques the first two weeks of school. These are small activities, almost incidental, but ones in which awareness and appreciation for diversity are fostered, laying out the foundation for teaching tolerance and erasing prejudice. These are examples of social studies happening all day in the classroom.

KEEPING THE ROUTINE FLEXIBLE

Sounds like an oxymoron, doesn't it? That's teaching sometimes. We need to be flexible, so even when we have created the perfect unit plan, we need to be ready to adapt, to change, to rethink. Routine, as I mentioned earlier, is a way to build safety into the school day. Kids like to know what is going to happen during the day, and when it will occur. I start each day with a "preview of coming attractions." This overview of the day (sometimes the week or the month or the trimester) helps the kids get a sense of the rhythm of our work and the cadence of what we want to accomplish.

In a self-contained classroom, make a deal with your class so those linear kids understand you may not adhere strictly to the schedule. Introduce the notion of "about" time: "About ten o'clock we'll move from math to reading." Writing the daily schedule on the board, including assignments that are due or projects that are ongoing, provides a positive organizational model.

CONSTRUCTING THE BRAIN-COMPATIBLE CLASSROOM

Students should go home each night with a positive attitude. When the kids are happy, the parents are happy. When positive school talk is happening at home, positive behaviors happen at school. It is the beginning of a cycle of success that pays big dividends later in the year. Setting up the "brain-compatible classroom" (Kovalik and Olson 1993) right from the first day, adding humor, changing the pace of activities, and insisting that an "action plan for peace" be followed are ways that work with my students. Kovalik identifies eight components in the brain-compatible classroom, which I discuss next in the context of my classroom.

Absence of Threat

Eric Jensen, in his book *Teaching with the Brain in Mind*, notes: "Threats activate defense systems and behaviors that are great for survival but lousy for learning" (1998, 57). Threats have long been used by teachers to control behavior. Threats can be as mild as not giving enough time to finish an assignment to as major as telling a student you are going to call his or her parents. Put-downs, bullying, and name calling from other students are threats. When the brain feels threatened, it can't learn.

I encourage my students to make at least one mistake a day during the first month of school. Some children get so uptight at the beginning of the year that they dig themselves a hole (of defeat, of self-criticism, of negativity, of poor work habits) and have a hard time coming out of it. When mistakes are made on purpose, they lose their power to embarrass or belittle. The children loosen up and they aren't so afraid.

Sometimes we take a "mistake break" at the end of the day, just so everyone has an opportunity to make one. The children and I talk about making mistakes. Risk-taking means mistake making. We talk about the kinds of risks we can take in the classroom and the kinds of things we can learn from mistakes. We identify how we can behave when we make mistakes and how we can support a peer who is mistaken. We begin to practice the art of informing people when they are wrong. Making mistakes becomes an expected part of learning and growing in our classroom.

Meaningful Content

The first day of school I try to teach my students at least one thing they've never known before that will last a lifetime. I use an international sign language the children can use in the classroom, when they travel or when they meet people who don't speak English. Connecting learning to the students' prior knowledge and experience and projecting it into the future makes it meaningful.

Choices

Selecting what to read, determining how our room is organized, and deciding how to demonstrate competency are some of the choices my students have during the first month of school. They determine, for instance, how many in-dependent reading books should be required and how the independent reading grade will be determined.

Adequate Time

I find this component much easier to accommodate because of our integrated curriculum. I don't have to stop the kids midstream in an activity just because it's time for social studies, or science, or art. Instead we can take the time for in-depth work using blocks of time at our discretion.

Timing Is Everything

Timing in teaching is critical. Some of the best lessons I've ever seen have imploded because too much or not enough time were given. Like good theater, it is better to leave the kids wanting more than it is to tell them more than they ever wanted to know. Teaching is much more fun if you are sensitive to the timing of activities. How many times has chaos erupted in a classroom due to lack of timing? More than once. Familiar senarios include not giving enough time for getting kids ready for the bus at the end of the day or to the lunch-room or library on time. Or giving too much time for an activity and watching the room slowly disintegrate as the kids hunt for something, anything to do, even if it means getting into trouble. If a planned lesson or activity isn't work-ing, stop—move on to something else. Maybe read to kids from a favorite read-aloud or take an extra recess. Don't blame the kids or get mad. Analyze what was or was not going on, and either fix it or drop it. Try it again later from another entry point, a different intelligence.

Enriched Environment

Reading stories aloud, finding patterns, examining artifacts, filling the room with books, and providing visual interest through student-made murals are pieces of an enriched environment. Speakers from the community, videos that fit and extend the curriculum, field trips outside the classroom, and movement within it are also part of enriching the environment.

Collaboration

Kovalik defines collaboration as students teaching each other and providing a sounding board for each other. In my classroom early in the year, students work together to achieve common goals, solving problems that matter. For example, my students create a mural of a Northwest forest as it was before the Europeans

Figure 2–5: An 1840s Northwest forest was created in our classroom by the Class of 2001.

arrived. The project is integrated with our study of Northwest Coastal Native Americans and the classification of plants and animals. The kids identify animals that would have been plentiful in the Northwest woods prior to 1840. They each research one animal and share the findings. In groups, they determine what plants would be indigenous. Working collaboratively, the students design and create a forest on our classroom wall (see Figure 2–5). The children each contribute a three-dimensional model of the animal they researched. Each animal is appropriately placed in the mural, creating a scene that becomes "Our Northwest Woods."

Immediate Feedback

I quit correcting most daily work years ago. When the assignment is short, I figure students should correct their work themselves. For example, in spelling, the single biggest factor in increased performance is self-correction. If kids don't "see" their mistakes, they seldom quit making them (see page 258 in the Appendix for spelling strategies). Most of the work in my room is long-term, comprehensive, and often project-oriented. To help students succeed, we spend time talking about what an outstanding product looks like. We create rubrics based on models that former students have produced. As students progress with projects, I frequently hold up partially completed work and ask: "What is particularly effective about this paper? What makes this look or sound so good?" Additionally, when kids are having trouble getting going, I encourage them to take a "walkabout" the room to look at what other kids are doing, not to copy others' ideas but to springboard from.

Mastery

Most of the time, I ask students to assess themselves. Often we develop rubrics before beginning the assignment. I want students to be able to identify particularly effective pieces of their work and to verbalize what they can do to improve. We use the notion of "personal best" in my classroom to get away from competitiveness.

Sometimes the students really want me to "grade" their work. They are interested in my opinion. I often choose to use symbols rather than numbers or letters. A plus (+) means I think the work is outstanding. A check-plus (✓+) means the work is quite wonderful but there are some inconsistencies. A check (✓) means I can live with it if the student can. A minus (−) means the student is volunteering to do the assignment over. I prefer to use a rubric or a continuum to indicate where they are in the process (beginning, developing, capable, strong, exceptional). Frequently, I write a note to each student, relating improvements in a paper or drawing to similar work in previous assignments.

Humor

Although Kovalik doesn't list this as a component of a brain-compatible classroom, I think humor and fun ought to be added. No one should learn without laughter.

CREATING A SUCCESSFUL SCHOOL YEAR

One of the things that took me a long time to learn is that there are certain things we can do at the beginning of a new school year to make the year successful and the classroom a positive place for both the students and the teacher. It is important to take time to develop a classroom community. The singularly most important thing that should happen the first week of school is to get the kids to like the classroom and the teacher. For most kids, and their parents, a new school year is like New Year's Day. It is time for starting over, for beginnings, for wiping the slate clean. Most kids come to school with the belief that

TARRY'S TEACHING TIPS: TEACHING THE ART PART

When students are asked to do drawing activities, many are reluctant because they feel artistically inadequate. Here are some techniques that will make every student's artwork look good:

- ◆ Make a frame for every drawing. This can be a simple black line, an elegant design, or a repetitive cultural motif.
- ◆ Color in everything.
- ◆ The only things that can be white are those things that are white (e.g., clouds, snowmen, salt).
- ◆ Outline everything with a darker color or with a black fine felt-tip pen.
- ◆ Write in pencil first, then go over edited writing in black fine felt-tip pen.

Using these simple rules makes artwork look better; and one more piece of advice, keep a sample of everything your kids do in the classroom. That way, next time you decide to do the activity again, you have a model to show other kids. It doesn't have to be the best one, just use it to set the standard for this assignment. Ask the kids, "What makes this effective (or attractive, or interesting, or acceptable)?" List the kids' comments. Then ask, "What could be done to make it more effective—attractive—interesting—acceptable?" The quality will go up. Your students will meet and/or exceed the model.

this year is going to be better. So do most teachers! Most parents have their fingers crossed that whatever went wrong last year will magically disappear and their children will have a successful and happy school year.

One of the ways teachers can foster that attitude is to make the first week of school a place where kids want to be. Little things, such as changing the activities several times during the day, providing lots of time for interaction, and letting them get acquainted, pay big dividends. Making crossword puzzles using everyone's name in the class, or playing Who Bingo (see page 217), helps the shy or new child gain confidence and feel comfortable in the classroom. Teaching the kids about the multiple intelligences or working in pairs to find out how much every student's name is worth (see Spelling Activities That Involve and Examine on page 258) creates an atmosphere in which kids can relax and learn. Imagine having an opportunity to learn to spell everyone's name in a new class . . . for fun! Planning for frequent breaks with stretches, movement to music, or chanting helps bring joy and energy to the classroom.

Another thing I do the first week is "take temperatures." At the close of each day, the students fill out cards with the following information:

One thing I did today:
One thing I learned today:
One thing I felt today:
One thing I'd change:

This information helps me to be sensitive to special needs and to see how the students are reacting to what we are doing to build community, self-esteem, and competence. Here are some sample responses:

> One thing I learned was the four A's. I started my storyboard and did some math. I felt good because people were nice to me. Tomorrow I hope we do an art thing and do another game.

> I learned about the International Communication System. I started my storyboard and practiced some math. I felt happy because I'm starting to understand this school better.

> Tomorrow I hope we have P.E. I learned the six elements of a story. I played kick ball at recess and started my storyboard. I felt sad because the day went by so quickly. Tomorrow I hope we play another game.

> I learned a lot, I mean "A LOT" about sign language. It's really cool. I made 3 new friends! If every day was like this I wouldn't even want summer to come. I would like to read more tomorrow.

ESTABLISHING A POSITIVE PLACE FOR LEARNING

Finally, try this. It's an activity to start during the first couple weeks of school, just before your kids go home each day. After taking the kids' "temperature" on cards, alternate that activity with verbal testimonials—a statement from each child responding to the question: "What's one thing you did or learned today that you enjoyed?" Go around the room and get a statement from each child. After a few days, limit the number of times students can repeat what someone else has said. Some days, as soon as children volunteer their statements, they get to put up their chair and leave. Some days I stand by the door and the kids line up as they make their statements. As they walk through the door, they give me a high five, a handshake, or a pinky tug. (Touching is important in this profession. The right kind of touching is more important. I let the kids initiate the hand gesture of their choice and I respond to their cues.)

What this process does is give the kids a knapsack full of answers for the question they'll hear when they get home, "What did you do in school today?"

67

Instead of the standard answer, "Nothing," they are primed to respond with their own positive response practiced at school or one of their classmate's . . . or maybe both! And the positive cycle about us and our classroom begins right there. The parents are more likely to be supportive of the teacher. Because the parents are supportive, so are the kids (and in some communities, the neighbors are too!). When parents and kids are happy, so is the principal and superintendent. It's a win–win situation. The kids feel safe in the classroom and so does the teacher! Good things happen when people feel safe. They are willing to take risks. They are more likely to accept responsibility. They respond positively to the environment they are in and the people they are with. What a great start!

REFLECTIONS

Intermediate-age students are quite self-centered in their point of view. Yet they are vulnerable, caring, and loving. They are also extremely concerned about fairness and equity. These seemingly contradictory attributes are the basis for building a successful school year for each child. Not long ago, I had a student teacher in my room; when he was leaving the kids wanted to give him a gift. I suggested that each child think of one piece of advice to give him so that he would become an outstanding teacher. Here's the advice my students gave:

FROM A FIFTH-GRADE CLASS TO A STUDENT TEACHER

Be fair.	Make fun projects.	Keep the classroom under control.
Laugh.	Use good methods.	Sometimes, let it go.
Be energetic.	Don't be sexist.	Have joy.
Explain thoroughly.	Make the kids clean up.	Smile.
Don't be afraid to say, "No."	Don't be afraid to say, "Yes."	Do fun things.
Don't say "try harder" when we don't understand.		Have down time during the day. AND Never have a sub!
Be thoughtful.	Treat everyone equally.	
Be enthusiastic.	Be kind.	
Change things.	Be firm.	

Chapter Three

IMPLEMENTING INTEGRATION

SOCIAL STUDIES TEACHING AND LEARNING IS POWERFUL
WHEN IT IS INTEGRATIVE.

—NCSS's "Vision"

CHANGING THE HIERARCHY

It seems as if a hierarchy of importance develops when we teach by subject. For instance, reading and math have driven the elementary school day for years. As teachers adjusted their schedules to meet planned contingencies, such as assemblies and field trips, as well as unplanned emergencies, like snowstorms and power outages—they would think, "I've got to get reading in first and then math. I can put social studies off until tomorrow." Today's teacher often feels pressure because of high-stakes testing; in many states, reading, writing, and math tests predominate. Few states are testing social studies, science, health, art, and music. Since teacher survival is often equated with classroom performance on state-mandated assessments, what isn't tested often gets short shrift.

It doesn't have to be that way. We know that the mind/brain innately seeks connections (Caine and Caine 1997, 105). Rather than choosing to spend a major part of the day on test topics in separate, unrelated periods, a teacher might decide to integrate learning. When the day is integrated, the teacher might think, "We'll continue reading our chapter book about the Inuit boy, make predictions in our reading journals, compile and classify data about life above the tree line, work in small groups to complete our mural of Arctic animals, and teach each other Yupik counting games." Instead of feeling obligated to get in certain subjects at the expense of others, the teacher in an integrated classroom looks at the amount of time available as a whole rather than as separate periods. Teacher and student stress is certainly reduced when one is not struggling to get in a subject fragment before the end of the day!

For me, the essential skills of social studies have been the primary means for integrating the curriculum. To apply and master these skills, a student needs to be able to "read, write, and do 'rithmetic." Rather than using subjects to order my day, I frequently connect data-gathering skills, intellectual skills, decision-making skills, and interpersonal skills across the curriculum. I use the term *block* to signal my students when we are working in an integrated fashion. Our local high school has a humanities/social studies core "block" class for advanced placement students. This class appeals to highly motivated and academically successful students. Because we live on a three-by-seven-mile island, everyone in the community knows about the block class. I decided if the high school could have a block, so could we.

Essential Social Studies Skills

No matter the content that needs to be taught, certain skills that are fundamental to social studies education need to be developed. According to the National Council for the Social Studies, they are (NCSS 1990):

1. Data-gathering skills. Learning to:
   - Acquire information by observation.
   - Locate information from a variety of sources.
   - Compile, organize, and evaluate information.
   - Extract and interpret information.
   - Communicate orally and in writing.

2. Intellectual skills. Learning to:
   - Compare things, ideas, events, and situations on the basis of similarities and differences.
   - Classify or group items in categories.
   - Ask appropriate and searching questions.
   - Draw conclusions or inferences from evidence.
   - Arrive at general ideas.
   - Make sensible predictions from generalizations.

3. Decision-making skills. Learning to:
   - Consider alternative solutions.
   - Consider the consequences of each solution.
   - Make decisions and justify them in relationship to democratic principles.
   - Act, based on those decisions.

4. Interpersonal skills. Learning to:
- See things from the point of view of others.
- Understand one's own beliefs, feelings, abilities, and shortcomings and how they affect relationships with others.
- Use group generalizations without stereotyping and arbitrarily classifying individuals.
- Work effectively with others as a group member.
- Give and receive constructive criticism.
- Accept responsibility and respect the rights and property of others.

Studying Cultures

My belief that every child can learn needs to be made real to my students. Therefore, I start with an interesting focus for study, not where the social studies text begins. The book suggests spending several days introducing the elements of social studies in a very didactic format. My experience tells me to get into some wonderfully engaging knowledge and to discover the elements of social studies by doing. Weaving in an application of the essential skills while integrating our day and the content of our learning, I can make sure that every single child succeeds. One thing I've learned is to begin with fabulous, luscious, incredibly delightful information and to choose an initial activity all children can do—and do well. Making it open-ended, giving plenty of latitude, and planning for diversity, in both the approach and the outcome of the assignment, invites every learner to succeed. Culture studies offer a wealth of interesting and intriguing information for all ages of students. I find culture studies an irresistible topic to engage students early in the year. Here is the blueprint I follow:

- Begin with a visual hook.
- Provide plenty of resources for information gathering.
- Develop a strategy for organizing data.
- Find literature that reveals different points of view to read aloud and read alone.
- Give an opportunity to compare or classify attributes on the basis of similarities and differences.
- Examine artifacts, bring in resource people, and/or go on field trips.
- Experience the culture through art, music, dance, and stories.
- Create a culminating activity to synthesize learning.
- Encourage student reflection: What did I learn? What did I do? How do I feel?

The remainder of this chapter discusses two culture studies I've used.

"ARCTIC ADVENTURE: AWARENESS AND APPRECIATION"

Children begin learning something new best by recalling what they know and by being presented graphics or pictures from which they can confirm what they already know or begin to store knowledge from.

Presenting the Visual Hook

"Today I'm going to start with a short film, *Across Continents*, on Inuit (Eskimo) people as an introduction to our early people's focus." My main goal is for the students to realize that there are many different groups of Inuit people, each having unique customs and traditions but whose culture has been shaped by the environment of the Far North. This goal also demonstrates the concept of unity and diversity. By sharing with them a visual image when being introduced to a new focus of study, I am also giving them a common storehouse of knowledge from which to draw. I usually use a picture book, but this particular film shows the connections between Siberian people and Alaskan indigenous groups. One of my objectives is for the students to be aware of the land bridge theory as we look at the inhabitation of the Americas. Before showing the film, I give the students five minutes to list everything they know about Inuit people. The stereotype of Nanook of the North runs deep, I see, as the students share the knowledge that all Eskimos live in igloos and ask, "What's an Inuit?"

Preparing Data Disks

After the film, I ask the students, "Is there anything you'd like to cross out on your list that you thought you knew but you've changed your mind about?" As the children revise their lists in small groups, I pass out a brief summary of the food, shelter, clothing, and language of fifteen different Inuit groups. The children learn that Arctic people in America called themselves Inuit, meaning "people." Eskimo was a name given them by the Abenaki Native Americans, meaning "eaters of raw meat" (Spizzirri 1989). Working in pairs, the students enter the information onto a "data disk" (see Figure 3–1). The data disk, round rather than rectangular, has proved to be an engaging way for intermediate students to gather data. Since the students are extrapolating existing data, everyone can accomplish this activity quickly and successfully.

When the data disks are complete, the students read a short informational article about the land bridge theory. Then each pair introduces their Inuit group to the class, sharing the information they have collected. I record the data on an overhead chart as the students share. Pretty soon, we have a graphic display

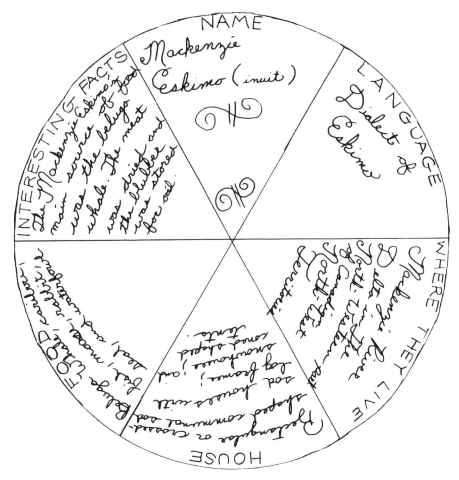

Figure 3–1: Rachael's data disk contains basic information about one Inuit group.

of data for comparing similarities and finding differences. We can hypothesize why some groups have developed differently and can form questions to be investigated.

Next, we begin to discuss the land bridge theory. I ask the students to compare it to the legend I read to them after recess about how Inuit people came to Alaska. During the discussion, one child comments on how it seems that all cultures have creation stories. Since we will study several cultures this year, we decide to test this: "Do all cultures have creation stories?" This generalization is the first of many threads that will weave our learning into a single cohesive piece throughout the year.

I share examples of Inuit art with the class. It usually intrigues the students because it is so unpredictable and seems humorous to them. We talk about the difficulty of living in such a harsh environment, using the atlas to verify our assumptions about climate and seasons. We hypothesize about the kinds of clothing, hats, and weapons that were used. Tomorrow will be a field trip to a local museum that has an Inuit display. We discuss things to look for and review the questions they raised—"Perhaps we can find the answers tomorrow. It's lunch time already!"

Building a Cohesive Classroom

After lunch is reading workshop. This sixty-five-minute period is devoted to reading and reading-related activities. Sometimes the children read anything they choose; sometimes they read material I assign them. Today, we begin reading *The Lamp, the Ice, and the Boat Called Fish* by Jacqueline Briggs Martin (2001). The central characters in this vivid retelling of a true story of survival and courage are an Inupiaq family. The narration provides pronunciation guides to help the children with the unusual Eskimo names—a perfect time for a quick pronunciation key minilesson. After about ten minutes of review and practice using the key to pronounce names, I begin reading the story aloud while the students either follow along or just listen. Getting the children into the rhythm of the story, answering their initial questions, and setting them up for success are important, particularly early in the year and especially when the story is required reading.

How much or how often I should dictate the reading material of my students is a question I ask continually. It's another balancing act. I want the students to have some shared knowledge so that our discussions can be inclusive. I've come to realize that reading the same material provides exactly the kind of community-based knowledge one strives for in today's classroom. No one is excluded from the common ground. In the integrated classroom, knowledge is the root of all the activities. Manipulating what is known—recalling it, analyzing it, putting it together in new forms, wondering about it, and making decisions about it—is what happens. Common knowledge is a club that everyone belongs to. Nobody is left out when we read the same story, discuss the same dilemmas, and evaluate decisions together.

Building Literacy Equity in the Classroom

Reading the same information also has to do with equity. All children have the right to have access to the same information. In a truly social studies–

integrated classroom, equity is the cornerstone of the democratic ideal. All children should have access to equal levels of foundational knowledge. That's why grouping in the social studies–centered classroom is cooperative, fluid, and often self-selected. Reading the same story acts as a common catalyst for a classroom. The story or article is often the springboard for examining issues, extending knowledge, and enriching appreciation.

Choice is also important. Kids can extend their knowledge based on interest and ability. Many of the latest recommendations for teaching reading suggest that student choice is a major key to reading success. I don't think it is horrible, however, for us to expect all children to read the same book, novel, or poem to promote greater comprehension about a culture or a social studies concept. What's to be done if a child can't read the assigned book? One strategy is to read the book aloud with the child. Another is to set up pair/share reading partners. Another is to use a T.A.R.P. (Tape Assisted Reading Program)— teachers can put books on tape for students to read along with. I have used parents and local high school seniors who need community service credits to put the books on tape to use in the classroom. (Books on tape can really help students with fluency difficulties. To promote fluency, students need to read the book with the tape multiple times.) Another source is Recorded Books, Inc., which distributes a catalog of more than 2,000 intermediate and middle school books on tape for kids that integrate social studies topics and concepts along with good literature. All are available for rent or purchase. (Both U.S. and Canadian teachers can call 1-800-638-1304 for a free catalog.) The problem with most tapes, both professional and amateur, is that they are read too fast for many struggling readers.

Reading a novel can become a central integrator, helping students personalize and activate knowledge. As Caine and Caine observe, "The problem is that a straight historical narrative often misses the power of story because it tends to be presented as additional inert surface knowledge" (1994, 122).

Getting Into the Story

Back to *The Lamp, the Ice, and the Boat Called Fish*: I read the first chapter aloud and then ask the students to write down at least one question and one prediction they hope to answer by the time they finish the book. When they have finished, students share their questions and their predictions. Now comes silent reading time. Early in the year, ten minutes is about as long as they can sustain the reading. Later, many can read thirty minutes at a "sit," though some still "fade" after ten minutes.

TARRY'S TEACHING TIPS: HOW TO HELP STUDENTS SELECT APPROPRIATE BOOKS

I introduce student-selected books by teaching my kids that good readers read three kinds of books: "Easy," "Just Right," and "Challenging." I probe for examples of books the kids have read in each of the three categories. As a student names a book and its category, I write it on the board. What we soon discover is that what one child thinks is a Just Right book, another child categorizes as Easy or Challenging. This awareness helps with that age-old problem of the least capable reader choosing the most challenging book so that no one really knows how limited her ability is.

The second tip I give my kids is to use the three-finger rule when selecting books to read. To use this rule, tell the kids to open to any full page of text in the book they have chosen. Read that page, putting a finger on each word that is unknown or impossible for them to read. If three fingers cover three words, then the book is probably too difficult and the child should choose to select a different one.

The final tip I give my kids is the "Just Because You Started It, Doesn't Mean You Have to Finish It" rule. This rule is predicated on the belief that independent reading should be enjoyable. Therefore, if a child starts a book and isn't enjoying it, that child should stop reading it and get a different book. The only caveat I have is that students need to read at least two chapters before "ditching" the book. I do give credit for partial books read in independent reading but my students do have to read complete books as well.

Taking out their literature response journals, the students then write for about fifteen minutes. Perhaps they will identify words, phrases, or paragraphs they find memorable. For this type of entry, I have them use a double-entry format that I learned from Patricia Hagerty. I find it encourages thoughtful exploration. The students draw a line down the center of their notebook page. On the left side they list interesting words, phrases, or whole paragraphs from the book. Adjacent, on the right side, they tell why they chose to record these particular words, phrases, or paragraphs.

The students have other options for journal responses: They can choose to write about what they know so far or how they feel. I try to open the door to all learning styles. They can write a poem about the family, or they can write a letter to any of the characters in the story. What they choose to write in the journals is essentially their own decision. But write they must. Over the year, I model additional forms of written communication and work with individual students to set goals that will enhance and extend their own knowledge and skill.

After about fifteen minutes, I ask the students if anyone would like to share what has been written. Several children usually do. I do this daily if I can, because I think it validates the writing, stimulates other students' thinking, and lets me know what's going on. More important, the kids hear what other students have written. This information provides future journal entry models that students can store to draw on next time we are journaling.

I read the journals once a week—seven a day for four days—and talk to each student once a week about the writing. I like this workshop approach because it facilitates the success of all readers in my classroom, regardless of ability. It promotes learning and prompts critical thinking by the reader as a writer and as a listener. I especially enjoy the autonomy it gives me. It's great not to have to lug a huge reading manual around anymore! The workshop format of read, respond, and share makes learning much more natural now— it flows. By supporting, connecting, and extending knowledge in reading and social studies, integration fosters a tapestry of learning, making the whole day significant.

Gathering Information

After the last recess, we begin a short, integrated language arts project. Many new vocabulary words and concepts are revealed as we learn about the Arctic and the Arctic people. I want to know what is "sticking" and what is not. I also want to discover what skills the students are using comfortably this early in the year. This strategy lets me observe learning orientation. Does the child tend to use words or pictures to communicate? Does he choose to work independently or does he gravitate toward groups? Does she take intellectual risks or does she play it safe with known information, familiar facts? Conversations about Inuits and Arctic life are spontaneous. I listen for understanding and misunderstanding.

An ABC organizer seems to be a perfect project for revealing this information and is an activity that will be successful for every child (see page 219 in the Appendix for detailed plans). We scour the library for resources: picture books, reference works, fiction and nonfiction books. After dividing a large sheet of white paper into squares, the students prepare an Arctic ABC chart. Using any of the resources, they are encouraged to begin finding words, ideas, or concepts that are a part of Arctic or Inuit life to place on the chart. Our challenge is to find at least one word for each letter of the alphabet. Some of the children, noticing the books of Inuit/Eskimo legends and accounts, such as *The Shaman's Nephew: A Life in the Far North* (Tookoome and Oberman 2000), placed around the room, begin perusing them. Others get out their copy of *The Lamp, the Ice, and the Boat Called Fish*. Others look back at the data disks. A couple of kids go to the encyclopedia while one girl heads for the computer, which has an electronic encyclopedia on disk. It's a scavenger hunt. Fun, but focused. And the day ends, too quickly—"We have lots to do tomorrow!"

The Little Book

Introducing a new kinesthetic organizer, I show the students how to fold a piece of paper into a little book for taking notes (see Figure 3–2). A strategy I learned from a primary teacher, I use the little book constantly in my classroom (see page 235 in the Appendix for extensions). Ubiquitous, versatile, and ecological, little books fit into every unit of study. They help organize observations for later reference and reflection. Today, the little book will serve as a notebook, where the kids will sketch, list, and collect interesting and/or important information about Arctic people. Everyone needs to collect at least five pieces of information and make at least two sketches. Thank you, whoever created the little book format! You've given a wonderful gift to teachers and students.

The field trip proves worthwhile. The students see many examples of the ways the environment shaped the culture of various Inuit groups. They marvel over the resourcefulness of the people of the North and are fascinated by their creativity. Many find the answer to questions they have posed. Several discover facts to add to the Arctic ABC chart. Their little books provide a

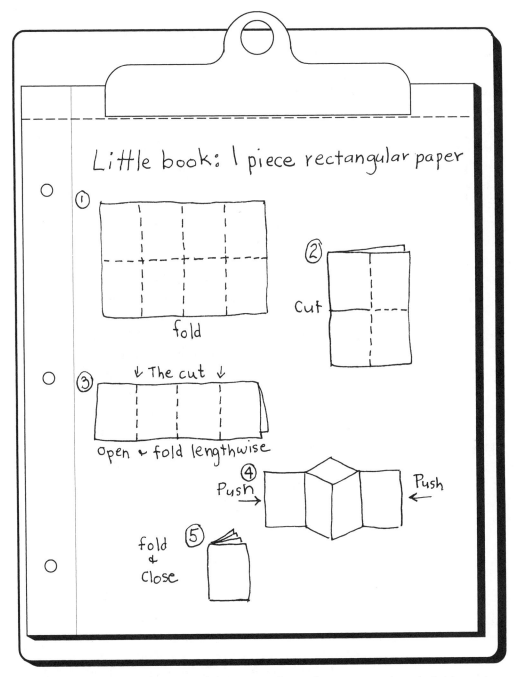

Little book: 1 piece rectangular paper

① fold

② Cut

③ ↓ The cut ↓
open → fold lengthwise

④ Push → ← Push

⑤ fold & Close

Figure 3–2: Little Book © 2002 by Tarry Lindquist from *Seeing the Whole Through Social Studies, Second Edition*. Portsmouth, NH: Heinemann.

reference for what the students observed, learned, or confirmed. The little books also reinforce the value of note-taking as the students share and compare their observations when back in the classroom.

Putting Out a Newspaper in a Day

We list everything we can remember on the board when we return from the field trip. Then we have a lottery. The first child whose name is picked from the "lucky lottery box" gets to choose what he or she wants to write about from the list. The second child gets second choice and so on, until every child has selected one of the items on the board to write about. Because this is our first writing assignment, I decide to use it as baseline data about each child's writing skill. A newspaper is an appropriate medium, since we have news to share about our trip to the museum. It's also a good way to share information with parents regarding the field trip. We need to take advantage of our community resources by moving our learning beyond classroom walls.

Newspapers in a day! The way real newspapers operate, not the old three-weeks-to-get-it-all-together kind of newspaper we used to do. I quit doing newspapers for about a decade because they were so boring and so out of date by the time we finally finished them. Today's copying-machine technology makes all the difference in the world.

By drawing on observations made during the field trip and by tapping the accumulated store of knowledge acquired by the class's reading and research, each student can successfully contribute. Over the years, I've come to understand that we don't need to ask intermediate-grade students to write "long"; we get more growth if we ask to students write "often." I've also noticed that if the shape of a piece of notebook paper is changed, students often find the writing task more engaging. For this activity, the students are each given a "column"—a half sheet of notebook paper, cut vertically.

In about an hour, the articles are complete. I encourage students who finish early to illustrate their work. We do shoulder-to-shoulder editing of the articles. Finally, the students go over the final copy in black felt-tip pen. Total time: about an hour and a half of class time and an additional hour of teacher time spent reducing the columns, taping the mock-up together, and running the copies.

The newspaper looks terrific (a page is shown in Figure 3–3). We have proof of the value of our field trip. We have an interesting piece to read as a class tomorrow, a piece that demonstrates how well the class can work cooperatively and productively.

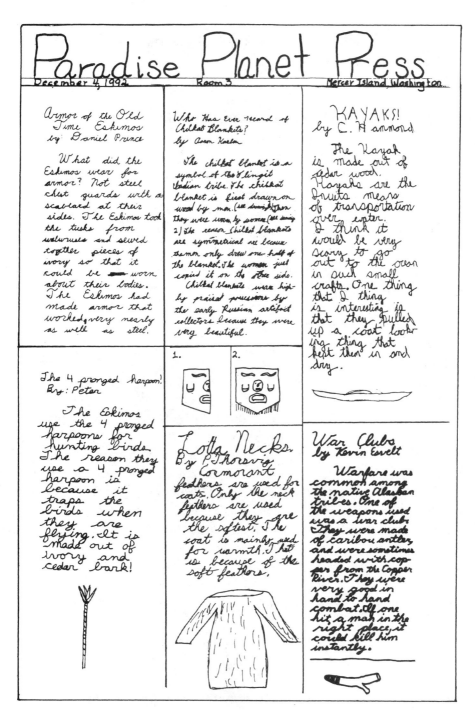

Paradise Planet Press

December 4, 1992   Room 3   Mercer Island, Washington

Armor of the Old Time Eskimos
by Daniel Prince

What did the Eskimos wear for armor? Not steel chest guards with a scabbard at their sides. The Eskimos took the tusks from walruses and sewed together pieces of ivory so that it could be worn about their bodies. The Eskimos had made armor that worked very nearly as well as steel.

Who Has Ever heard of Chilkat Blankets?
by Aaron Koslen

The chilkat blanket is a symbol of the Tlingit Indian tribe. The chilkat blanket is first drawn on wood by man. (see drawing) Then they were woven by women (see drawing 2) The reason chilkat blankets are symmetrical are because the man only drew one half of the blanket. The woman just copied it on the other side.

Chilkat blankets were highly praised possessions by the early Russian artifact collectors because they were very beautiful.

KAYAKS!
by C. Hammond

The Kayak is made out of cedar wood. Kayaks are the Inuits means of transportation over water. I think it would be very scary to go out to the ocean in such small crafts. One thing that I think is interesting is that they pulled up a coat looking thing that kept them in and dry.

The 4 pronged harpoon!
By: Peter

The Eskimos use the 4 pronged harpoons for hunting birds. The reason they use a 4 pronged harpoon is because it traps the birds when they are flying. It is made out of ivory and cedar bark!

1.   2.

Lotta Necks
By P. Korsvig

Cormorant feathers are used for coats. Only the neck feathers are used because they are the softest. The coat is mainly used for warmth. That is because of the soft feathers.

War Clubs
by Kevin Esvelt

Warfare was common among the native Alaskan tribes. One of the weapons used was a war club. They were made of caribou antler, and were sometimes headed with copper from the Copper River. They were very good in hand to hand combat. If one hit a man in the right place, it could kill him instantly.

Figure 3–3:   Thanks to a classroom full of reporters, we have a newspaper in a day!

Implementing Integration

I can also use it for evaluation. The students identify their strengths and comment on what they might improve next time. The editing process points to what needs to be emphasized next. I can also see where content knowledge has been misunderstood and plan for clarification.

Using Picture Books and Stories to Teach Traditional Cultures

A new day. The students continue working on their Arctic ABC charts as they read books about Inuits and their environment from the library. Many of these books are picture books, so the students often pair-read, enjoying stories together, gathering information in tandem.

After recess, I read another legend. Sharing literature and stories of the people we are studying is my way of trying to instill appreciation for similarities and differences among cultures without reinforcing old stereotypes or inventing new ones. I try to find stories written by members of the groups we study. More often than not these days, collections are written by native authors or retold by indigenous speakers. Many new picture books feature native stories and legends. Be aware, however, that the illustrations are not always accurate.

Seeking Authenticity

As a social studies educator I think it is very important to portray cultures in the classroom as accurately as possible. No one has firsthand experience with every culture. We need to rely on experts. Because literature permeates our social studies–centered program, I have learned to be wary. Just because a book is an old favorite or fits the topic we're studying doesn't mean it is culturally accurate or sensitive. Teachers can look for recommendations from reliable groups. *Through Indian Eyes: The Native Experience in Books for Children*, edited by Beverly Slapin and Doris Seale (1992), critiques more than 100 children's books that have Native Americans as the main characters. I think many well-meaning classroom teachers would be surprised at the evaluation these two Native American authors give books such as *The Double Life of Pocahontas* (Fritz 1983). While I still use this book in my classroom, I certainly use it differently now. I ask the students to evaluate the character of Pocahontas in relation to their understanding of Native Americans at that time and the role Native American women played in their particular society, pointing out discrepancies and inaccuracies from a different point of view.

Using Picture Books and Stories to Teach Contemporary Cultures

Too often we leave cultures on the museum shelf, rather like the Native

American in *The Indian in the Cupboard*. In the story, a young boy finds a magical cupboard that brings to life a miniature of a Native American permanently fixed in the past. So, too, classroom studies often focus on the exotic and the unusual of a culture, the old, or the archaic. I think we have an obligation to share with our students the authentic life of native people today—members of dynamic and vibrant cultures, they are a part of today's world. It doesn't matter whether we are studying Native Americans, African Americans, or Chinese immigrants. Each culture needs to be studied in a contemporary context, not treated as an artifact to be taken out, examined, and put away again, folded within the pages of history.

Picture books provide vivid and contemporary glimpses of life today in many cultures. So often, the cultures in these kinds of resources are revealed through the eyes of children, as in "The World's Children" series published by Carolrhoda/Lerner or the "A Day with . . ." series published by Runestone/Lerner. Each book provides insightful text and superb photographs that introduce the history, geography, and culture of ethnic groups around the world. A wonderful U.S. history resource is *We Were There, Too!* by Phillip Hoose (2001). Not only are different cultures represented but so are different times in history, through the eyes and experiences of young people.

Using Picture Books to Model the Six Traits of Writing and to Correlate to National Social Studies Standards

I have found that picture books make wonderful models for teaching the six traits of writing as described in Ruth Culham's 1998 book, *Picture Books: An Annotated Bibliography with Activities for Teaching Writing*. It occurred to me a few years ago that, charming as most picture books are, I could be choosing models from the Notable Social Studies Trade Books for Young People and the Outstanding Science Trade Books for Children lists that connect with my curriculum. That way my kids are experiencing books that not only model writing traits but also extend their knowledge and appreciation of social studies and science topics.

The sections that follow contain a sample of models that I have compiled from extensive lists published annually by the Children's Book Council, the National Council for the Social Studies, and/or the National Science Teachers Association. (The books selected from the Notable Social Studies Trade Books for Young People also correlate to national social studies standards. They are identified by Roman numerals at the end of each entry. The ten NCSS Curriculum Standards for Social Studies thematic strands are:

I. Culture

II. Time, Continuity, and Change

III. People, Places, and Environments

IV. Individual Development and Identity

V. Individuals, Groups, and Institutions

VI. Power, Authority, and Governance

VII. Production, Distribution, and Consumption

VIII. Science, Technology, and Society

IX. Global Connections

X. Civic Ideals and Practices

Ideas

For the writing trait of *ideas*, which Culham describes as "The heart of the message, the content of the piece, the main theme together with the details that enrich and develop that theme." To provide practice, suggested activities might include making a list of things to write about from ideas found in picture books or to compare the way two authors write about the same idea.

Cole, Henry. 1998. *I Took a Walk*. New York: Greenwillow. (VIII)

Curley, Lynn. 1999. *Rushmore*. New York: Scholastic. (III)

Heide, Florence Parry, and Judy Heidi Gillian. 1999. *The House of Wisdom*. New York: D. K. Publishing, Inc. (II, III, IX)

Medearis, Angela Shelf. 2000. *Seven Spools of Thread: A Kwanzaa Story*. Morton Grove, IL: Albert Whitman and Company. (I, III, IX)

Ryan, Pam Munoz. 1999. *Amelia and Eleanor Go for a Ride*. New York: Scholastic Press. (II, III)

Tarpley, Natasha Anastasia. 1998. *I Love My Hair*. Boston: Little, Brown and Company. (I, IV)

Vogel, Carole G. 1999. *Legends of Landforms: Native American Lore and the Geology of the Land*. Brookfield, CT: The Millbrook Press. (III, VIII)

Canadian Books

Kiarostami, Taghi. 2001. *Amoo No-Rooz*. Vancouver, BC: TABAS.

Owens, Ann-Maureen. 1999. *Canada's Maple Leaf: The Story of Our Flag*. Toronto: Kids Can Press.

Schaefer, Carole Lexa. 2001. *Two Scarlet Song Birds: A Story of Anton Dvorak*. Toronto: Random House.

Organization

Culham describes the trait of *organization* as "The internal structure of the piece, the thread of central meaning, the logical and sometimes intriguing pattern of ideas" and suggests practice activities like writing a new ending for one or more picture books or creating your own ABC book.

Ammon, Richard. 1999. *Conestoga Wagons*. New York: Holiday House. (II, VII, VIII)

Fraser, Mary Ann. 1997. *A Mission for the People: The Story of La Purisima*. New York: Henry Holt and Company. (I, II, III)

Gherman, Beverly. 2000. *Norman Rockwell: Storyteller with a Brush*. New York: Atheneum Books for Young Readers. (I, II, III)

Gibbons, Gail. 1998. *Soaring with the Wind: The Bald Eagle*. New York: Morrow Junior Books. (VIII)

Guthrie, Woody. 1998. *This Land Is Your Land*. Boston: Little, Brown and Company. (II, III, IV)

Singer, Marilyn. 2000. *On the Same Day in March*. New York: HarperCollins. (III, VIII, IX)

Canadian Books

Manson, Ainslie. 2001. *House Calls: The True Story of a Pioneer Doctor*. Toronto: Groundwood.

Nichol, Barbara. 2001. *Trunks All Aboard: An Elephant ABC*. Toronto: Tundra.

Voice

"The heart and soul, the magic, the wit, along with the feeling and conviction of the individual writer coming out through the words" (1998, 2) is how Culham identifies the trait of *voice*. She suggests activities such as comparing the voices of two different authors exploring the same idea or two different characters sharing their point of view about the same event.

Bunting, Eve. 1998. *So Far From the Sea*. New York: Clarion Books. (II, III, IV, V)

Bruchac, Joseph. 2000. *Sacajawea*. New York: Silver Whistle. (I, II, III)

Grutman, Jewel H., and Gay Matthaei. 1994. *The Legend of Thomas Blue Eagle*. Charlottesville, VA: Thomasson-Grant, Inc. (II, III, IV, V)

Lester, Julius. 1999. *From Slave Ship to Freedom Road*. New York: Dial Books. (I, III, V)

Sinnott, Susan. 2000. *Charley Waters Goes to Gettysburg*. Brookfield, CT: The Millbrook Press. (II, III, VI)

Tookoome, Simon, with Sheldon Oberman. 2000. *The Shaman's Nephew: A Life in the Far North*. Toronto: Stoddart Kids. (I, III, V)

Younger, Barbara. 1998. *Purple Mountain Majesties: The Story of Katharine Lee Bates and "America the Beautiful."* New York: Dutton Children's Books. (II, III)

Canadian Books

Savage, Candace. 2001. *Born to Be a Cowgirl: A Spirited Ride Through the Old West*. Berkley: Greystone Books.

Trottier, Maxine. 2001. *There Have Always Been Foxes*. Toronto: Stoddart Kids.

Word Choice

Word choice is "The use of rich, colorful, precise language that moves and enlightens the reader" (Culham 1998, 2). This trait can be explored by highlighting active verbs or making a list of interesting, exciting, or striking phrases or words that you find in picture books.

Balit, Christina. 2000. *Atlantis: The Legend of a Lost City*. New York: Henry Holt and Company. (V, VI)

Fleming, Candace. 1999. *A Big Cheese for the White House: The True Tale of a Tremendous Cheddar*. New York: D. K. Publishing, Inc. (III, VIII)

Garland, Sherry. 1998. *My Father's Boat*. New York: Scholastic Press. (I, II, III, IV, V)

Gollub, Matthew. 1998. *Cool Melons–Turn to Frogs*. New York: Lee & Low Books, Inc. (I, III)

James, J. Alison. 1999. *The Drums of Noto Hanto*. New York: D.K. Publishing, Inc. (III, V)

Canadian Books:

Khan, Rukhsana. 1998. *The Roses in My Carpet*. Toronto: Stoddart Kids.

Martin, Rafe. 2001. *The Twelve Months*. Toronto: Stoddart Kids.

Sentence Fluency

"The rhythm and flow of the language, the sound of word patterns, the way in which the writing plays to the ear, not just to the eye" is how Culham describes the trait of *sentence fluency* (1998, 2). She suggests using choral reading to practice hearing where and how sentences and phrases begin and end or listing sentence beginnings to see how much variety authors use.

Burleigh, Robert. 1998. *Home Run: The Story of Babe Ruth*. San Diego: Harcourt Brace & Company. (I, IV)

Katz, Bobbi. 2000. *We the People*. New York: Greenwillow Books. (I, III, IV)

Kurtz, Jane. 2000. *River Friendly, River Wild*. New York: Simon & Schuster Books for Young Readers. (I, II, III)

Laufer, Peter, and Susan L. Roth. 2000. *Made in Mexico*. Washington, DC: National Geographic Society. (I, III, VII)

Canadian Books

Highway, Tomson. 2001. *Caribou Song*. Toronto: HarperCollins.

Kusugak, Michael Arvaarluk. 1998. *Arctic Stories*. Toronto: Annick Press.

———. 1999 (reprint). *Baseball Bats for Christmas*. Toronto: Annick Press.

Conventions

Conventions, last but not least, are "The mechanical correctness of the piece: spelling, grammar and usage, paragraphing, capitals, and punctuation" (Culham 1998, 2.) Try using cartoon bubbles or the one-page play format in the Teacher's Notebook. Both of these activities act as scaffolds to writing dialog.

Bial, Raymond. 2000. *A Handful of Dirt*. New York: Walker & Company. (Science)

Bruchac, Joseph. 2000. *Crazy Horse's Vision*. New York: Lee & Lowe Books, Inc. (IV, V)

Leedy, Loreen. 2000. *Mapping Penny's World*. New York: Henry Holt and Company. (I, III)

Simon, Seymour. 1998. *Bones: Our Skeletal System*. New York: Morrow Junior Books. (VIII)

Canadian Books

Bourgeois, Paulette. 2001. *Oma's Quilt*. Toronto: Kids Can Press.

Gorrell, Gena K. 2000 (reprint). *North Star to Freedom: The Story of the Underground Railroad*. New York: Delacourt.

Walters, Eric. 2000. *Rebound*. Toronto: Stoddart Kids.

Introducing Points of View

During block, the students watch a Cousteau video of an Eskimo village. The thrust of the film is how compatible the life is with the environment and how it is changing as technology and contemporary life become more and more a part of the culture. I read the book *Baseball Bats for Christmas* by Michael Arvaarluk Kusugak (1999 reprint) to the students to give them yet another point of view. We discuss how Inuit life appears to have changed in our contemporary world: "Has our life changed as well?" The children decide to interview their parents or grandparents to find out what changes technology has made in their lives.

Working in groups of four, the students eagerly compare their lists of changes with one another looking for similarities. Eliminating repetitions, they compile a new list. Then each group shares with the whole class. Obviously, technology is a powerful agent for change, regardless of the culture. We discuss the costs and benefits of technology in society. The discourse is thoughtful, energetic, and spontaneous. No conclusions are drawn, but I ask the students to tuck this conversation into their memory banks because we'll revisit the effect of technology on cultures throughout the year. We've identified another "thread" in our integrated curriculum.

The Arctic ABC charts are nearly finished. Many are hanging around the room (see the example in Figure 3–4). Students enjoy looking at one another's work. I'm continually amazed by the diversity such a rudimentary assignment generates. In our evaluation session, the students decide that when they do an assignment like this again they'll make some presentation improvements—outlining the squares, writing more legibly, and illustrating as well as listing words.

Replicating Inuit Art

Copies of illustrations from legends and folktales depicting Inuit life in more traditional times are hung around the room. Calling attention to the wildlife, the activities of the people, and the lines of the landscape, I show the class a block print of Inuit life done by a former student use tagboard and printer's ink. I then demonstrate how to make a similar print.

Figure 3–4: Alexa collects Arctic words on her ABC Chart.

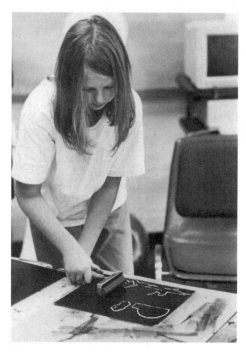

Figure 3–5: Lindsey brings Inuit
images to life through block printing.

Having the copied illustrations available keeps the students more focused on the goal, which is to replicate Inuit art—a certain discipline is imposed. In many cultures, artists learn by copying: They are required to reproduce traditional form, line, and color. This is good practice for my students as well. Those who are insecure feel free to trace various shapes directly from the models. Others re-create the art through observation. Once children have tried to authentically reproduce the art of another culture, most of them internalize a respect and regard for that culture (see Figure 3–5).

Reading to Learn

"Reading to learn" is an important skill to master in fifth grade, as is reading in a wide variety of genres. Now that the students have a sense of and a connection with the people who live in the North, it's time to integrate earth science. Using an existing curriculum, I select particular chapters or sections of chapters from our earth science textbook as the foundation of our study. To

90

give the students practice in becoming capable readers for information, this will be a reading-based study. Much of what we will do the rest of the year will reflect an ability to learn from reading.

Extracting and interpreting information will be modeled by me and remodeled with peers. Sometimes we'll work in guided-reading groups, and sometimes we'll work as a whole class. Sometimes we'll be using literature circles or book clubs as structures to comprehension and enjoyment. To learn from reading, according to Opitz and Rasinski (1998, 14), the successful reader accomplishes five tasks:

- Predicting
- Forming mental images while reading
- Using what they already know about a topic (prior knowledge)
- Monitoring how well they are comprehending during reading
- Fixing problems as they occur while reading

Our next few days are divided between working on the block prints and reading to learn about land formations on earth. Beginning with a "visual walk" through the chapter, students predict what we are going to learn. They share their prior knowledge and recall experiences they've had related to the topic. Each section of the chapter is headed by questions. We talk about the importance of reading the questions first so that we will know what to look for. Later, I'll teach the kids the kinds of questions there are and the level of responses they are meant to elicit. We discuss why the editors add pictures or graphs, and what a boldfaced phrase or italicized word might signify to the reader.

I begin by reading aloud, having the kids follow along. Using a technique called Think Aloud (Opitz and Rasinski 1998, 14) to help students realize that the purpose of reading is to understand a message, I verbalize my thoughts as I read, demonstrating to the kids what experienced readers actually do to ensure comprehension. As I read, I make sure to stop at trouble spots, stop and think aloud so that the kids have a model of one or more of the tasks successful readers do almost automatically.

Making the Community Connection

A parent comes in to show us her collection of Inuit clothing and artifacts. She and her husband lived in an Inuit village several years ago. She shares some of her thoughts and observations about how she has seen technology influence Inuit life-styles. She even brings her new husky puppy so that students can see a real sled dog. Sending thank-you cards to her provides a real-life reason for writing.

Culminating Activities for the Story

Everyone has finished their reading. Early in the reading, the students wrote letters as if they were members of the family in *The Lamp, the Ice, and the Boat Called Fish* as they joined the scientists at the beginning of the story. Now they write letters as if they were the same family member reflecting on what happened at the end of the adventure. The block prints are done. They write poetry to share their feelings and knowledge about the Arctic and Arctic life (see Figure 3–6).

The final activity is a classic short story, *Call It Courage* (Sperry 1940), about a boy's survival and courage in a South Pacific setting. Some years I read it aloud to the class; some years each student reads an individual copy. Some years I show the video, some years I don't. The students compare the family's situation with the South Pacific Islander, Mafatu, sorting similarities and differences. They identify a common theme of courage. Sharing comparisons in a class discussion leads to inferences and conclusions:

- ◆ "Courage is challenged by the environment."
- ◆ "Courage is from the inside out."
- ◆ "Anyone could be full of courage."
- ◆ "Any environment can become a matter of survival."
- ◆ "Good luck and good thinking make survival possible."
- ◆ "Anybody can have hard times."

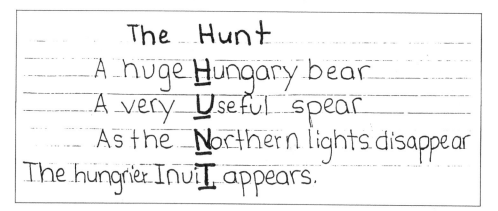

The Hunt
A huge Hungary bear
A very Useful spear
As the Northern lights disappear
The hungrier Inuit appears.

Figure 3–6: David's acrostic poem.

The students know that we are going to move on to another culture and they are reluctant to leave their friends, the Inuits. I hope this interest in studying cultures becomes lifelong.

"PEOPLE OF THE NORTHWEST COAST: PAST AND PRESENT"

A large wooden crate dominates the table in the back of the room. As the children enter, they poke it and question each other about the contents. I observe their interest but start the day out routinely. By midday, many have forgotten the crate's existence.

Introducing Artifacts

"Who knows what an anthropologist does?" Many guesses—some close, some far afield, one right on! "Today, you are going to be anthropologists. In the box are artifacts from another culture. Each of you will choose an artifact, sketch it, and develop a hypothesis about how it is used. Let's plan how you might do your work."

By sketching the artifact, the students will observe it carefully, look at the colors, and feel the textures. In speculating about its use, they will call on their prior knowledge and make assumptions about the culture the object came from. We practice making some hypotheses and assumptions about common articles around our classroom (the chalkboard eraser, the clock, and the overhead). When the assignment seems clear, the box is opened. The artifacts are objects on loan from a local natural history museum specializing in Northwest Coastal Native American groups. Each child gets one artifact to examine. It's a quiet room right now. All their energy is concentrated on the artifacts. As the students finish, they hang their Artifact Find sheet (see Figure 3–7) on the bulletin board and place their artifact on the display table that sits beneath the bulletin board.

Relating Reading

During snack and story time, I begin reading legends dealing with Raven, a very powerful figure in Northwest Coast lore. A trickster, a changer, often a troublemaker, Raven is mirrored in many cultures. Coyote, Anansi, Brer Rabbit, and Monkey all play similar roles in Southwest Native American, African, African American, and Chinese folklore. Trickster tales are another cultural "thread" we will follow throughout the year.

Beginning with the geography and geology of the Northwest Coastal people, we review some of our earth science knowledge and add information about

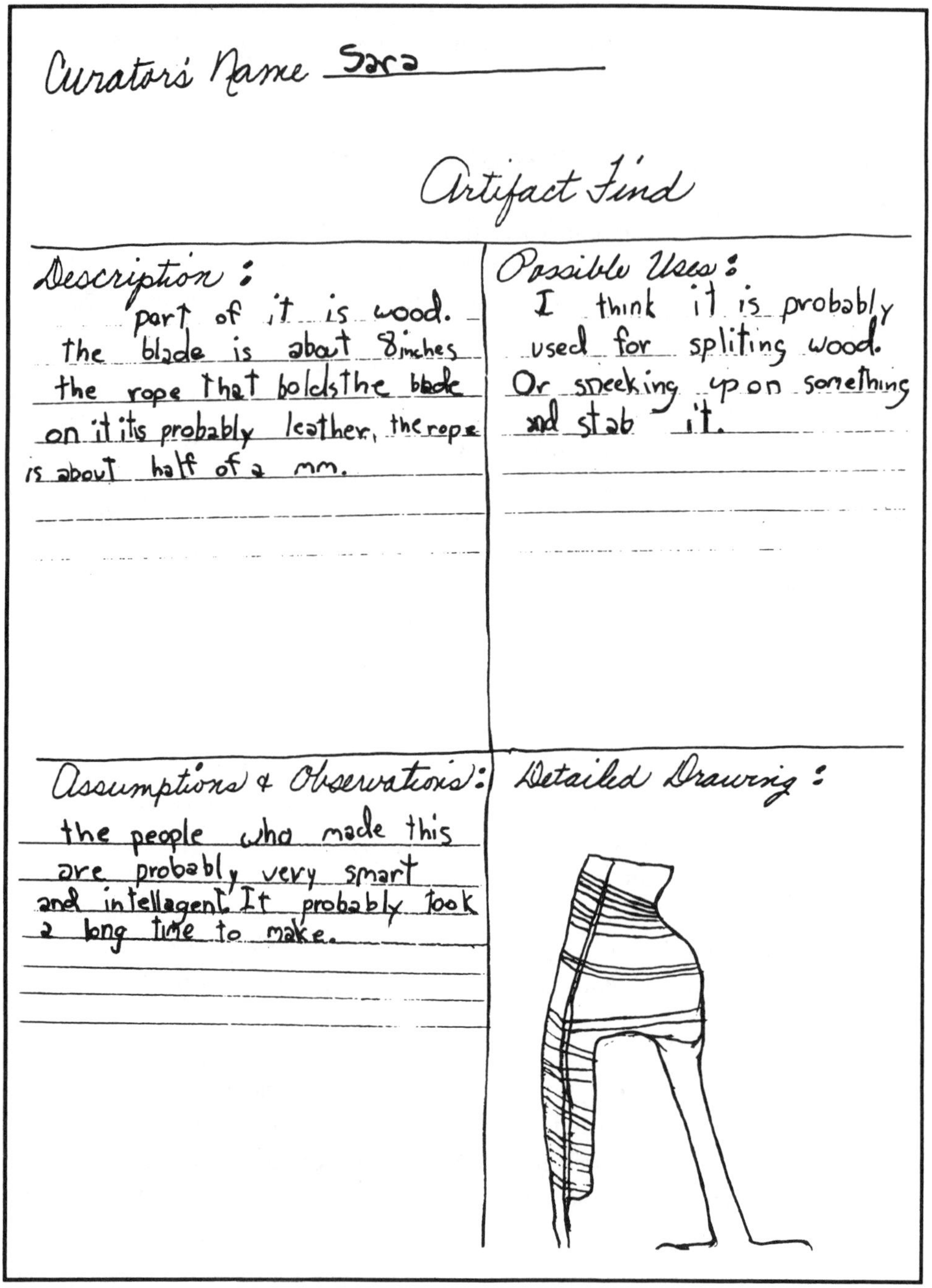

Curator's Name **Sara**

Artifact Find

Description:
    part of it is wood. the blade is about 8inches the rope that holds the blade on it it is probably leather, the rope is about half of a mm.

Possible Uses:
    I think it is probably used for spliting wood. Or sneeking up on something and stab it.

Assumptions & Observations:
the people who made this are probably very smart and intellagent. It probably took a long time to make.

Detailed Drawing:

Figure 3–7: Sara's Artifact Find sheet.

the coastal climate. We have no single piece of literature featuring Northwest Coastal people. Instead, I provide a list of potential read-alone books featuring Native Americans from many different nations:

> Here is a list of books that feature Native Americans as main characters. In the next three weeks, read at least two of them. You may work in groups of no more than four, but you must work with someone. I'll help you find your group members and set up a schedule for reading the first book. If we have three weeks to read two books, how many days do you have to read the first one?

After that I do a book talk about each book. There are enough copies so that each child can choose a title right away, even though it might not be a first choice. After the books are selected and groups are formed, the kids have a choice: Do an independent reader's response to prompts provided by me each day and then discuss those responses in a group of four, or complete an Important Idea Disk with a buddy. Capable, confident readers will usually select the four-person response group. Those who are less confident find the paired relationship of making a disk a more comfortable assignment. In addition to those read-alone books, there are also several reference books about Native Americans available around the room.

The next day, I become the guide and take the students on a "tour" of the artifacts. After discussing each object, describing its use, and pointing out unusual or common characteristics, students reclaim their objects and fill out an Artifact Fact sheet (see Figure 3–8). Hanging the Fact sheet over the Find sheet, we discuss how anthropologists might make errors. We also observe how they can be incredibly accurate. During block time, we begin using Frank Staub's *Children of the Tlingit* (1999) as our "textbook," in order to explore and examine Northwest Coastal Native American life specifically.

Teaching Peers, Reaching Across Ages

The students now prepare to become guides themselves. First, we decide to invite their kindergarten buddies and the third graders. They'll be our practice groups. Younger students are easier than peers, less intimidating. After that, we'll invite the other fifth-grade classes because they study Northwest Coastal people too.

Practicing speaking clearly and loudly enough to be heard, keeping the presentation coherent and informational, maintaining poise and eye contact, each student presents his or her piece eight times. Those listening practice being

95

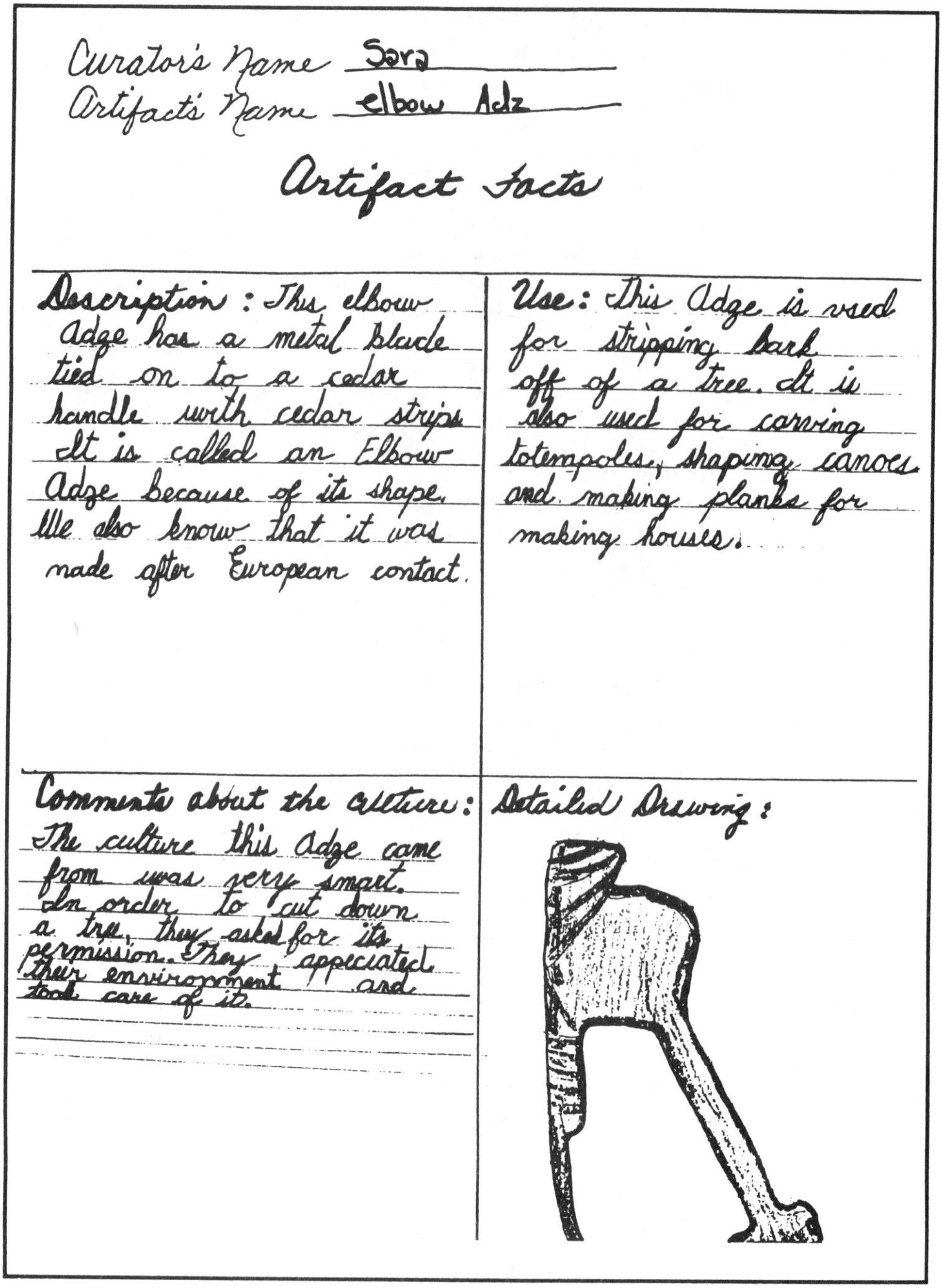

Curator's Name **Sara**

Artifact's Name **Elbow Adz**

Artifact Facts

Description: This Elbow Adze has a metal blade tied on to a cedar handle with cedar strips. It is called an Elbow Adze because of its shape. We also know that it was made after European contact.

Use: This Adze is used for stripping bark off of a tree. It is also used for carving totempoles, shaping canoes and making planks for making houses.

Comments about the culture: The culture this Adze came from was very smart. In order to cut down a tree, they asked for its permission. They appreciated their environment and took care of it.

Detailed Drawing:

Figure 3–8: Sara's Artifact Facts sheet shows that she has moved from "maybe" to "knowing."

good and supportive listeners. By the eighth round, each child in Paradise Island knows each artifact, how it's used, and its special characteristics. When asked to identify each artifact on a paper-and-pencil test, there's no problem. Students can describe the artifacts' functions and tell why they had value to the people of that time and place. Everyone earns 100 percent. Fifth graders should practice taking tests, and they should be successful in their practice. I don't want to teach test phobias or practice test failures.

After the test, we discuss why they did so well. One student observes that they had "done" it eight times. Their conclusion? If a person really wants to know something, teach it the right way eight times! We do remember most of what we teach others. It's not a bad rule to figure out if you're a student, and it's great strategy to use if you're a teacher!

Teaching Your Passion

Teaching about Northwest Coastal people is one of my passions. I've taken classes, gone on trips, and read voraciously to deepen my keen interest in these diverse and talented people of the Northwest. It's not so surprising, then, that I cheat just a little and stay with the topic just a little bit longer than planned each year. There is such a wealth of information: Northwest Coastal art, in particular, seems to strike a chord with fifth graders. They, too, identify strongly with animals and have a sense of kinship with all living things.

Throughout our study, we recall our initial threads: creation and trickster stories, technology and ecology, and how environment shapes culture. We look, again and again, at the multicultural nature of societies; the interaction of humans and the environment; and the culture, geography, and history of diverse societies. Through it all is woven the foundation of social responsibility and the meaning of democracy for that is how we work with each other on a daily basis.

Whether we are drawing Northwest Coastal animals or learning how to make a cedar canoe with a stone adze, I want the students to appreciate the strength and the ingenuity of these amazing people. I want them to recognize the symbols of the culture so that when, later in their lives, they see something of Northwest Coastal origin, they will recognize it and have positive feelings about it. One of reasons I teach is to bring about in my students an openness to different things, ideas, and people. This openness springs from knowledge and appreciation. How else can we make the world a better place?

We replicate Chilkat dancing blankets using the traditional Northwest Coastal design elements—line, ovoid, S and U shapes—and appreciating symbolism,

Figure 3–9:   Christopher displays his Chilkat blanket.

like the hatch marks of a beaver's tail or the blowhole of a whale (see Figure 3–9). We create coppers and name them using Chinook trade jargon. We try splitting cedar into planks, noting the smell and the feel of this wood that is so central to the Northwest Coastal people's spirit. We raise salmon and release them into local streams with the help of local Native American fish hatchery personnel, providing an enriched environment that meets the needs of all learning orientations, all intelligences.

Making Books of Knowledge

As a culminating activity, the students make Books of Knowledge—collections of information the children have learned throughout our course of study. Rather than giving a final test, the students demonstrate their knowledge by creating books about Northwest Coastal Native Americans. They must collect at least twenty things they know about their lives. To tap both sides of the brain, they will draw a picture and describe it in writing, telling about its origin or function (see Figure 3–10). The book must be organized by categories that can be

98

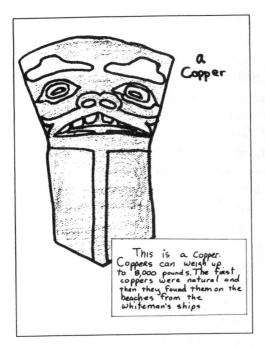

This is a Copper. Coppers can weigh up to 8,000 pounds. The first coppers were natural and then they found them on the beaches from the whiteman's ships

a Copper

Figure 3–10: Lindsay adds a page to her Book of Knowledge about Northwest Coastal Native Americans.

determined by the author; a table of contents is required, a dedication is optional. Resources are used in the best possible way—to remind, to verify, to extend. The students do all the work in class. I'm interested in what they know and how they go about their work. They do their initial text in pencil and let me or a peer do shoulder-to-shoulder editing. Some students choose to use the class computer to write their descriptions. (See page 224 in the Appendix for a detailed plan for the Book of Knowledge activity.)

It takes a week of concentrated work to complete the task. Everyone is tired, but everyone feels good as arms stretch over heads and backs flex. It feels good because a solid piece of work has been accomplished. A really worthwhile project is complete. "Is this something you're going to keep to show your own child the kind of work you did in fifth grade?" The answer is always "YES!"

Penning Personal Narratives

Writing is a vital part of literacy. In many states, high-stakes testing places a great deal of emphasis on writing, especially at the intermediate and middle levels. It is possible, in fact desirable, to pair writing for a purpose with social studies content. I frequently use models in my classroom, often using picture books. In the late 1900s, some seventy Cherokee, Kiowa, and Cheyenne men were put in a Florida penitentiary for their refusal to accept life on reservations. Using the only available materials, they purchased ledgerbooks from the prison store on which to create pictographs chronicling their history. Many of these books were destroyed when the men were finally released, but a few have survived, capturing the essence of days now gone.

In response to the need for writing practice to prepare for state-mandated testing, as well as interest in providing an entry for my students into history, I created the ledgerbook lesson. After reading *Warrior Artists: Historic Cheyenne and Kiowa Ledger Art* by Herman J. Viola (1998) to inform myself, I read *The Ledgerbook of Thomas Blue Eagle* by Jewel H. Grutman and Gay Matthaei (1994) to the class. This book is a facsimile of a ledgerbook, telling the story of a young Sioux boy who is taken from his parents on the plains and moved to the Carlisle Indian School in Pennsylvania. I used *The Ledgerbook of Thomas Blue Eagle* to set the stage for discussion: first about the content, and second about the way in which it was presented. Using the format of the book, the students became quite entranced with the challenge to create their own ledgerbooks. Brainstorming what they wanted to capture in a book about their lives, we came up some broad topics: Early Years, Family, Elementary School, Family Story, and Future. Referring to *Writer's Express: A Handbook for Young Writers, Thinkers, and Learners** (Kemper et al. 1995)* the students discovered that they were embarking on a journey to write personal narratives. Since a personal narrative is story about a personal memory, I find this assignment a perfect time to practice expanded sentences, word choice, and personal feelings.

Depending on a student's interest, writing expertise, developmental level, and comfort, the kids pick one of the brainstormed topics or come up with one of their own, for example: When I Was Born, Preschool: My Early Years, A Celebration I Remember, Where I've Been. They write their rough drafts, share them, enlist editing help from peers, revise, and polish. When they have written three to five narratives, they are ready to create the book. After writing and revising the drafts, the kids write using real ledgerbook paper that I pur-

---

* (*Writer's Express* is one of a series of language arts handbooks for all different grade levels that is published by Write Source, a Houghton Mifflin Company. I use it frequently to help me give more direct help to kids in their writing across the curriculum. What I particularly like are the clear models that are given and the possible steps that kids can use to achieve the kind of writing assigned. U.S. teachers can call 1-800-289-4490 and Canadian teachers can call 1-800-268-2222 for a sample copy.)

chase at an office supply warehouse. We do this because the kids decide a ledgerbook, like Thomas Blue Eagle's, should be handwritten in their best cursive. After writing, the students draw pictures to enhance and illustrate their narratives. We used colored pencils because markers bled through the ledgerbook paper. Besides, crayons didn't have the look of ledgerbook art. Additionally, we had to use both sides of the ledger paper because I could only afford three pieces for each child.

Before we started, however, the students helped develop a rubric for this strategy. Each student assessed his or her own work and then asked for my input. These rubrics were bound with the ledger papers. (To see the rubric we used, go to page 225 in the Appendix.)

A couple of years ago I made a promise: I would not be the only person to read my students' writing. To complete the activity, we spent one period reading each other's ledgerbooks and adding personal positive comments. (It takes some practice to get the kids to respond positively to their peers. Praise, I've noticed, does not come naturally to intermediate or middle school kids. We practice writing encouraging and positive comments early in the year for just this kind of situation.)

To facilitate the process, I give each child several blank file folder labels. They are inexpensive and limited in space. As a student finishes reading a peer's ledgerbook, he writes the author's name, jots down a positive comment, and signs his initials. Holding up the ledgerbook, signaling he's ready to trade for another, he waits for another student to trade with him. At the conclusion of the reading/sharing period, the students each put their ledgerbooks on their desks. Then, all the kids move around the room affixing their labels to the back of the ledgerbooks they read. I used to have the kids write directly on the back of each student's book they read, but what I discovered was that after the first comment or two, all the following comments were basically "ditto." Having the rubric focuses responses for the peer readers. Now readers must respond personally, not piggyback on peers. This organizational structure honors the kids who read slowly as well as the nimble readers. A child can read one or two or twelve or thirteen peer ledgerbooks during a sharing time organized like this. Plus, a harmonious classroom is maintained.

REFLECTIONS

Powerful social studies is not only integrative in the way topics are treated, but it is also integrative across time and space. Content is linked to past experience and is projected into the future. One of the true strengths of integrating around social studies is that respect for different points of view is encouraged. Multicultural appreciation and awareness is ongoing, an interwoven part of the day, not a unit or a special event to celebrate a holiday.

The mind makes meaning when it sees patterns and relationships. All learners don't make the same meaning, however, nor see the same patterns and relationships. Nevertheless, just by telling my students I'm trying to organize the year so things connect seems to ignite the process of personal integration. We know the mind retains information better when it is placed in a larger context or framework. It seems to me that the social studies–integrated classroom is more like real life. It's not terribly tidy, seldom fits into a square box or behind a rectangular desk, and something always seems to come along to modify it!

I love social studies because the students are such an important part of the learning. The dynamic quality of a social studies–integrated classroom has as much to do with the interaction the kids have with the content, with the teacher, and with each other as it does with concept and skill acquisition. It's the *social* in social studies that makes it so much fun to teach. I also love the idea that I can be on Level 1 integration when facilitating our explorer's investigation, approaching Level 4 integration when we study Pacific Northwest Coastal Native Americans, and at Level 3 during our Inuit work. As my awareness, appreciation, knowledge, and resources grow, my level of integration changes. This keeps teaching dynamic for me and learning exciting for the kids. Who could ever be bored?

Chapter Four

MAKING IT MEANINGFUL

SOCIAL STUDIES TEACHING AND LEARNING IS POWERFUL
WHEN IT IS MEANINGFUL.

—NCSS's "Vision"

Making learning meaningful is the core of teaching. If children don't connect what's going on in the classroom with their minds, their hands, and their hearts, then it seems to me that not much learning is going to occur. How do we know when teaching and learning is meaningful? Some of the best thinkers and teachers in the National Council for the Social Studies addressed this question and identified elements of meaningful social studies (NCSS 1993, 216):

- Rather than memorizing disconnected bits of information or practicing skills in isolation, students learn connected networks of knowledge, skills, beliefs, and dispositions that they will find useful both in and outside of school.
- Instruction emphasizes depth of development of important ideas with appropriate breadth of topic coverage and focuses on teaching these important ideas for understanding, appreciation, and life application.
- The significance and meaningfulness of the content is emphasized both in how it is presented to students and how it is developed through activities.
- Classroom interaction focuses on sustained examination of a few important topics rather than superficial coverage of many.
- Meaningful learning activities and assessment strategies focus students' attention on the most important ideas embedded in what they are learning.

◆ The teacher is reflective in planning, implementing, and assessing instruction.

I've observed that what clicks with one learner may leave another confused or frustrated. Therefore, deliberately devising multiple ways for students to experience and demonstrate "knowing" helps me make learning meaningful for all students.

LITERATURE-ENHANCED INSTRUCTION

I'm concerned about two ends of a continuum involving literature, social studies, and the classroom. On one end of the continuum we find the teacher who makes literature the base of social studies instruction in the intermediate grades. This teacher reads one historical fiction novel centered on an event, such as the Civil War or immigration, and that's that. Social studies is done. The teacher on the other end of the continuum never takes time to read a story or share a related picture book with her students. Often this teacher is too busy teaching to "The Test." We know kids are not born with history genes. We have to reach our kids, stimulate their interest, capture their imaginations, and imbue them with questions, concerns, and comments. Story has long been used to scaffold this meaningful kind of learning, providing a secure platform from which to explore new ways of thinking about one's self and the world. In classrooms in which "the story" has become the sum of the learning experience, not much social studies learning is accomplished.

I am a strong proponent of using literature to enhance classroom instruction and suggest that teaching near the middle of the "To Use Literature" or "Not To Use Literature" continuum provides not only balance in social studies instruction, but also provides a powerful entry point for novice learners, an extension for the more experienced, and an enrichment for all.

Sometimes, literature leads instruction. The literature, often in the form of a picture storybook, an historical novel, or a nonfiction reference picture book, may directly correspond with a goal or objective or is chosen for the values it represents, the perspective it reveals, or the questions it stimulates. Sometimes, a concept, a skill, or a generalization drives learning and the companion book selected may be social studies oriented or language arts based. Picture books can be used as models for the students to replicate, using content from the social studies topic being studied. Many times, literature in the form of picture books sets the stage, giving students a visual picture of the time and place about to be studied. Literature and the essentials of social studies are almost always blended together to create an integrated learning experience for my students.

INTEGRATION INVITES MEANING

Teaching an integrated curriculum invites meaning. The action in the classroom needs to be meaningful to both the students and the teacher. From our earliest methods' classes we've been told that if we, the teachers, act interested then they, the students, will be interested. It seems to me that teachers have to *be* interested, not just *act* interested. The interest, the concern, and the passion of the teacher spills over into the strategies selected to teach the content, choose the resources and materials, allocate time, and communicate expectations.

Teachers not only need to see the connections between content areas, they also have to be willing to push themselves intellectually, physically, and emotionally to find the connections that dispose children to certain knowledge, attitudes, and beliefs. In addition, they need to be open to the connections their students make. This kind of collaboration is more powerful than teaching in isolation, more meaningful than confining learning to specific subjects. Disconnected facts and fragmented ideas do little to change the world. Building a network that supports important ideas is critical to today's teacher and learner.

Developing ideas in depth invites the class to spend time, not only in investigation and verification, but also in reflection. How content is presented is as important as what is presented. The kinds of activities chosen to apply or reshape information are significant. If the activities are not worthy of the ideas, if the events planned to broaden and deepen understanding trivialize learning, we have shortchanged the learner and sold our own efforts short as well. Meeting goals, while considering developmental appropriateness, cost, and feasibility, is part and parcel of making learning meaningful.

Essential Participation Skills

When the classroom is connected to the community, meaning is enhanced. To become effective participants, our students need to learn basic participation skills, which include the following (NCSS 1994, 149):

◆ Working effectively in groups—organizing, planning, making decisions, taking action.

105

- Forming coalitions of interest with other groups.
- Persuading, compromising, and bargaining.
- Practicing patience and perseverance in working for one's goal.
- Developing experience in cross-cultural situations.

Intellectual Engagement

The things we study must matter, must be based on common understanding, and must be approached through worthwhile activities that promote application and encourage independent thinking. Social studies invites multilevel intellectual engagement. There is a rich array of content and ideas to choose from, whether one is focusing on U.S. history or modern Japan. Students can be encouraged to find connections on their own, to develop generalizations to test, and to recognize the "a'ha's" in their own understanding of how the world works. The beauty of a social studies core is that students do not always have to start with facts before engaging in higher-level thinking. Instead, they can process on several levels at once, relating new knowledge to prior experiences, thinking critically and creatively, or making decisions based on well-founded reasoning (NCSS 1993, 216).

After all these years, Bloom's (1956) taxonomy of cognitive objectives (knowledge, comprehension, application, analysis, synthesis, and evaluation) still helps me plan. Working backward from my goals, I constantly check for balance between the application of concepts, skills, or generalizations. Planning is multidimensional rather than linear—that realization is one of the biggest differences in my planning today compared with when I first started teaching.

"EXPLORERS AND THE EXPLORED"

Sometimes I need to teach a unit in a compressed amount of time. Perhaps I've spent too much time on an earlier theme or the way the school calendar is laid out demands it or it's a topic that doesn't need to be dealt with deeply, as long as the important ideas are emphasized. This doesn't happen often, but when it does I make careful choices. "Explorers" is a topic often included in the fifth-grade curriculum, which can be compressed without losing meaning.

The first thing to determine is what are the important ideas:

Teaching Important Ideas
- More than one point of view about historical "facts."
- A historical chronology in exploration.

- ◆ Conflicting emotions between the explorer and the explored.
- ◆ Controversy about Christopher Columbus.
- ◆ The dilemma inherent in the word *discovery*.

My goals are for the students to realize there is more than one point of view about historical "facts," to have a notion of when explorations occurred chronologically, to do independent research, and to empathize with the conflicting emotions of the explorer and the explored. Also, there is controversy about Christopher Columbus and his "discoveries"—can people be discovered?

Class discussions often reveal that students have some pretty strong stereotypes about Columbus and some confused notions about other explorers. By way of the lottery box, each student picks an explorer from a list. Given blank data disks, each student spends a short time researching information. (For a detailed plan see page 221 in the Appendix.) This research is a bit more complex than that for the Inuit data disks. This time the students need to read short factual description, which may or may not contain all the desired information. I read books aloud that share diverse perspectives of Columbus—for example, Jane Yolen's *Encounter* (1992), and *Christopher Columbus* by Peter and Connie Roop (2000). As the students complete their data disks (one is shown in Figure 4–1), we talk about these different perspectives and what they might mean. I read them excerpts from Columbus' log.

Living Time Line

When the data disks are complete, the students line up in the order of the date of their particular explorer's death. (Death dates more nearly approximate explorations than birth dates do.) The student who researched the explorer who died first stands at the head of the line, the student who researched the last to die goes to the end. Each student then introduces his or her explorer and shares information from the data disk, creating a living time line of explorers and their explorations. (After we finish, we hang the disks in sequence around the border of the room as a paper time line we can refer to often.) The students peek up and down the line, looking at their friends. Identifying the French, the Spanish, or the Italian explorers triggers the students' understanding of which countries pushed frontiers and why they later claimed certain land in colonial America as their own.

Later each student introduces his or her explorer to just one other student. Practicing the art of introductions, they mention one interesting thing about the explorer. It's fun and funny. It's the first layer in learning about time lines.

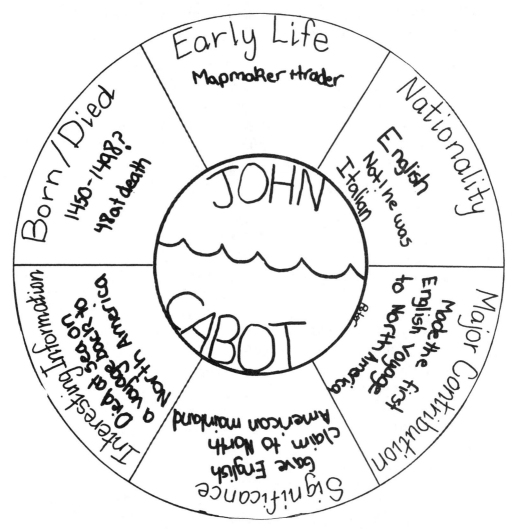

Figure 4–1: Peter's data disk about John Cabot shares important information. See page 221 for the Data Disk and the Reveal Disk directions.

Kinesthetic, visual, logical, and interpersonal intelligences are tapped in this strategy. It's an introduction to names and events, the first threads of knowledge in a network of knowing.

Making Math Connections

The time line activity lends itself to a natural math extension—the human graph. The students who represent explorers who sailed between 1500 and

1599 take two steps forward. The question, "Why is this period referred to as the Golden Age of Exploration?" takes on graphic and numerical meaning. More than half the class has stepped forward. Other directions that stimulate this human graph include: "All who sailed for Spain, go down on one knee. What does this tell you?" "All who sailed to Central and South America, raise your hands." "All who sailed to North America, shake your leg." Cognition is enhanced through kinesthetic and visual manipulation of the living time line.

Writing Connections

By this time the students have read Michael Dorris' evocative book *Morning Girl* (1992). Among the most lyrical of books written for children, it describes the life of a Taino family before the arrival of Columbus. As our study of explorers draws to a close, the students write a letter to Morning Girl in which they tell her what they learned from her story (demonstrate comprehension), alert her how contact with the Europeans will change her life (synthesize the information they gleaned from the reading and research), and share their feelings about what happens to the Taino people (include an affective). Alexa, who has a twin brother and one older brother, wrote:

> Dear Imaginative Morning Girl,
>
> Hi! You've taught me some very interesting things. One truly great thing you taught me is how important brothers and sisters are. The sentence "Without him the silence is very loud" made me realize what a gift my brothers are. You taught me many other things too. But, overall this is the most important.
>
> Boy, did your lives change after contact with explorers and other people who came. Didn't your lives change? From [what] I heard and learned, you got metal and tools, diseases, etc. The diseases really swept out your villages. I'm sorry!
>
> I have mixed feelings about what happened. I really disagree with the idea of slavery! You aren't a people to be owned by others! You're a kind and gentle group in my opinion. But Europeans and other foreigners did give you useful things. I wish those first explorers would have been nice to you! You were very kind to them, and that proves you are lovable people.
>
> Yours always,
>
> Alexa Nicole
>
> P.S. You've made my imagination stretch!

This letter made me feel as though Alexa had realized the goals for the unit. She was able to discern positive and negative points regarding early exploration. She recognized more than one perspective.

Morning Girl models several valuable writing traits and skills. First, the book is structured so that Morning Girl narrates the first chapter. The second chapter is narrated by Star Boy, her younger brother. This pattern of Morning Girl, Star Boy continues throughout the book. Voice, an important writing trait for intermediate and middle school learners, is vividly and repeatedly demonstrated, forming a model that the kids can go back to throughout the year. Second, when Morning Girl speaks, she tells of an event in the family or the village. When Star Boy speaks, he relates the same incident from his point of view. Here is a vital social studies concept—perspective. I think it's the most important social studies concept we have to make our students aware of. Additionally, in terms of writing, the kids are experiencing point of view. Finally, Dorris peppers his prose with figurative language; *Morning Girl* is filled with metaphors and similes. What a good place to introduce this literary device to young authors and readers, especially those who are still very literal readers. What an excellent place to provide the opportunity for more experienced learners to identify, analyze, and create their own metaphors and similes.

Although only a seventy-six-page book, *Morning Girl* is packed with reading, writing, and social studies. Yet it is fiction, and it tells the story that no social studies text tells. How can we provide a more referenced source? I often use a technique called twin texting. As the students are reading *Morning Girl* as a reading assignment, I am reading Francine Jacobs' 1992 nonfiction book, *The Tainos: The People Who Welcomed Columbus*, aloud to the kids during social studies block. This book, written for middle school readers, is an excellent resource book about Columbus and the Taino people. Hoose's book, *We Were There, Too! Young People in U.S. History* (2001), also has an interesting section on Taino life. The research stimulates discussion and provides a background that we can refer to as we study the westward expansion of Europeans in the New World. Pairing, or twin texting, scaffolds the scholarly nonfiction piece with the often more palatable fictional representation. In addition to the information provided, twin texting stimulates what some label "historical literacy." Myra Zarnowski, in an article in *The New Advocate*, suggests when selecting and using children's literature to teach history that the challenge elementary and middle school teachers face is to identify books that both fit educational goals in terms of content and make the process of historical thinking visible. This means we want our students (1) to pay attention to sources of

TARRY'S TEACHING TIPS: GETTING STUDENTS TO *REALLY* REVISE

My students are reluctant revisors when it comes to the writing process: prewriting, drafting, revising, editing, proofreading, and publishing. My students are happiest when prewriting, drafting, or publishing. Getting them into revising, editing, and proofreading is a challenge. In fact, some evidence indicates that primary students are not conceptually prepared to go about the business of revising. Perhaps that's why it's a real struggle for many fourth and fifth graders. The computer has helped nudge the students into really trying revision, not just looking at their papers, shrugging and saying they're done.

Thumb back to the letter to Morning Girl that Alexa wrote. Notice that she's word processed the letter. Doing it took a couple of times at the computer and her efforts are saved on disk. Now it's time for something I call forced revision. It goes like this: "Make a copy of your letter. Rewrite your first paragraph, making it more descriptive. Add one new sentence. Take away one old sentence. Underline your revisions." Rewriting (re-visioning the text) and using the word processor are combined. When Alexa is ready, new directions await: "In the second paragraph, make sure you have at least three facts that you have learned from our study so far. Underline the three facts." Comprehension and recall are woven into the act of revising. And finally, "In the third paragraph, use a metaphor or a simile to describe how you feel. Underline the metaphor or simile. Do not erase your first draft. Save this as draft 2. Make a copy of each draft. Put your initials on each copy. Be ready to share and compare with a writing buddy."

When the final copy is due, the student can return to the first draft, choose the second draft, or continue with self-initiated revisions to a third. Forced revision aids those kids who are convinced that their first effort is their best effort. I use this strategy more at the beginning of a year, rarely past the first semester. Second semester, I tend to do more peer editing (see Lindquist, *Ways That Work*, 1997). Conversations about which letters or parts they end up liking best are humorous. Often, they are surprised to discover that their first draft is not their favorite!

information, (2) to recognize conflicting accounts and interpretive decisions, (3) to identify powerful concepts and generalizations, and (4) to discover connections between past and present. (Zarnowski 1998, 345–57).

"COLONIAL AMERICA—LIFE, LIBERTY, AND THE PURSUIT OF HAPPINESS"

To enhance meaning, I try to connect ongoing generalizations and values all year long. As we shift to pre–Revolutionary America, a Native American thread weaves back into our tapestry of learning. No more do my students experience the "inoculation" principle of learning, "once you've had it, you never

Making It Meaningful

get it again." Instead, common threads continue to weave throughout all we study. To do this, the whole class reads an historical novel.

Reconnecting

I read the first chapter of *Our Strange New Land: Elizabeth's Diary* (Hermes 2000) while the students follow along and we discuss the contents. I also show a filmstrip and bring in additional books and illustrations. Referring back to the explorer's data disk time line, the class connects exploration to colonization. First, we pinpoint the century Jamestown was founded and discuss the gap between Columbus' arrival and the first settlement at Jamestown. Historical time is a very difficult concept for intermediate-grade children. I encourage the students to develop graphic evidence of chronology by creating pictorial time lines of historical benchmarks that they will be able to use as reference points as they mature. Graphic representations, combined with literature, are a powerful educational tool. Certainly this pairing is more meaningful than memorizing a list of dates. The combination is also a very age-appropriate way to create meaningful links during historical studies.

Teaching Each Other

The history of indentured servants is intriguing to fifth graders. The notion of apprentices and master craftspeople is conceptually interesting to ten-year-olds. Using the lottery system again, the students each select a colonial trade, such as tinsmith, cooper, hat maker, or carpenter, to investigate. The students use various resources to identify the craft, the tools needed, and the product produced. Each student creates a poster to display his or her research. In addition to a picture of the craftsperson at work and a depiction of the tools used, the poster contains a "broadside" advertising for an apprentice in colonial America. There is also a letter to a friend or relative in Europe, as if written by an indentured servant or apprentice working in that trade in the colonies (see page 227 in the Appendix for a detailed plan).

Why an advertisement? I begin this way because one of the major pieces of study later in the year is how advertising influences choices and decision making, especially when it comes to drugs and alcohol. Our students are bombarded with advertising from the minute they get up and turn on their radio until they click off the television at bedtime. I think students need to thoroughly understand the techniques of persuasion. So I begin gently, asking them to create an ad for an apprentice. This is the first step in becoming aware of propaganda techniques using persuasive writing.

Why letters? I think letters are one of the most interesting forms of communication we have. It's also the form most likely to be used by the students throughout their lifetimes. Letters are often persuasive or informative and frequently illustrate point of view. Letters let me know what the writer is thinking. I often use letters as a way to check comprehension. I agree with Mem Fox, noted Australian children's author and educator, who writes in her book *Radical Reflections* (1993, 18):

> Isn't it incredible how often writing means writing stories? I can't stand writing stories. Honestly!—What's wrong with letters, for instance? Clarity, voice, power, and control are much more easily developed through letter writing because, perhaps, the audience is so clearly defined and will, if all goes well, respond.

As the posters go up around the room, the classroom environment is permeated with interesting information. Exchanges among the students are frequent and lively as they comment or ask questions about each poster. The kids learn from one another as they listen to their peers' presentations and observe how differently each poster is organized. They notice what seems to work. Because this is our first poster piece, we discuss the effectiveness of students' work and why it is so appealing or informational. The students point out qualitative differences in a positive light. They reveal what they would do again or what they would change next time.

Deepening the Learning

This strategy has continued to "grow" over the years in my classroom. While the Early American Trades poster is very engaging as well as being a vehicle for revealing the students' comprehension of the life and times in colonial America, a deeper and more integrated study has evolved.

When studying colonial America, it is quite common for teachers to ask students to compare and contrast life in the New England, Middle and Southern colonies. A tremendous resource for this exercise can be found in Jody Potts' book, *Adventure Tales of America: An Illustrated History of the United States: 1492–1877* (2000). Using the PERSIA acronym, she provides not only a print response but a graphic one as well while comparing the three colonies with regard to their political, economic, religious, social, intellectual, and artistic institutions. Additionally, graphs, which compare ethnic populations in 1790 and contrast black populations to white in 1750 and 1790, are provided, (Call 1-800-494-2445

Making It Meaningful

to order a copy of this unique resource/textbook written with both sides of the brain in mind. The book is a wonderful aid for elementary teachers who teach U.S. history and an outstanding textbook for middle school students.)

Armed with this information plus other books we read, the kids decided they wanted to build houses that would reflect the character of the region. Students could choose any of the three regions and they could choose to work independently, in pairs, or in groups of up to four. Using empty cereal boxes, opened, flattened, and turned inside out, construction and research dominated several days. Doing projects that require students to build three dimensionally is valuable and worthwhile. So much of what our students do is two dimensional. The manipulation, experimentation, visualization and problem-solving skills required to build a period house out of cereal boxes embodies the best kind of integration: math, social studies, and art (see page 228 in the Appendix for a detailed plan).

When the students completed construction on their houses, they couldn't let go of them. We had to do something with these wonderful representations of knowledge, so we decided to write a journal from the point of view of the house. This gave us an opportunity to practice the "voice" writing trait as well as provided a platform to display both knowledge about the era and region we were studying and our own creative prowess.

Using the little book concept (see page 235) as a kinesthetic organizer, the class came up with possible topics: page 1—Title and author, page 2—Introduction, page 3—Description of house when built, page 4—Currently, what is my condition and who lives in me, page 5—What are some of the good or happy things that have happened in me, page 6—What are some of the sad things, Page 7—What my future will bring, and page 8—About the author. By using 18"-by-24" construction paper to create the little book—we call it the Little Bigger Book!—students are encouraged to illustrate their writing.

My students became so engaged with their houses that they created paper dolls to people their buildings. These were the people who were described in their Journal of a House writings. Many of the kids used fabric to "dress" their paper dolls. These dolls, handled like puppets without a stage, had long conversations with each other, discussing the concerns of pre–Revolutionary America. Definitely, a deepening of learning displayed.

Putting Literature in Place

As the posters are being created, we begin reading Scott O'Dell's *Sarah Bishop* (1980). Even though it was written many years ago, the story is engaging to both boys and girls. It does a good job of bringing out multiple perspectives about the Revolutionary War and provides a setting for the more historically driven information the students will need later to understand the Constitution and the Bill of Rights. Sarah's father is a Tory and suffers abuse because of his beliefs. The threads of witchcraft and religion are also "sewn into the fabric" of the book. There is a richness to the story that encourages many connections as well as historical scholarship. The whole notion of justice, law, and order is fundamental as well, initiating still another thread we'll continue to follow throughout the year. It's also a challenging book. When used early in the year, I often read it aloud. Sometimes the kids listen. Sometimes they follow along with me. I've also put it on tape so that those kids who need it get the support they need to read this book. Making sure they get to "read it with the tape" at least once before we actually begin reading the book in class scaffolds greater success for struggling readers.

Some teachers may not be comfortable with this selection, however, because there is one episode in which Sam Goshen, a less-than-admirable character, attempts to molest Sarah. She handles the situation effectively and efficiently. Depending on their reading maturity, some children never "get it" and others do. I use the scene to discuss what Sarah does to get herself out of an uncomfortable, possibly dangerous situation. Personal safety is one curriculum we teach and this seems like a natural place to insert a discussion about it. Today's students certainly need to be well aware of danger signs and what to do, and we need to open up lines of communication so that they can talk about uncomfortable things if they need to. Other teachers may find *Sarah Bishop* too difficult for many of the students to read or too long to fit into an overstuffed schedule.

Books from the "Dear America," "My America," or "My Name is America" Scholastic series are excellent choices for many classrooms and schedules. Written by experienced children's authors, these series of books are written as journals from either a boy's point of view of a time or event in history or a girl's. The narrative is accompanied by Historical Notes and an About the Author section, the study of which promotes historical literacy.

It is important to offer alternative choices. We have so many pieces of literature to choose from now that every school topic can be enhanced through more than a single piece of literature. Teachers who feel their community would find the scene with Sam in *Sarah Bishop* unacceptable can use other historical novels. Perhaps that is one reason *Johnny Tremain* (Forbes 1943) is often used. I find it rather ponderous and dated, so I show the *Johnny Tremain* Disney movie instead, and we watch it after reading *Sarah Bishop*. It is a good companion piece, providing a rich background about how some people dressed, talked, and lived, spurring a series of comparative activities and discussions (Sarah and Johnny, Boston and New York, the Loyalists and the Patriots).

A twin text that works well with this topic is *The Liberty Tree: The Beginnings of the American Revolution* by Lucille Recht Penner (1998). Organized in two-page segments of important and interesting events leading up to the Revolutionary War, accompanied by charming illustrations, this nonfiction book encourages students' exploration of history. To reinforce newly acquired knowledge, I created a floor-to-ceiling tree trunk out of brown butcher paper, all scrunched up, on the back bulletin board. It was fall so we used brown, red, and yellow construction paper to make oak leaves. At the end of each day, the students each cut out three oak leaves and wrote one thing they had learned that day about the American Revolutionary period that was important or interesting. As they left for the day, they'd hand me their three leaves. Then I hung the leaves from the three branches I had fashioned off the trunk. This turned out to be a terrific kind of exit pass because I was able to keep track of what the kids knew and what they were misunderstanding or just plain missing. Also, each day the tree "grew" more and more leaves, visually demonstrating the volume of knowledge they were learning to the kids.

Two other picture books that add to students' understanding of this period in history are *Revolutionary War* by Rebecca Stefoff (2001) and *Colonial Times; 1600–1700* by Joy Masoff (2000). When we finished studying the American Revolution, we moved to studying the Constitution. The Liberty Tree on the bulletin board morphed into a visual metaphor for the Constitution and the three branches of government.

TARRY'S TEACHING TIPS: TEACHING THE SIX ELEMENTS OF FICTION

Years ago I was taught this strategy for teaching the six elements of fiction. Another teacher who had attended a Writers Northwest workshop showed me and I never forgot. I don't know who to cite but I am grateful for the Little Miss Muffet analogy:

◆ Little Miss Muffet—main character
◆ Sat on a tuffet—setting
◆ Eating her curds and whey—situation or condition
◆ Along came a spider—problem
◆ Sat down beside her—conflict
◆ And frightened Miss Muffet away—resolution

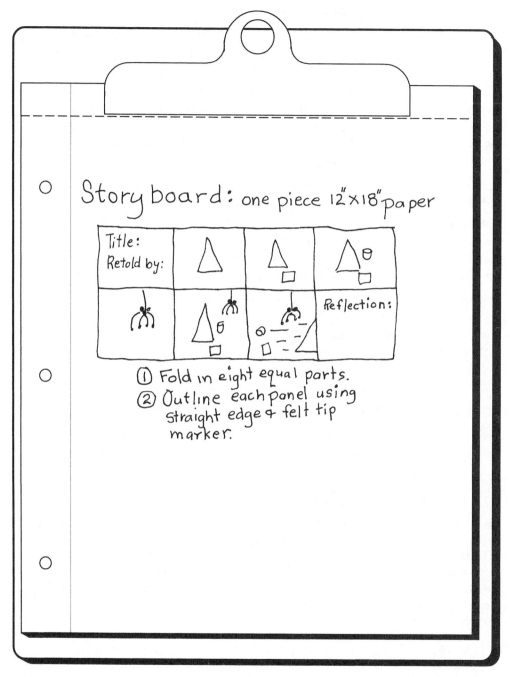

Figure 4–2: Storyboard © 2002 by Tarry Lindquist from *Seeing the Whole Through Social Studies, Second Edition*. Portsmouth, NH: Heinemann.

Creating Picture Storyboards

After reading *Sarah Bishop*, we create a group storyboard identifying the six elements of a story. The students work in pairs, creating a panel that becomes part of the whole storyboard.

Like all good novels, there are several subplots woven into the main story of *Sarah Bishop*. The students work in groups to present their ideas to the class. Talk centers on the novel and I hear students questioning each other about parts they didn't quite understand or verifying an understanding with a friend. This kind of conversation is rich because it is child-centered.

Above the occasional inaccurate assumptions and conclusions, I hear children sharing their understanding and insight. I know that children, developmentally, need practice talking about what they read. Like many adults, they often don't really know what they believe until they say it out loud. It seems critical to me that students not be judged by the correctness of their responses, but rather by their growth and thoughtfulness in understanding and appreciating literature. By using literature and encouraging conversations enriched with engaging activities, we foster increasingly complex levels of comprehension and appreciation of life through language. My friend Paula Fraser, puts it well: "Literature is a way to entice and engage students initially so that they are motivated to discover the substance and the facts."

HOW IT WORKED FOR ME—LYNN, 14 YEARS OF EXPERIENCE

Facts and Stats: fifth grade, 27 students, self-contained, heterogeneous class: some bilingual, some inclusion, small town/rural, mixed demographics

Storyboards aren't just for stories anymore! This is how serendipity met a good idea and changed science. The first week of school, we used storyboards with picture books to learn the basic elements of fiction. These fifth graders loved rereading some of their favorites "from when they were little," and it was fun for me to share the newer titles they hadn't seen before, too. Students concentrated on the big ideas and mastered the terminology before we began our fall quarter novel—a real plus when tracking a much bigger story line! It was heartening to hear them explain these key concepts from the storyboard display to their parents at Open House. They were proud of their mastery, and I was too!

It seemed like a real shame to abandon such a useful learning tool, especially since its beauty lies in its simplicity. All students can be challenged and successful, regardless of ability. So, I started looking for ways to apply this scheme elsewhere in the curriculum. As we approached the end of our spring earth science unit, the idea hit me like a earthquake: provide a choice of earth science topics to present as a culmination of a final research project in a storyboard format. Reviewing the objectives for our unit, we brainstormed a list of possible topics to review and investigate further. Using the eight-panel storyboard layout,

---

we identified eight corresponding areas to cover in both research and to represent on the 'board itself:

1. Topic—example: Recycling plastics. Bad news—acid rain. Effects of pollution. H_2O. Visit the wastewater treatment plant. Life of an igneous rock.
2. Introduce Topic—Main "character"; definition of terms.
3. Setting—Where on earth?
4. Situation or Condition Before the Problem—Life as it was
5. The Problem—Explain it
6. Conflict—People versus nature
7. How Can the Problem Be Solved–Recommendations—"Caretakers of the earth"
8. Resolution—How your solution will change the world for the better

I set a one-week due date and was delighted with the focused, creative action that followed. Students were thorough and inventive in using text and Internet resources to prepare their storyboards. The hardest part was learning to write concisely so that the information and illustration could fit in the panel—several students wanted to use poster board to fit more in, which may be an option in the future.

We shared the now retitled "Earth Boards" on Earth Day in April with another class, and then made a hallway display for the school. The projects reinforced goals for student research—using cross-curricular reading and writing, identifying main ideas and supporting details in informational text, synthesizing information, presenting orally, and making connections to the real world.

I saw students learn more deeply and devote more time on-task than for any test they'd prepared for earlier in the year—a real plus!! And the results were *excellent*. It's become a staple of our spring curriculum, garnering compliments from parents and positive feedback from staff (How *did* you do these?), and the kids are so proud of what they have accomplished. Some of them sent their recommendations to public officials as a follow-up, which I plan to incorporate for all students this year. And to think all this great scientific research started with *Danny and the Dinosaur!*

Taking Notes

The hook is in, the kids care. Ready now for more factual information-gathering, we move to the textbook and other resources, reading to learn. We compare textbook information to the novel *Sarah Bishop* and the movie *Johnny Tremain*. The students meet General Gage, Samuel Adams, John Hancock, Reverend Clark, and Dr. Warren in print. The pieces of colonial life and pre–Revolutionary America connect in meaningful ways. Note-taking is arduous for intermediate students. I help my kids get started by copying isolated pages of information from various sources, including our textbook. Instead of writing

Figure 4–3: Dasha and Chris present a class storyboard created after reading *Sarah Bishop*, a Revolutionary War story by Scott O'Dell.

out notes, which can take some kids forever, we start by highlighting important information. I teach my kids Stephanie Harvey's (1998, 76) steps:

- Scrutinize the first and last line of each paragraph.
- Highlight only necessary words and phrases.
- Don't get misled by details.
- Try to highlight less than half of any paragraph.

Philip Spencer wrote a wonderful resource for fifth graders titled *Day of Glory: The Guns at Lexington and Concord* (1955). The book recounts the twenty-four hours surrounding the battles of Lexington and Concord, a chapter for each hour. To check comprehension and encourage discussion, I pair the children by reading speed and require them to create a "Very Important Idea" disk. First, both students read an agreed-on chapter. When finished, these reading "buddies" discuss what they have read and come to an agreement as to

Figure 4–3: *continued*

what was the most important or significant part of that chapter and they record their decisions on a "clock" face that they have created using a disk (see Figure 4–4). I can monitor their comprehension by walking around the room, reading their disks. Those who are demonstrating their understanding can continue on to the next chapter, reading and discussing at their own speed. Those who need assistance, get it from me, up close and personal!

Listening to Unheard Voices

I ensure that diverse perspectives are visited and validated, that information is extended and enriched, that learning and teaching is meaningful to all students in my classroom, not just a favored few, that cultural connections and ethnic origins are recognized and studied. This is not accidental but deliberate and is guided by my personal belief that historical studies should be inclusive. In the past, textbooks and other easily accessible materials have tended to be monocultural. Nowadays, there may be a mention or two of minority contributions, but it is more often tokenism than anything else. If we truly value a pluralistic

Figure 4–4: Cailen's "pocket watch" records significant information by the hour as she reads *Day of Glory*.

society, we must provide more than passing mention of the roles diverse people played in our past.

In my classroom, valuing multicultural America permeates the day, week, month, and year. It is not something I teach for a week or two. I don't do a multicultural unit. Instead, over the years, a learning environment has developed that touches, recognizes, and values the diversity of our classroom and in our community. We don't "do" Native Americans on Thanksgiving and African Americans on Martin Luther King, Jr. Day. Ethnic literature, games, and songs fill the classroom all year. I've moved away from the Tacos-on-Tuesday Syndrome, a term coined by Mako Nakagawa. A multicultural education specialist formerly with the Washington State Office of the Superintendent of Public Instruction, Mako was referring to those classrooms whose total multicultural education program consists of recognizing a culture (e.g., Mexican) in a one-day celebration centering around food (e.g., tacos). While food is important, certainly there is more to cultural understanding than a single dish, and most certainly understanding a culture takes more than a single day.

122

Presenting a Microlecture

Picture the poor patriots—broke, disorganized, and basically alone. There were small-scale riots and neighbors who harbored grudges against each another. What is this fledgling country to do?—*If You Were There When They Signed the Constitution* (Levy 1987) is a quick read-aloud to set the stage for more learning. What would you do? Get a group of respected people together and work out the problem. Does that seem logical? It does to the kids. Why weren't there Native Americans, women, Hispanics, or African Americans involved? The students know. They have knowledge about colonial society.

Not having a particularly engaging resource for the students to read about the "founding fathers" and the history of the events leading up to the actual gathering in Philadelphia, I decide to use a microlecture. Seldom more than ten minutes in length, the microlecture is a strategy I choose when nothing else seems like it would be as effective or efficient. (*Beware!* It's a seductive strategy. The sounds of our own voices are music to our ears, and we often forget to stop in time. Inevitably, we end up telling students too much!)

I choose a microlecture when there aren't any appropriate student materials available and/or when there is little time in which to disseminate the information. I make sure my presentation is upbeat, interesting, and accurate. I model the elements of engaging public presentations. My goal is to quickly inform by pointing out specific steps or identifying key elements. Moving from a lecture-style presentation to a story format means I need to know what I am talking about and have a global view of the topic. I need to be aware of my own bias and opinions, taking care not to let my personal response color the information that is being disseminated. And, I always follow up with an engaging kinesthetic organizer so that the kids can show me what they know!

Practicing Taking Tests

During our study of Revolutionary America, facts, concepts, and generalizations are woven into a comprehensible pattern. At the close of our study, we are ready to practice test taking. There's a certain amount of specific information students need to have at hand about the colonial period. I am particularly interested in their understanding of the events leading to the Revolutionary War. It's important for them to be aware of the issues involved. We start with a review. Using a study guide, and working in groups, the kids think it's fun. Their interaction is lively and focused. They can ask anyone for assistance, but they have to assist someone else before they can request help again. The process jogs memories and encourages students to share their interpretations of what we have read, viewed, and discussed. Believing that laughter stimulates the memory, I encourage humor as we work. Learning should be fun! (See Figure 4–5 for another kinesthetic organizer.)

Setting a tone for collaboration among the students, their parents, and me, I alert the parents about our "examination." We have discussions in class to clear up any confusion or misunderstanding. I use this opportunity to explicitly teach test-taking strategies, showing the kids how to identify overarching statements, look for categories, or use graphic organizers. Study buddies are selected and time is provided for shared studying. Activating pre-learning strategies, I demonstrate techniques for answering true/false and multiple-choice questions and writing an essay. We develop mnemonic devices and create visual clues to prompt the memory and stimulate thinking.

I never test on a Monday. Sunday evenings are too precarious for many students. The test is Tuesday. We are ready. The students are focused, serious, and intent. This is practice in self-discipline. And I want every student to *win*. Knowing quantifiable information is a valid activity, but certainly not an end in itself.

In addition to recalling a few facts, the students have an opportunity to show their understanding of cause and effect, their grasp of relationships, and their ability to predict what might have happened if a different verdict had been found at the Peter Zenger trial or King George had been of a different character. The most creative part of the test is a takeoff on—*If You Lived in Colonial Times* (McGovern 1964). Choosing from several hypothetical scenarios, the students choose one and write what their lives would have been like.

I grade these paper-and-pencil tests quickly, using scoring we've agreed on beforehand (see Chapter 8 for a discussion of assessment strategies). Doing a version of the think-aloud strategy, I show the class how I read the papers and what I think as I score their papers. I invite the kids to share their reactions. We talk about why one answer "works" and another doesn't. They figure the mean, median, and mode. In essence, I try to demystify testing for my students and unlock traditional, almost genetic, test phobias. Haven't you had parents tell you they aren't surprised that Johnny can't do math or social studies because "I was always awful in math" or "I never liked history"? Instead, my students have a model for test preparation, test taking, and test evaluation. Testing in a supportive, happy environment occurs several times throughout the year, until every child feels confident.

Ending with a Song

The students have a solid understanding of colonial times, Revolutionary War issues, and the people and events important to that historic period. Now we

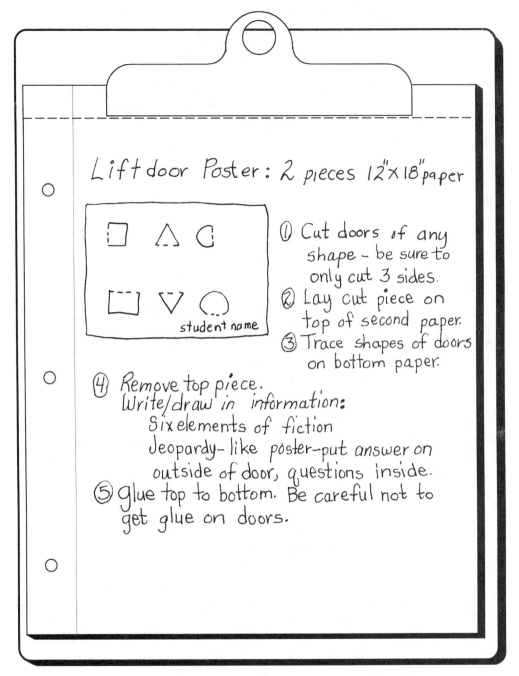

Figure 4–5: Lift Door Poster © 2002 by Tarry Lindquist from *Seeing the Whole Through Social Studies, Second Edition*. Portsmouth, NH: Heinemann.

Making It Meaningful

need to synthesize and personalize it into a whole. Music is one way to do it. First as a whole group, we try writing lyrics summarizing the events surrounding the Revolution to the tune of "Yankee Doodle"—a song associated with that time. The verses might deal with things like taxes, the Boston Tea Party, the Minutemen and Paul Revere, the shot heard 'round the world, Bunker Hill, the Declaration of Independence, Hessians, Washington crossing the Delaware, or the first stars and stripes, to mention a few. I familiarize the students with the tune and the form, then brainstorm all the possible events, people, and issues. The children, working alone or in small groups, create their own verses and write them on overhead transparencies. Many draw scenes to accompany their lyrics. When everyone is ready, each verse is placed on the overhead and we all sing and laugh and share our knowledge. The pictures, drawn on the overheads with permanent marking pens, create a "slide show" as well as illustrate the kids' comprehension of the events.

Piecing It Together

Quilting, a common craft in colonial times, is quite engaging to intermediate-grade students. While I once had a student's mother come in and teach quilting to my students, I am more pulled to the color and form of quilts than to the stitchery. We usually create personal quilts out of paper (see page 230 in the Appendix for detailed plans). We begin by looking at quilt patterns and listening to quilting stories. *Eight Hands Round* (Paul 1991) is an especially delightful quilt book because each page gives a brief history of the pattern, shows one square in detail, and then shows a series of squares, making the overall pattern apparent. Another is *The Quiltmaker's Gift* (Brumbeau 1999), which is filled with traditional quilt patterns. The mathematical repetition of quilting is intriguing. The memories and history of the "fabric" that makes up a quilt evokes wonder and special feelings.

After looking at and talking about quilt designs, color, and form, my students each create a personal quilt. Felt-tip markers make bright, sharp colors. Colored pencils bring a soft, pastel feeling to the design. Colored crayons add texture. Using paper lightly lined in one-inch squares, the students create their own memory quilt. I encourage them to draw on knowledge as well as experience to fill in their squares. Some choose to make a series of one-inch designs—others work in four-inch or nine-inch patterns. Math applications occur as the students use symmetry, fractions, or tessellations. We've discovered over the years that outlining each square with a solid color brings out the design more clearly. Children are urged to share their designs: "piggybacking" is the best form of flattery. The quilts project wraps up our colonial study by appealing to the kinesthetic and the visual, locking in memories, and providing a vehicle for self-expression. When the students are finished, I laminate their work because the process heightens and intensifies the colors. It also protects the project until it reaches home. So much work and careful detail needs to be ensured safe passage. (Michele's quilt, shown on the cover of this book, is a memory of our year.)

HOW IT WORKED FOR ME—MARIE TOBUREN, FIRST YEAR OF TEACHING

Facts and Stats: fourth grade, 25 students, self-contained classroom. Many students struggling with reading and writing competencies, some repeating the same grade.

The first strategy I tried was an artwork and writing piece to use as an assessment after reading aloud the picture book *Sweet Clara and the Freedom Quilt* by Deborah Hopkinson. We were doing the unit from our social studies textbook on slavery and the underground railroad. I wanted to evoke strong emotions from my students regarding these issues and I knew the textbook alone could not do it. I chose to read aloud this story about a young slave girl who listens carefully to what visitors say when they come to her plantation and then uses the information to sew a quilt that contains a secret map and directions for how to follow the Underground Railroad and escape to freedom.

After reading the story and sharing reactions, we set to work creating our own quilts with small quadrants in one large one. Up to this point in the school year, I had not been specific in my requirements about how artwork was to be done, and, unfortunately, this showed in the quality of the work students turned in.

This time I used Tarry's guidelines and instructed the kids to draw in pencil first, then outline everything in black, and then color *everything* unless it was naturally white. Initially, my students were unhappy about all this "extra" work but that changed when they saw the results. They were truly impressed and proud of the artwork they had created and wanted to display them in the hall for others to see!

Along with the artwork, I instructed the students to write a one-page response to the read-aloud story and artwork activity. Again, I followed Tarry's suggestion and gave my students a simple outline of what I wanted in each of the three paragraphs—write about what they did, what they learned, and how they felt. When I read their responses, I could easily assess whether they had learned the main ideas and then modify my next lessons accordingly. As I think about this activity, I definitely feel it was worth the time and I plan to incorporate it into the unit again. Here are two excerpts from student work:

> "When I heard this book I learned overseers could be black. I learned slaves lived in shacks and were shackled." (Jamie, 10)

> "What I learned was that it was just that hard to be free. I also learned that you have to take a certain path or you'll get lost . . . I would have felt sad if I were a slave. I'd die for my family! I think that if slavery were still here I'd pay their owner for them to be free. I felt mad and angry." (Andrew, 10)

REFLECTIONS

I think intermediate-grade students need to experience learning with all of their intelligences. Although teachers may not need to teach through every single intelligence every single day, we should provide an environment that encourages children to explore or expand their own learning orientations. Multiple ways to become knowledgeable, as well as multiple ways to demonstrate knowing, mean that more children will experience success.

Teachers who incorporate the multiple intelligences into their planning use words like *networks, connections, sustained, authentic,* and *reflections.* Students *read, participate, relate, write, invent, design, interpret, construct, chart, illustrate, describe, conduct, demonstrate, generate, laugh,* and *share.* This kind of vocabulary characterizes meaningful teaching and learning. Integrating parts and fashioning them together makes it possible for children to experience their education wholly.

Jesse Jackson (1988) once likened our country to a blanket woven from many threads, many colors, but one cloth. He went on to say that sewing together pieces of cloth, patches of wool, silk, and gabardine, with sturdy hands and strong cord creates a quilt, "—a thing of beauty, power, and culture." The fabric of our country is made up of individual and unique pieces, just as classrooms are made up of individual and unique students. Together, these pieces form a strong cloth that will "wave" forever. Ours are the hands, our planning the cord, that contribute to the character and knowledge of students. Acknowledging, appreciating, and accommodating individual differences within classrooms makes learning meaningful, it makes it whole.

Chapter Five

EXPLORING VALUES
AND POINTS OF VIEW

SOCIAL STUDIES TEACHING AND LEARNING IS POWERFUL
WHEN IT IS VALUE-BASED.

—NCSS's "Vision"

MAKING MULTIPLE PERSPECTIVES REAL

Gary Howard, director of the Respecting Our Ethnic and Cultural Heritage Center (REACH), likes to explain the concept of multiple perspectives in the following way. He describes an accident occurring at the intersection of five streets: On one corner stands a young man who has recently been arrested for driving under the influence and has had his license revoked. On a second corner stands an elderly woman with cataracts who has never had a driver's license. On the third corner is a middle-aged career woman hurrying to an appointment. On the fourth corner is a recent immigrant who is used to driving on the left side of the road. A trained insurance investigator stands on the fifth corner.

How do you think their stories might differ when each is asked to describe the accident? Their point of view—where they were physically standing at the moment of the accident, as well as their awareness, their interest, their past experiences, their knowledge, and their ability to accurately describe what they saw—will influence each story. This is what multiple perspectives are about, and it is an incredibly important concept to teach children.

Those who teach nine- to twelve-year-olds know just how egocentric they are. It has never occurred to many of these children that they are not the center of the universe. Nearly every event is personalized. Almost all action is a stimulus or response to self-gratification—not in a greedy or grasping way, but in a naive, unconscious way. Yet intermediate-grade children also are openly sensitive to the plight of others, want to rescue the weak and protect the innocent, are masters of righteous indignation. Their sense of justice is highly developed and the worst epithet they can utter is, "It isn't fair."

Literature brings multiple perspectives to life in the classroom better than any other resource I know, whether legend, folktale, novel, or true story. Diverse perspectives are most vividly realized through narrative.

Children need to connect with heretofore unexamined issues, unexplored thoughts, and unexplained rationales. Caught up in a story, we care about the characters and experience their problems vicariously. The bond between reader and story creates a friendly foundation for age-appropriate discussions, debates, simulations, and research.

UNEARTHING ETHICAL DIMENSIONS

Opening children up to other perspectives is one of the most delightful tasks a teacher has. Kids are so adept at learning how to look at issues from more than one side. Paradoxically, they are not so quick to apply the notion of multiple perspectives if the issue involves them. One of the true strengths of powerful social studies teaching is that it encourages respect for opposing points of view, sensitivity to cultural differences, and a commitment to social responsibility and action (NCSS 1993, 218).

Recognizing that it's easier to talk about something than it is to do it, the democratic classroom encourages students to apply multiple perspectives, not just give lip service, to the concept. Considering the ethical dimensions of topics can become a routine part of learning. Controversial issues can be addressed maturely and readily. The realization that anything can be talked about leads to deeper reflection and more engaged ways of being in the real world.

The classroom should be a safe forum for trying out ideas and suggesting solutions. The teacher's role is to encourage the students to respect the dignity and rights of others while ideas are being tested and shared. Teaching children the language of multiple perspectives is necessary at this age—some people think this way, other people think that way. Sharing strategies for weighing the costs and benefits of choices with them is an important part of value-based teaching. Through the teacher's questioning and modeling, students begin to internalize basic democratic concepts and principles when making personal decisions or finding solutions to public problems. Surrounded by people who demonstrate they care about the common good engenders an environment for prosocial values and social responsibility.

Intermediate-grade students are ready to look at the implications of social action and to think critically about social issues. Too often, there isn't enough time to examine persistent social issues in our classrooms. The integrated curriculum buys the time we need to identify and analyze relevant information about an issue; to measure the merits of various arguments; and to make thoughtful, reasoned decisions.

ACHIEVING BALANCE

As teachers, we need to be keenly aware of our own values. We need to think about how these values affect the teaching strategies we use, the resources we suggest, and the questions we ask. Then we need to adjust our planning to achieve balance. Our responsibility is to make sure the students are aware of the many points of view inherent in an issue. Students should remain unaware of our personal views on an issue, at least while we are studying it together. We should help children identify the positive and negative attributes of decisions. Weighing the advantages and disadvantages is an important undertaking at this time in a child's development.

Once again, how we do something is as important as what we do. Promoting positive human relationships while acknowledging opposing perspectives models mature behavior. Demonstrating respect for well-reasoned positions rather than accepting shoot-from-the-lip responses helps children develop a more critical habit of mind. Displaying sensitivity to cultural differences and similarities validates every child in the room. Demonstrating a willingness to compromise, to listen carefully, and to search for the common good provides a springboard for student reflection and subsequent positive behavior. The notion of perspective nudges children toward a deeper understanding of themselves and others. It begins the process of empathy and sets students up to become "bigger than themselves," to live more widely than their young lives can allow. Looking at multiple perspectives at this age is incredibly freeing. Seeing two, three, or more sides to an issue is evidence of growth, intellectually and emotionally.

Exploring Values and Points of View

TARRY'S TEACHING TIPS: DOUBLE DIPPING, AKA TEACHING CURRENT EVENTS AND READING SKILLS

Trying to get in current events in some kind of routine way is often difficult. I find that using a weekly magazine, like *Time for Kids*, is helpful. Not only do we keep current in terms of what is happening outside our classroom, but we also have a resource to use to work on reading and writing skills. For example, when targeting comprehension, I ask the kids to look at a picture and *predict* what they think the article is about. After reading about an event, I ask the kids to take turns telling a buddy what they picture in their minds about the event, working on *mental imaging*. Before beginning the lead story, I probe for *prior knowledge*. I also use the current events magazine later with guided reading groups, focusing on fix-it strategies in reading comprehension. For example, what to do when a student is incorrectly pronouncing words (have her point and slide, physically touching each part of the word as she says it), not recognizing alternative forms of words (have him analyze the word, identifying the root, and then any affixes), or substituting similar words (encourage her to stop, adjust, and reread all the while making sure that what she says sounds like language—"My family is building a white horse?" "No. My family is building a white house.")

News magazines are a wonderful way to introduce students to note-taking. Any experienced teacher knows that this is a very laborious exercise for most young readers. Skip the kids' copying words and phrases! Instead, give them each a highlighter and use the current events magazine as the worksheet. Have the class highlight the main idea in each paragraph. Have them identify the main character, mark active verbs, underscore powerful adjectives, number details or leave them blank. Teach kids to really look at the first and last lines of each paragraph to find main ideas. Congratulate those who highlight less than half of any paragraph!

Even using the current events magazine as a reading tool does not mean that we spend actual class time every single week on current events. I balance using class time with passing out the magazines during silent reading time, letting the kids choose to read it independently or take it home. Sometimes I save an issue for later distribution if a topic that we are going to study later in the year is featured. Having spent the money, some teachers feel they have to use every single copy, every single week. Sometimes that causes stress and the weekly news magazine becomes a burden. News magazines are a tool. Much of the adult population buys magazines they don't read every single word of every single week. It's okay to vary the use and attention these kinds of resources get on a weekly basis.

Note: If you don't order a news magazine, try this website if you'd like to add a current events component to your reading/social studies: *www.cnnsf.com/education/education.html*. Here you'll find a newspaper reading experience provided in a weekly "featured story, both in full text and edited text (shortenend and simplified)." Additionally, extensive learning activities are provided to build skills (vocabulary, comprehension, and standardized-test practice).

STRATEGIES FOR SEEING MORE THAN ONE SIDE

In our classrooms, we can make it a point to expose students to multiple perspectives. We should give children the opportunity to experience multiple ways of looking at knowledge. The very strategies we choose to use convey our appreciation for diversity. Providing formats that encourage students to share their own perspectives helps students grow.

Story Ladders

New year, new beginnings! As a transition to new studies, we begin thoughtful read-alouds, exploring democracy and other forms of governance through science fiction. Some thoughtful read-alouds I use include three books by Margaret Peterson Haddix, *Running Out of Time* (1995), *Among the Hidden* (1998), and *Among the Imposters* (2001). I also like *The Last Book in the Universe* (2000) by Rodman Philbrick very much. Using a strategy I call the story ladder, another kinesthetic organizer (see Figure 5–1), I ask the students to depict the four most important parts of the story (see page 252 in the Appendix for a detailed plan). It is interesting to note the way one child will use mostly words and sketchy pictures, while another will choose pictures only. Each is effective. Each is affective. Both demonstrate unique yet shared interpretations of the story, record comprehension, and encourage personal connections.

Historical Context

Although many students have had an opportunity to learn about Martin Luther King, Jr., it is usually fifth grade when what they know is placed in a historical context. So often, we "do" the Civil War but leave African Americans "enslaved" in children's minds, treating great black leaders as anomalies rather than the norm.

I like to introduce civil rights in my classroom immediately after we study the Constitution and the Bill of Rights. While his birthday frequently accents our study, it is not treated as a one-day spectacular. Instead, we investigate ideas the kids have about violations of rights. Inevitably, a child will cite racism or segregation as a civil rights violation. With that impetus, we begin our study.

I like to begin with King's stirring words using *Martin's Big Words* (Rappaport 2001). After this introduction, each student memorizes a small section of one of his many well-known speeches. I have combed his speeches and selected particularly memorable or powerful pieces, each one beginning with a concept that illuminates his life and values. Then we present an oral "ABC of Martin

Exploring Values and Points of View

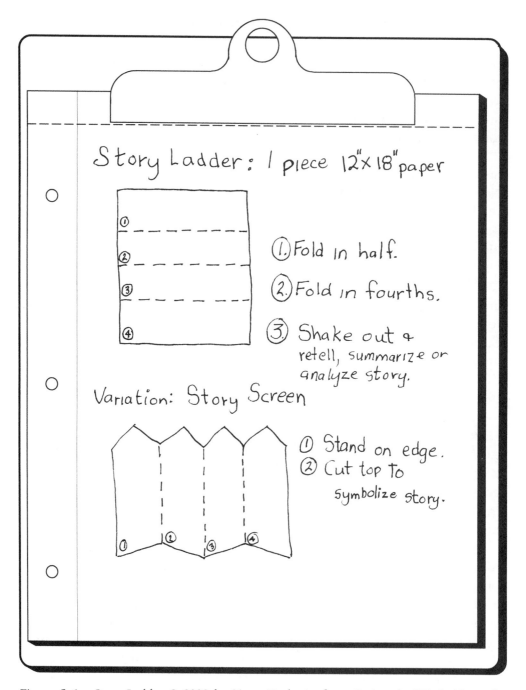

Story Ladder: 1 piece 12"×18" paper

① ----
② ----
③ ----
④

①. Fold in half.

②. Fold in fourths.

③ Shake out &
   retell, summarize or
   analyze story.

Variation: Story Screen

① ② ③ ④

① Stand on edge.
② Cut top to
   symbolize story.

Figure 5–1:   Story Ladder © 2002 by Tarry Lindquist from *Seeing the Whole Through Social Studies, Second Edition*. Portsmouth, NH: Heinemann.

Luther King, Jr." Each child repeats words about concepts ordered alphabetically, that this great man spoke (all together, brotherhood, cooperation, and so on). We spend time looking at the issues and events that inspired the words. We investigate the meaning of the words and appreciate the way in which King used language. We practice delivering the words in a way he would have admired, enjoying the solemnity and grandeur of the English language. We identify issues he would probably be involved with today. And as we sing "We Shall Overcome," I hope the students will remember this ten years from now, standing hand in hand, reviving old promises and making new ones about life, liberty, and the pursuit of happiness for all.

Literacy License

Moving on to the Civil War, we start with literature. We begin by studying slavery and the Underground Railroad prior to the Civil War. Civil rights, the Civil War, and slavery are topics rich in values and points of view. They are a source to be "mined" as the children try on different perspectives and learn the language of opposing viewpoints.

All the kids read the same historical novel, *The Story of Harriet Tubman: Freedom Train,* by Dorothy Sterling (1954). They compare it with information in the social studies textbook and other resources about Harriet Tubman. They verify or repudiate the information that conflicts with their expanding repertoire of historical issues and events. They discuss the notion of "license" in historical fiction, finding examples and hypothesizing why the author chose to illuminate some information accurately and other information not as accurately.

Zarnowski (1998) reminds us that as we teach history, we also need to teach for historical literacy. We need to remember that history writers select what they think is important or interesting to incorporate into their works. Their books reveal how they, the authors, think of the past. Zarnowski reminds us that as time passes, the focus of what is of historical significance often changes. We need to help our students consider the author's reasoning. We need to discuss whether we agree or not, to analyze whether we think the events portrayed are worth knowing. Zarnowski urges us to "bring the ideals home" by exploring whether something similar could happen to us or if the events portrayed remind us of other events. With assistance from us, our elementary and middle school students can deal with historical significance. Using source notes, reading one or two primary documents, looking for bias, and becoming aware of slanted or emotional language are clues we can introduce to students to help them develop historical literacy.

Letters from the Heart of History

I think it is the combination of scholarship and appreciation for conflicting points of view that reaches to the heart of history and touches the mind of the intermediate-grade learner. Writing helps us know what we think and think about what we know. Letters are one of the most age-appropriate and engaging strategies I use to encourage my students to reveal their knowledge and engage in personal reflection (see page 254 in the Appendix for a detailed plan.)

When we begin reading the novel about Tubman, the children choose a character in the book, and write about Harriet to a friend as if they were that character. Meghann, as the plantation owner's wife, Mrs. Sara, writes the following letter after reading the first three chapters:

> Dear MoJo,
>
> My husband has died, and I have to take care of the slaves. They are all stubborn but there is one slave named Harriet that I particularly hate. She is extremely stubborn and will not listen to me. A while ago she was somewhere and got hit in the head with a two lb. weight and ever since she's had sleeping spells.
>
> I think she is useless and is a cheap excuse for a slave. She is strong but terribly useless with all those sleeping spells. I cannot afford all the slaves so I think I will get rid of her.
>
> Harriet will probably be sold to a cotton plantation in the south. If I don't sell her, I will get no money and [she] will probably run away. I hope people will buy her even though she has sleeping spells. Hope to see you soon but so long for now.
>
> Sincerely yours,
>
> Mrs. Sara

Further along in the reading, the kids change perspectives, writing as Harriet to some other character. Meghann writes as Harriet communicating with William Still, a Quaker conductor on the Underground Railroad:

> Dear William,
>
> How are you? Can you remember the first time we met? I can. I was looking at the Liberty Bell but I could not read it. So I looked around and there was a proud looking man so I asked him If he could read the bell to me. That man was you.
>
> I can remember my first journey to the north and how so many people helped me. It was cold but I kept on moving. I can also re-

member the day my own [master] died and how we were all afraid of being sold.

It's weird but I feel like Moses because I also lead my people to freedom. But the one main difference is I can't part water. I am going to keep on doing what I am doing now but It's getting harder to take them all the way up to Canada. I hope to see you soon.

Sincerely yours,

Harriet Tubman

Finally, after finishing the book, they write to Harriet from today, as themselves, telling to her what they admire most about her, what she'd find surprising today, and what she might do if she were here now. Here is Annie's letter to Harriet Tubman:

Dear Harriet Tubman,

My name is Annie and I have always looked up to you as an inspiring role model. Recently my class has been studying you in school and your life fascinates me. I admire you for so many reasons. Some of them being your extreme bravery and amazing courage. To go back over and over to free your people. I think it is amazing how many slaves you freed and lives you saved. I don't think I could ever have performed such bravery with both sleeping spells and not knowing how to read. Judging from what I learned about you, I can tell you were an extremely strong woman. And to spite not ever going to school, you were smart and clever. I think you were probably the kindest, smartest, and bravest woman of your time.

My feelings about slavery are so entirely awful I can't even begin to describe them. I mean, it's unbelievable! To make others work in a strange land for no pay. And only because of the color of their skin. It's simply outrageous! I have read many stories about slaves who worked in houses on plantations and I must say I certainly share your opinions on it. I wish it could never have happened. All those poor people forced to work against their will. It makes me feel happy that great people like you have attempted to save them and many time succeeded.

I am sure you would be happy to know that here is no slavery in the United States any more. The United States itself has probably tripled in population. Now, all different races work together, talk together, and go to school together. Women also have equal rights to men. Basically, everybody now has equal rights and free choice. But it wasn't like this right after the Civil War. It took years for African

Exploring Values and Points of View

Americans to earn respect. Martin Luther King was a black man who spoke for equal rights during that time. People working together has certainly proved to be a better way of life. During the nineteen hundreds, peoples' lifestyles have changed quite a bit. Most people drive in fast moving vehicles called cars, which run without horses. People fly in airplanes and have even gone to space. I listen to music on a small box called a radio and watch news and entertainment on television. I like to talk to my friends who are miles away with a telephone. Though all these things are wonderful, they cause pollution and litter. Even so, I think you would be very pleased with the way things are going these days.

From,

Annie

Poetry with a Purpose

"Poems for two voices" is a technique for revealing what I call the *smart heart*—the combining of knowing and feeling. This strategy encourages children to respect the dignity of others and illuminates their ability to incorporate basic democratic concepts and principles into their own lives. Marj Montgomery of Day Junior High in Newton, Massachusetts, first shared this idea with me, using Paul Fleischman's *Joyful Noise: Poems for Two Voices* (1998) as a model (see page 240 in the Appendix for a detailed plan). Pairs of students write a joint poem, a dialogue for two different points of view (see Figure 5–2). Each voice speaks individually, but the two voices also speak together, offering comments about which they agree or about which they agree to disagree. Luke and Sarah wrote the following poem for two voices after reading the book about Harriet Tubman. The characters are Thomas Garret, a Quaker, and Daddy Ben, Harriet Tubman's father.

Thomas Garret	*Both Characters Together*	*Daddy Ben*
	Why does the color of our skin matter?	
I'm white.		
		I'm black.
	We both love the thought of freedom for each and every person.	

Figurte 5–2:   Darby and Alyssa create a poem for two voices.

Our worlds are
separate.

                                                    But just as
                                                        equal.

Why should skin
matter?

                                                    The color of your
                                                    eyes don't
                                                            matter.

The color of your
hair does not matter.

                                                    We both work long
                                                    hard hours.

I get paid for
what I do.

I don't get a
single dime.

Why does the color
of our skin matter?

INVESTIGATING PERSONAL PERSPECTIVES

When I want to focus on a single perspective, I use a strategy called "interior monologues," which I also learned from Marj Montgomery. To introduce this integrative strategy I ask the class if they ever have conversations inside their heads. The students are often surprised to find out they aren't the only ones who "head talk." We discuss how interior monologues give us incredible freedom to hop around mentally from idea to idea and provide a way to practice how we will express ourselves in public. (For a detailed plan, see page 242 in the Appendix.) The students then write as if they were a character in the book carrying on an interior monologue.

Jon wrote the following as if he were Jim, the slave Harriet tried to protect from the overseer's brutality. Instead she was permanently injured.

> I really wish I was the one that got hit by that two lb. weight instead of Harriet. She doesn't deserve to have sleeping spells, but I do. Please let me suffer and not Harriet. Gosh Harriet you shouldn't have held me—then again maybe it was sort of her fault, too—what am I think- ing it was all my fault. I should have stayed at the master's planta- tion and gone without tobacco or told Harriet to stay and not to warn me, but I think Harriet will do just fine—or she might be sold "down river." Oh Harriet, how I wish you had stayed at the plantation be- cause I can take a whipin' and keep on tickin'—Oh, Harriet—Oh, Harriet you foolish girl, you.

BLENDING RESEARCH, RESOURCES, AND LITERATURE

In this unit, the students also investigate the lives of Lincoln and Davis. As we did when we studied the Revolutionary War, we try to identify issues. We com- pare life in the North with life in the South. We look at the geography, the economy, and the society of Northerners and Southerners. Sometimes we draw megamaps—large-scale representations of the eastern third of the United States. These maps are approximate rather than precise. We do them as pictorial representations rather than replicas. Locating strategic places and identifying important sites helps keep history grounded.

There are many Civil War books out now for the intermediate and middle school classroom. Encouraging students to read from a list of Civil War novels and nonfiction books expands their comprehension of the period and the people. Creating a storyboard with a zoom lens, or a flip book analyzing the six elements of fiction, provides students an opportunity to represent their understanding through a graphic kinesthetic organizer (see Figure 5–3).

Reporting from a Bias
During readers workshop, we learn more about different perspectives from various resources. As our study of the Civil War draws to a close, we turn once again to the newspaper. This time the class is divided into three groups. One group is designated Southern whites; another Northern whites, a third free blacks. Each group is responsible for creating a newspaper from their specific point of view. The groups each choose an editor, who then assigns reporters a specific space to fill and kind of article to write (see page 244 in the Appendix for detailed plans). The variety of writing—editorials, news reports, special features, religion, sports, horoscope, obituaries, comics, classified ads, crossword puzzles, political cartoons, and advertising—within a newspaper makes it possible for every child to contribute positively to the group work. It is also imperative that each child *does* contribute or the paper will be incomplete.

The editor checks each article and sends the reporter back to rewrite if necessary. In less than a week, the papers, culminating the children's study of the Civil War, are hanging in the room. Each group reads their paper to the rest of the class (see Figure 5–4). I hear the generalizations, check the facts, and have a very good idea of what the children know, what they can do, and how they feel about the Civil War and the people of that period.

Investigating Immigration
Our next focus of study is usually immigration. Our region is particularly influenced by Asian immigration, so we compare the Asian American experiences on Angel Island with European American experiences on Ellis Island. I often read *Journey to Topaz* by Yoshiko Uchida (1971) aloud to the class. This book helps students understand institutionalized racism through the story of a Japanese American family in Berkeley, California, at the time of Pearl Harbor. Just as many

Exploring Values and Points of View

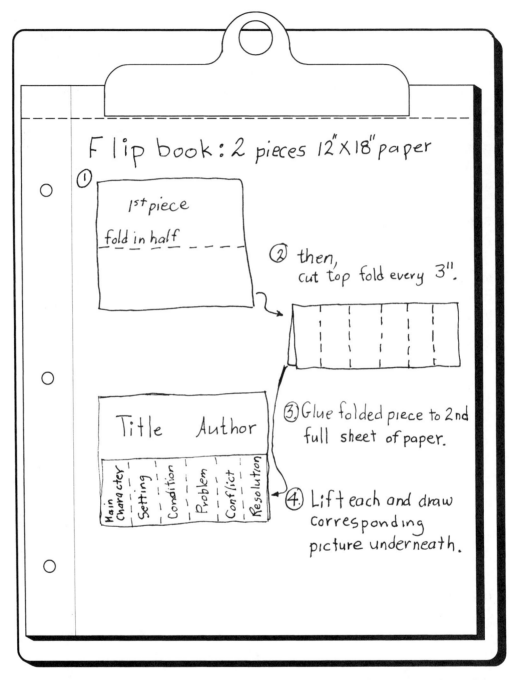

Figure 5–3: A flip book is a variation of the storyboard. © 2002 by Tarry Lindquist from *Seeing the Whole Through Social Studies, Second Edition*. Portsmouth, NH: Heinemann.

Figure 5–4: Stacy, Dan, and Julia display perspective newspapers from the Civil War.

children know nothing about the Holocaust, many know nothing about internment. Every year I have Japanese American children in my classroom, and some of them know little about internment, either. Just because children are of a particular race, teachers cannot assume they are ethnically and historically literate.

It's easy to move from fiction to nonfiction by sharing the history of Gordon Hirobayashi. He is one of three Japanese Americans who refused to follow Executive Order 9066, which required all Japanese Americans to keep a curfew and to relocate to camps inland during World War II. His experience connects to our study of civil rights. Gordon Hirobayashi, born and raised in the Seattle area, was a University of Washington student when he was incarcerated. Later, he took his lawsuit through the courts to the Ninth Circuit Court of Appeals in Seattle.

We re-create another courtroom scene. This time our knowledge base is not literature but real life and primary documents. It is important to make sure that the students understand the tenor of the times. The children study photocopies of Executive Order 9066. We read archival copies of newspapers and diaries

Exploring Values and Points of View

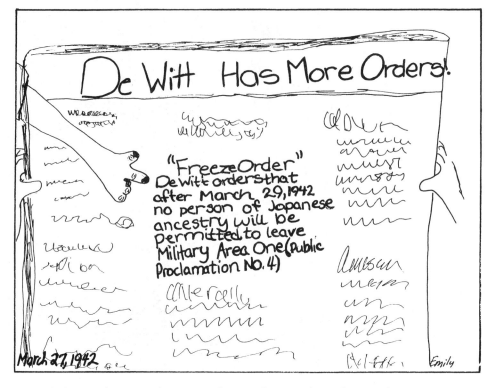

Figure 5–5: Emily's contribution to the Gordon Hirobayashi time line.

of internees. We view old newsreels and watch videos depicting America during World War II. We discuss the courage it takes to stand up for what is right. The students culminate their study with a time line of Gordon Hirobayashi's life, created in a coloring-book format. We print a copy of the completed book for each child to take home and share with his or her family (see Figure 5–5).

Popping Up with Pop-Up Books

The thread of justice continues to weave throughout our studies all year long. In connection with our immigration theme, the whole class often reads *In the Year of the Boar and Jackie Robinson* by Bette Bao Lord (1984). This story of a Chinese girl who immigrates to Brooklyn in 1947 is perfect for the spring—baseball season is about to begin. The students already have a good grounding in immigration. Now they meet a girl who tells about her confusion with English, her misunderstandings at school, her friendships, and her family. Is it a variation of the theme from one of the thoughtful read-alouds? Maybe. That's also for the students to determine. But one strong message is that America is the land where dreams can come true, where people of all races can find freedom and justice. Is that true? Maybe. That's for the students to determine.

It's time for a really kinesthetic activity. The students make pop-up books highlighting each chapter of the Lord book. Using *How to Make Super Pop-Ups* (Irvine 1999), the students depict their comprehension in a new format. The tie-in with Jackie Robinson weaves back to the civil rights study we began in January. Three picture books—*Teammates* by Peter Golenbach (1990), a story about Jackie Robinson and Pee Wee Reese; *Baseball Saved Us* by Ken Mochizuki (1993), a story about a boys baseball team in an internment camp, and *First in the Field: Baseball Hero Jackie Robinson* by Derek T. Dingle (1998)—bring us to a sense of closure. By gathering and analyzing information and assessing the merits of diverse points of view, the students become more aware of social policy decisions such as internment and desegregation. They begin to demonstrate the ability to think critically as they explain reasons for their decisions and their solutions.

HOW IT WORKED FOR ME—MARTE, NINETEEN YEARS OF EXPERIENCE

Facts and Stats: fourth and fifth grade, 25 students, alternative public school program, inclusion, heterogeneous social economic status and abilities

After the attacks of September 11, 2001, I knew my students needed reassurance and hope. Yet never had I felt so hopeless or lack more confidence. I knew it was important for me to give them a future. Writing provides catharsis, allowing authors to get down on paper those scary, awful thoughts that lips can't shape nor voices sound. The events of that day were so devastating that tomorrow seemed an impossibility to many of my students. How could we use letter writing to provide a hopeful future? Write to our grandchildren!

The kids and I talked about how we were participating in history. We discussed how, years from now, we would be asked about what we were doing and how we felt on September 11. This conversation led to the listing of things the kids knew (facts) and things they thought they knew (suppositions). Using the *Time for Kids* magazine, we highlighted the information we thought might change during the days and months to follow; listing these on butcher paper, we would refer to this list many times over the next few months.

As a culmination of our discussion and research, each student wrote a letter to a future grandchild, describing what had happened, what people were doing about it, and how they felt. These letters embodied hope, revealed secret fears, and spanned generations of Americans yet to come. We mailed those letters to each student's family. I added a note, asking the parents to put these letters away in a safe place so that someday, grandchildren really could read a first-hand account of "history." The letters did brighten my students' lives as they realized that to become grandparents they would survive this tragedy and leave a legacy of their own.

Exploring Values and Points of View

DEALING WITH DIFFICULT ISSUES

"A Vision of Powerful Teaching and Learning in the Social Studies" presents three steps to include when dealing with difficult issues in the classroom. According to the NCSS, teachers should make sure that students (1993, 217):

1. Become aware of values, complexities, and dilemmas involved in an issue;
2. Consider the costs and benefits to various groups that are embedded in potential courses of actions; and
3. Develop well-reasoned positions consistent with basic democratic social and political values.

They then can be confident that they've provided sound guidance regarding value-based decision making in a democratic classroom.

Asking students to role-play different positions of an issue is one way. For example, we have held "senate hearings"—three or four students become senators on a fact-finding committee to seek input on a current issue or problem. They represent diverse states and interests. The students, usually by drawing a position out of a hat, take one of the sides of the issue. Working in small groups, the students prepare a presentation for the senate committee. This preparation might include signs, scientific data, and expert witnesses. The groups present their side of the issue to the senate committee. They include a solution to the problem posed or a resolution to the issue being examined. When each group has made a presentation, usually within an agreed-on time limit, the senators adjourn to discuss the proposals. They choose one or come up with a compromise. Meanwhile, the rest of the class listens to the senators discuss the presentations and make their decision. When the role-playing is over the whole class debriefs, identifying what techniques and arguments were particularly effective and which ones didn't seem to work. By role-playing, students "take on" different personalities, often making it easier to deal with difficult issues.

Creating a Math Connection

My friend, Marte, teaches in a neighboring school district. Recently, her district made a curriculum change and adopted a new math program. The first time through any newly adopted curriculum is filled with potholes and "woulda, shoulda, couldas" (wish I would have . . . , know I should have . . . , what I could have . . .). The first year of adoption, Marte had to do an exercise that required the students to spend one million dollars. The purpose was to help intermediate students conceptualize "million." She was horrified by the results. "Million" got lost in the avarice and greed displayed by the kids as they spent their make-believe money. All the table talk and the research centered on who could buy the most expensive cars, take the most expensive vacations, and purchase the most expensive toys. Her classroom deteriorated into a "Me-generation" blowout; she was determined not to let it happen again. The next year when the same assignment came around, Marte reshaped it. She shared her revised unit with me and it has become one of the most socially conscious activities we do all year.

MARTE'S HOW TO SPEND $1 MILLION AND MAKE THE WORLD A BETTER PLACE: A MATH, READING, WRITING, AND RESEARCH INTEGRATED PROJECT *

Ask the class to begin by dreaming of who they could help if they had unlimited amounts of money. Brainstorm potential beneficiaries, (e.g. environment, children's welfare, animals, and health issues). Working in small groups, list places, people, and problems they could give money to, large and small.

Now, set up a scenario: "You have just been given $1 million by an anonymous donor. The only 'string' to the money is that as much of it as possible must be spent to make the world a better place." Some key vocabulary words the students will need to know are *planned giving*, *charities*, *grants*, and *foundations*. I add my own *string*—students must identify at least ten organizations they could possibly give money to.

Now is the time to identify sources of information about real places in your community or county to whom your kids could give money to make the world a better place. The City of Seattle gave us a free booklet that listed each charity in the city and gave a little bio as well as a phone number. United Way programs often have local listings. The Internet has a wealth of information. I just typed in "planned giving" and went from there. I was able to share a list of agencies in our state that receive charitable contributions with the kids.

With each child having a copy of the brochure, I do a think-aloud so that they all experience a model of how to read and interpret this kind of information. It won't take long for the kids to discover that all the money one gives to a charity does not go directly to their cause or beneficiaries: There are administrative or overhead costs. I invited a speaker from a charity to explain why these expenses are necessary and how they are determined.

Remember the string—as much of the money as possible must be spent to make the world a better place. It is important to find out the administrative fees of the charities they are interested in. Fees often run from 15 to 45 percent of the gift, some even higher. To find out, the kids need to write letters requesting more information. To write letters, they need the address of the charity. (Writing business letters or persuasive letters is often called for in real life and on state-mandated tests.) Time to use the phone. Having a parent or an instructional aide help oversee the phone calls is very helpful. We discovered that it's best to have the kids use the teacher's name and school address and to use the school's phone number. Parents aren't always thrilled to have charities calling them at home!

It's time to teach the kids how to set up two spreadsheets on the computer: one lists the original amount and the kids note how much they plan to give and subtract that amount; the other lists the organization, the administrative costs, and the amount given. I have the kids work in pairs so that there is lots of conversation and support, otherwise this project can be overwhelming.

We find it helpful to set up a "pool" of information on a table at the back of the room. That way kids who don't get enough responses from their inquiry can sift through other kids' stuff and use what they need. The kids receive lots of information from the different charities they contact. We also keep a running chart of charities we hear from.

Creating bar and/or circle graphs to depict their giving adds another math application. We used the ClarisWorks graph-making program. My friend, Marte, uses Data Wonder, a graph-making program; or the kids can create their own graphic representations of the money that was spent.

At the end of the project, I ask the kids to reflect on what they have learned and why it is important to them: "Learning about this project taught me many things, for instance I learned how to complete a spreadsheet, percentages, and how much one million dollars is." They thoughtfully describe what they value about the project: "This learning experience was worth it in many ways. Now I know more about charities than I ever had. I know about administration costs and what they are." Often kids also share their feelings: "I liked this project because we made and received business letters by having fun. This project includes art, math, and of course, charities, making it enjoyable and educational."

Some of the kids created an accordion-fold book with construction paper to keep all their documents and research in (see Figure 5–6). Each pair was required to have the two spreadsheets, a graph, and a reflection. Others created "pockets" in the books to save their collections of materials received. Most of the kids used pictures from the brochures they received to visually highlight their choices in these books. This project takes about a month when done in class.

Note: Some of the kids, with no prompting, did actually donate to a couple of the charities they had chosen. One child gave his birthday money, another turned in aluminum cans. A third used money earned from doing odd jobs around the neighborhood.

* Thanks to my friend and colleague, Marte Peet, Northshore Public Schools, Bothell, Washington, for sharing this wonderful, value-laden integrated activity.

REFLECTIONS

Layer upon layer, thread intertwining with thread—what we know and how we feel permeates the pattern of our lives. It is our responsibility to give students the opportunity to become aware and informed about diverse points of view.

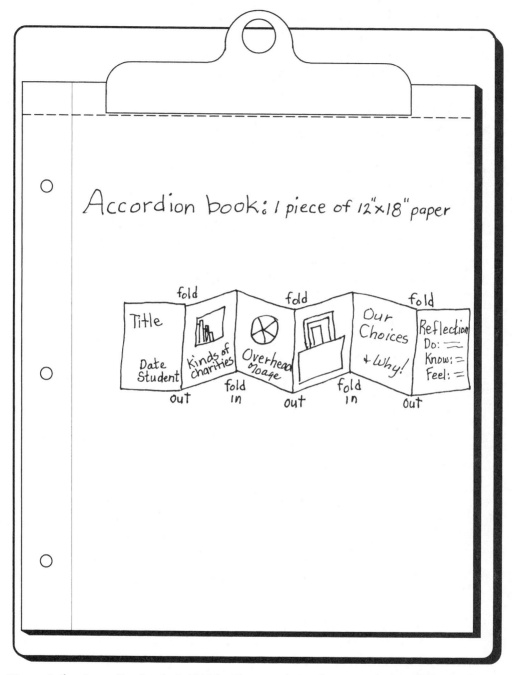

Figure 5–6: Accordion book © 2002 by Tarry Lindquist from *Seeing the Whole Through Social Studies, Second Edition*. Portsmouth, NH: Heinemann.

Exploring Values and Points of View

We need to help them discover that solutions reflect values. We need to provide them with avenues for exploring their own personal values as well as those of a democratic society. Developmentally, our students are moving from self-centeredness to other-centeredness, physically, intellectually, and emotionally. They need frameworks for making decisions. Learning to assess the costs and benefits of a plan of action, whether public or private, is smart. Practicing in the classroom predisposes students to use a similar decision-making model when not in the classroom.

Becoming aware that different people may see the same event or issue in very different ways is often a revelation for the intermediate-grade student. Connecting their behavior on the playground (Why am I always in trouble?) to the classroom (Let's weigh costs and benefits. Let's look at that from someone else's point of view.) is as far removed from students' comprehension as the Civil War was prior to our studying it, unless we provide the ways to make these connections. We are the cord that connects content to self-knowledge. We shape the student as a citizen of today's classroom and tomorrow's world.

Salmon

Chapter Six

ACTIVATING LEARNING

SOCIAL STUDIES TEACHING AND LEARNING IS POWERFUL
WHEN IT IS ACTIVE.

—NCSS's "Vision"

When I started teaching more than thirty years ago, my desk was front and center, the children's desks faced it in neat little rows. I was the star and they were the audience. These days my desk is at the back of the room, where it is used for storing things in, putting things on, and hiding things under. Since I have started integrating the curriculum around social studies, I find I no longer have to carry the whole responsibility of teaching and learning. Sometimes I teach, sometimes my students teach. We all learn. Learning is as much my students' responsibility as it is mine. In fact, one of the most interesting things I've observed is how my students and I gradually shift roles over a course of study. They wean themselves away from my authority and become autonomous learners. I laughingly call this the bonbon approach to teaching, after those moments when the students are so intent in their own investigations that I feel I really could put my feet up and eat bonbons while the children carry on independently.

When children are investigating genuine questions, ones that neither they nor I know the answer to, I have as much to learn as they. Open-ended activities that have the flexibility to extend student knowledge in areas of real interest often enrich both teacher and students.

MEETING MULTIPLE LEARNING STYLES

We know that children don't always get stuff when they are told. Education is not a process of being stuffed. Instead, it is an active process that invites children to explore, to question, and to verify. Social studies is very rich. There's so much to get into. Children need to make sense of what they are learning by manipulating information, investigating questions, checking what they know, and identifying what they don't know.

The activities teachers plan for students can greatly enhance this learning process or impede it. Activities that rely on rote work seldom bring great rewards. Activities that encourage students to develop individual expertise, construct a cooperative group project, or modify an inaccurate belief are much more effective. An activity that helps a child gain self-confidence is a good activity. One that nurtures creativity; spotlights strengths; or eases a child down an intellectual, physical, or emotional path not taken before is a very good activity indeed. And, I think we get more "bang for our buck" when those activities are connected.

Active learning and teaching are multifaceted. It seems a natural extension for teachers who are interested in incorporating the theory of multiple intelligences into their classrooms to direct their own creativity and problem-solving abilities toward establishing integrated learning in their classrooms as well. As a teacher, I love the challenge of trying to devise useful, worthwhile, stimulating, connected opportunities for students "to apply existing knowledge to questions about new content, to learn new content with understanding, to synthesize and communicate what they have learned, to generate new knowledge or creative applications, or to think critically about the content and make decisions or take actions that relate to it" (NCSS 1993, 219).

We should not engage students in artificial activities. You know the kind I mean, the ones when the students look up at you after completing the assignment, a big "So what?" in their eyes. I think activities should matter. They should invite the student to develop a social understanding applicable to the real world around them. They should have an opportunity to "try on" new modes of behavior, whether it is watching a television advertisement critically or volunteering to work with the kindergarten students during recess. I also think it's more than okay for teachers to provide leadership, models, knowledge, and approaches for gathering data, organizing information, posing questions, and searching for answers. I think it is essential.

LEARNING ABOUT RESEARCH WRITING

A common language arts goal in the intermediate grades is to provide experience and develop skills in research writing. Rather than invite the students to choose any topic they wish, I prefer to focus their research and their writing on subjects connected to social studies. My students have had quite a bit of practice extrapolating data from various resources by using the data disk. Now it is time to scaffold a move to a second, or higher level of complexity: the data sheet. Data sheets are organizers I developed several years ago to help all children in my classroom write research papers successfully. I have always had several children on individualized education plans (IEPs), many of them identified as attention deficient disabled or learning disabled. I feel that too often students are asked to do research but are not given the support needed to develop a lifelong strategy. Data sheets, which facilitate note-taking, are my attempt to give all learners a process that will be reliable and replicable. Remember, this is still early in the year and for some kids, the first time they have been asked to research and write a multiparagraph report.

To model how to use data sheets, I use the overhead. I give the kids copies of the nonfiction material I am going to take data from. After discussing the format, the kinds of information provided and the kinds of information required by the assignment, the class and I complete one data sheet together. The general data sheet is quite easy because the information requested is graphically organized into a chart. The students, to be successful, simply move the information from one format to the data sheet. After modeling how to use the general data sheet, I ask my students to choose one of the original thirteen colonies to research. They can work with a partner or alone, but each student needs to take notes on the data sheets, and find information regarding some general, cultural, and economic aspects of the chosen colony. Note-taking strategies include using only short phrases, not complete sentences, and jotting down only the most important information. I will model strategies for completing the cultural and economic data sheets on ensuing days. These are more difficult as more reference information is given and more decisions have to be made about what is important. I expect the work to be done in class and give enough time for it to be completed. This is not homework. It's important in-class work. I want to be able to supervise and to support each student as they try out their research "wings." (Pages 264–66 in the Appendix show suggested data sheets.)

Some teachers may find this way to teach research writing too prescriptive. Over the years, I've found that every single child in my classroom can complete this activity at a satisfactory level. In doing so, the children greet the next, more independent nonfiction writing exercise with confidence and a choice of strategies that work. And that next nonfiction writing will begin with questions posed by the students.

USING QUESTION/ANSWER RELATIONSHIPS

Keene and Zimmerman (1997) remind us that proficient readers ask questions for a variety of reasons ranging from clarifying meaning, to locating specific answers, to predicting what's yet to come. Whether using questions to focus on important parts of the text or determining an author's style, intent, content, or format, questions guide and shape comprehension. Knowing what kind of answer is needed, where to find it, and how to find it are skills the proficient reader employs regularly (119).

Questioning is also a key to unlocking social studies topics. Questions guide research and help writers frame their inquiry. So how do we facilitate student acquisition of the question/answer relationship? We teach it. Researchers and observers of educational process have been codifying the kinds of questions for more than twenty years. Raphael identified three levels of questions (1982, 32):

Right There (also known as **Here** or **On the Line** questions)

Answers can be found directly in the text

What are Cinderella's jobs?

Think and Search (also known as **Hidden** or **Between the Lines** questions)

Answers are stated in the text but in different places

Why did Cinderella get treated so awfully by her stepsisters?

Author and You and **On My Own** (also known as **In Your Head** or **Beyond the Lines** questions)

Answers are not stated explicitly in the text

If you were Cinderella, would you have forgiven your stepsisters? Why or why not?

When I was doing a workshop in Des Moines a while back, the teachers shared with me their titles for these levels (see notes in parentheses). These are the ones they found resonated with students as they taught their classes the kinds of questions and the responses each kind requires.

Fogarty, in her book *Brain Compatible Classrooms,* dices the question continuum in another way (1997, 77):

Fat Questions
Require lots of discussion and explanation with interesting examples

Take time to think through

May not have a single correct answer

Skinny Questions

Require a simple yes/no/maybe or one-word answer or a nod or head shake

Take up no space or time

May need to skim back to answer

Usually have a single correct answer

Early on in my teaching career, I learned a third way to look at questions while attending a workshop given by the Northwest Regional Education Lab from Oregon. I've used this organization to teach all my students not only what kind of answer each question elicits but also the reading mode and speed that each usually calls for. Unlocking the question/answer relationship is vital to our young learners, especially with high-stakes testing lurking around the perimeter of our classrooms.

Description or Data (often answers who, what, where, when); reading speed: SKIM

Answer is directly in the text

Usually one word or two

May need to skim back for answer

Explanation (often answers how, why, explain); reading speed: SCAN

Answer can be pieced together from different parts of the text

May need to reread a couple of times to "get it"

May take a sentence or two to answer

Evaluation or Supposition (make a decision and give reasons, examples, or proof; reading speed: STUDY

Answer may come from combination of sources within and outside the text and/or prior knowledge

May not be one correct answer

Often takes longer, more thoughtful answers

To help my students get comfortable with question/answer relationships, I start by introducing the concept. Often I read a short story to the kids and then, using the overhead, share a series of questions. First, we try to identify different questions, then we attempt to describe how we know they are different. We practice generating each style of question. I give the kids practice questions, using the overhead, board, or copy machine, asking the kids to mark what kind each is. We discuss each and I probe for what clues the kids used to determine the relationship. Then we put the concept into practice. During reading, I devise questions. Just a few, not many. At first I label each, and the kids strive to answer them appropriately. Soon, I am able to drop the labels. I always give the kids choices during this learning time. While I may write twelve questions, four for each level, the kids are instructed to choose two data questions, three explanation and one evaluation or supposition to answer. Kids don't need to answer reams of questions to demonstrate their comprehension of the material or the questioning levels. Short practices, daily at first and then becoming more intermittent, will do the job. Question/answer relationships will be internalized and used for a lifetime.

INTEGRATING CIVICS AND SCIENCE

Perhaps no single topic lends itself more readily to active, connected, and purposeful activities than environmental education. I have trouble seeing environmental education as a science-only issue. I find there is a civics side to the environment that puts it squarely into the social studies arena as well. Anyway, for a teacher in a self-contained integrated classroom, it doesn't really matter what discipline it is. It is a topic tailor-made: science and social studies integrated for a common purpose—to save the earth. I love it!

We start with the science side of environmental learning. Working with local Native American hatcheries, my students raise fertilized coho salmon eggs. They care for the salmon as the fish develop from egg to fry to fingerling. They keep charts on water temperature, take daily tests for pH, change the water, clean the tank, and watch their salmon grow. They solve problems like what to do when power goes out during a storm or when the refrigeration unit stops working. The students examine the eggs with microscopes, make little books about the development of the salmon egg, and trace the life cycle of the salmon from stream bed to the Pacific Ocean and back. They know what salmon need for survival and they can list the problems salmon are having in the Northwest. Early on we integrate the science of salmon, first with language arts and then with social studies. As my knowledge and experience with salmon raising increases, I am able to see where connections exist and how we raise not

Figure 6–1:   Raising salmon in the classroom integrates science with civics.

only fish but also ten-year-olds' awareness of the plight of salmon and the
widespread ramifications of this local issue (see Figure 6–1).

We are the first class to raise salmon on our island and we want to share
our knowledge and our fish with others. The students decide to write one-
page plays about the problems (see page 247 in the Appendix for a detailed
plan) and to create the Sockeye Salmon Theater using my husband's widowed
athletic socks (see Figure 6–2). Not only do the students demonstrate their understanding of issues relating to salmon but they also have an opportunity
to practice reading fluency because they do the plays in a readers theater format. They give their plays to most of the classes in the school so that all the
students learn about salmon and the concerns related to the salmon's return.

This is a real issue in our area. Salmon are critical to the economic health
of our state. Many families earn their livelihood from the fishing industry, either
directly or indirectly. The students are very aware that there is a problem because local broadcasts and newspapers seldom go more than a week without

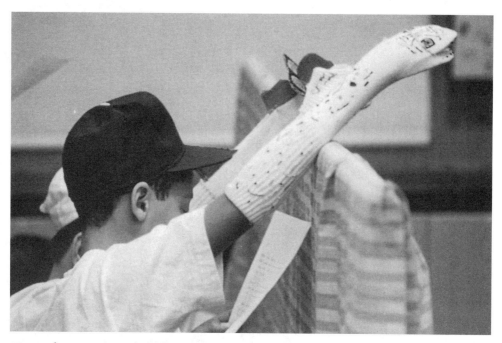

Figure 6–2:   Widowed socks turn into sockeye salmon puppets, as the students create one-page plays to teach others about the plight of salmon.

some salmon-related headline. Using the puppet play as a medium to educate others about the problems of salmon is very effective.

The students also create a huge comic book describing the plight of the salmon and hang it in the front hall of the school for all to see and learn from (see Figure 6–3). Their book is based on their classroom activities and the information in a similar book prepared by the Department of Fisheries.

"The Return of the Salmon Chief"

As the students connect the salmon historically with the Native Americans of the Northwest Coast by learning about fishing lore and fishing expertise, the Native American thread reappears in our tapestry of learning. The kids describe different styles of fishing used by the Native Americans until treaties forced them to stop. They become aware of the historical politicization of the salmon industry, especially in Washington state, when Judge Boldt ruled that the Native Americans had the power to grant non–Native Americans fishing rights, not the reverse.

158

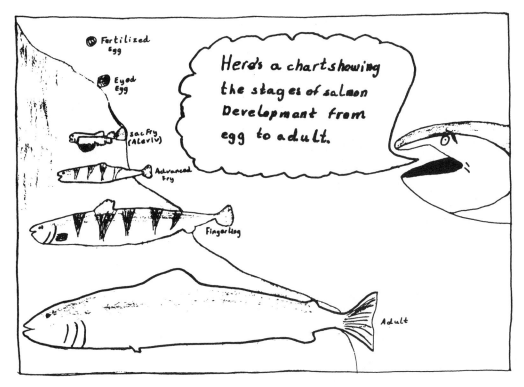

Figure 6–3: Andrew's comic book page helps the whole school learn about salmon.

Local Native American lore relates that each year the salmon chief sends a scout to see how things are. If the salmon scout is treated respectfully by the people, he will go back with a positive report and the salmon chief will lead the fish on a return to the rivers and streams. However, if the scout is treated poorly, the salmon will return no more.

The pivotal question for students becomes, "How can we ensure the return of the salmon chief?" They have deduced that if the salmon can no longer return, then the life on this planet is in pretty miserable shape—streams fouled, rivers blocked, oceans overfished, and development unbalanced.

Connecting Through Commercials

We begin looking for answers. First stop, *Fifty Simple Things Kids Can Do to Save the Earth* (Javna 1990). Each student chooses one of the fifty things to share with the rest of us. After discussing these environmental problems in class, we decide to put together some "Saturday Night Live"–type commercials to address them. Each student takes responsibility for one problem. The goal:

159

Produce a sixty-second commercial stating the problem and suggesting one thing kids can do about it in an engaging and entertaining way. Some students immediately enlist others to work on their "spot."

Others decide to handle it by themselves. All over the room, different kinds of activities are going on. I hear tunes being hummed, see posters being made, watch faces screw in concentration as text is composed. Another bonbon moment!

I see the need for some limits, however—three boys are now using the length of the room and half the hallway for a river race. "Don't forget, you are going to present these as if they are inside a television set. Let's say that it's a really big-screen television, about the size of the blackboard. Keep your action within that width and height. Yes, you can bring in costumes. No, you can't throw candy."

After the first dress rehearsal, we discuss problems: some kids talk too fast, some kids don't "stay in character," some kids talk too softly. But overall, it's pretty entertaining and surprisingly effective. We make out a schedule and invite other classes to sign up for when they'd like us to perform "30 Minutes Live to Save the Earth" for them. Notes go home to parents to invite them to drop in. We decide to make a videotape so that we can enjoy it and have it available for families who can't come to school during the day.

Conducting Independent Investigations

Working outside of class with a friend or with their families, each student researches an environmental topic independently. Choosing any related topic that interests them, they can use any medium or combination of media: poster, essay, debate, video, demonstration, play, poetry. The presentation should take no less than three minutes, no more than five.

We brainstorm possible topics, ranging from deforestation, the spotted owl controversy, and the demolition of dams, to chloroflorocarbons, recycling, low-flow toilets and the weatherproofing of houses. The assignment is made just before spring break to allow plenty of time. This is one of the few true "homework" assignments all year. Most often students are simply finishing work at home that they didn't complete in class. But I know if we really want to make a difference, it will take more than the good intentions of my students. I want to enlist their families and their friends as we try to make the world a better place.

Guided by different levels of questions that they have posed and then researched answers for achieves spectacular results. Charts inform about the rainforest, graphs show the growth of the ozone hole, and videos demonstrate the environmentally sound home. Still photographs of a student inside a paper recycling bin show what other stuff people have thrown into it. A "TV talk show" interviews experts (one student's high school sister, another student's neighbor) about saving the earth. Poetry explores the population explosion and the cycle of hunger. Posters list steps to "Save the Salmon Chief." Ecotrivia games teach and surveys report products people use that harm the environment. The diversity of the kids' interests is astonishing. The integrity of the information is impeccable. The presentations range from okay to awesome. The students are very pleased with themselves, deservedly so.

Becoming Community Activists

The students feel impelled to do something for Earth Day, so we brainstorm some ideas. The local recycling station is run by a high school environmental club. Called "The Committee to Save the Earth," they helped fund the refrigerator unit for our salmon tank. Now, they invite us to help them raise our community's consciousness about Earth Day. My students decide to "Picket for the Planet." Bringing in a parent who is in advertising is the first step. She shows the students how to make effective informational placards, helping them see that size, message, and color are all important considerations. After creating placards and mounting them on cedar laths, all the fifth graders march four miles from our school to the local recycling center in the middle of our business district. When they arrive, they are greeted by the mayor and the city manager, who recognize their dedication to the environment. Then the students go to work. Some work at the recycling center. Others take up positions in grocery stores around town, helping with demonstrations about wise consuming, composting, and precycling. Working with secondary students is very powerful. Fifth graders enjoy linking up with older students as well as leading younger ones.

Becoming Environmentally Conscious Entrepreneurs

Our class is buddies with a first-grade class. The fifth graders want to make something that will help their buddies learn, so they create an *A,B,C 1,2,3 Coloring Book to Save the Environment*. It is a series of black felt-tip drawings of beneficial environmental practices, and a single copy costs fifty cents to produce. We borrowed fifty dollars from the PTA and printed 100 copies. Giving one to each of our first-grade buddies, we sold the rest for one dollar at open

TARRY'S TEACHING TIPS: FOSTER REFLECTION WITH QUARTILES

Don't forget to leave time for clean-up and reflection. For years I planned all our presentations so that they fell on Fridays. And I can't tell you how many Friday afternoons found me cleaning the room and getting it ready for a new start on Monday, by myself! I've learned to schedule class events on Wednesdays or Thursdays. That way, if we run late and clean-up with the kids can't occur on the day of the presentation, the next morning works just fine. Plus, reflection takes place more powerfully for some kids if they personally assess it soon after the activity is over. Frequently, waiting for a response to the activity after a weekend garners lackluster and shallow reflections. Kids associate Mondays with new beginnings. What happened on Friday is old news, done, finished, kaput!

One kinesthetic organizer that supports student reflection is the quartile. Just ask your kids to take a piece of notebook paper and fold it in half, a hamburger fold. Then fold the hamburger in half. You'll have a four-page booklet, a quartile, perfect for thinking about learning (see Figure 6–4). Imagine announcing at the end of a wonderful activity like wax museum (see page 167), "Class, guess what? We have had such a great time. Now it's time to really have fun! Take out a piece of notebook paper and write three paragraphs reflecting on the wax museum." And what would be the class response— "Do we have to?"

Instead, lead the kids through the folding and then ask them to put a title, date, and author on the first page. On the second page, ask them to write about what they did. On the third page, ask them to share what they learned. And on the fourth page, encourage them to identify how they feel. They will end up with three paragraphs of metacognitive response to the recently completed activity and you'll end up with an assessment of the worth of the activity.

house and sold out. We paid off our debt and financed a second printing, which nearly sold out as well. We made a profit of ninety dollars, which helped another fifth-grade class buy some of the equipment needed to set up their own salmon tank. Culminating learning becomes an economics lesson and a real-life application of citizenship.

Making the Native American Connection, Again

Reweaving the Native American thread provides a vehicle for reflection. (Jan Hoem created this very special activity our first year of integrating.) The students pretend to be a Native American elder: "Recall something from your past, share something from the present, and predict something for the future." In character, wearing the Chilkat blanket we have made in class, each child makes a speech. Tony integrates knowledge and values in his:

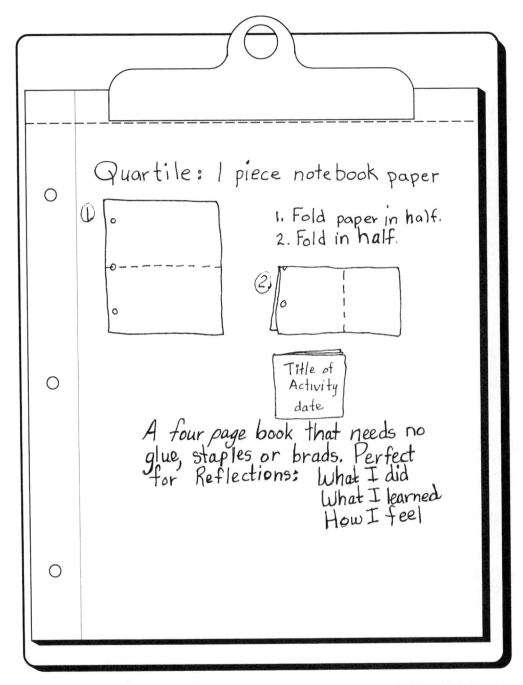

Figure 6–4: Quartile © 2002 by Tarry Lindquist from *Seeing the Whole Through Social Studies, Second Edition*. Portsmouth, NH: Heinemann.

Activating Learning

How, my name is Big Hawk, which is my sacred name but the name I go by is Tom Hawkson. I have lived on the great spirits land for one hundred winters and ninety-nine summers.

I remember as a boy climbing many hills and viewing the Great spirit's land. I saw no skyscrapers. I could breathe the clean air and could see Mt. Rainier, or as we call it Mt. Tahoma, in all its beauty. There were hundreds of trees. It was beautiful. I could see and smell many beautiful flowers. I was able to observe many, many animals building dens or homes and scouting out food. I could see many deer frolicking in the meadows. We had no worries of pollution on the land. I do recall fishing in the river and catching many fish in the wonderful, sparkling-clean, unpolluted water. We had enough in one catch to feed two longhouses full of people. Now we catch very few. Now those that have crossed the land and call themselves Americans have come and taken over. Everywhere I look, the fresh clean air and water have been polluted by machinery, chemicals, waste, and the smoke from big factories. Where I saw hundreds of trees, giant skyscrapers have been built.

I would like all the people to remember we must control what waste we dump in our waters, in our air, and on to our land. We must also control the amount of logging we do and the areas we do the logging. We need to have controls on building skyscrapers. We have to protect our land from pollution and overdevelopment if we want our grandchildren and their children to use and enjoy the land the great spirit has given us.

Tapping the Power of the Pen

Active learning also means activism. My students, using their skills in letter writing, write letters to legislators and corporate officers. They learn how to write persuasively and passionately about things that matter to them. For instance, after studying the effects of oil spills, they wrote a letter to one of our senators, to support a bill for double-hulled tankers.

I always send a copy of each letter that "goes public" home so that parents are informed. I once had a parent ask me whether his child would receive a lower grade if she didn't sign one of our public letters. My response? "Of course not." One of the cornerstones of my teaching is respect for individual decisions. Certainly, this class activity honors that respect. That respect has been accomplished when a child does decide not to sign and does so comfortably. More often, though, the letters are individual, personal, and based on solid knowledge. The classic format of a persuasive letter in my room is:

Figure 6–5:   Michelle writes a letter to express her opinion.

1. Identify the problem.
2. Discuss alternative solutions, including costs and benefits of each.
3. Suggest the best solution and support it with further detail.
4. Be accurate, succinct, and respectful throughout.

MAKING QUICK-AND-QUIET BOOKS

Active learning includes creating learning materials for the class. We frequently create our own books. "Quick-and-quiet books" usually culminate a field trip or are created after we have heard someone speak at our school. I named them that because they capture the essence of some recent class activity quickly and quietly. For example, at the end of our study of immigration, we often take a field trip to the International District in Seattle. While less than thirty minutes away from our school, many children have never visited this unique neighborhood in our metropolitan area. Our suburban island tends to be rather insular and hooked on car pools rather than public transportation, so the first thing we do is use the city bus system to get to the International District. Once there, we spend the day visiting historic sites on a walking tour—the students see the first Chinese school in Seattle and learn how racism kept the International

District from being an integrated part of Seattle until quite recently. The students appreciate the outdoor sculptures and visit exhibits at an Asian American museum named in honor of the first Chinese American to become a U.S. legislator. We eat lunch—in six courses!—in a Chinese restaurant at large round tables that seat ten. We invite parents who work downtown to join us. Chopsticks, tiny cups of tea, and fortune cookies highlight the meal. It's one of the few times that we spend an hour over food, talking and sharing the adventures of the day.

After lunch we break up into small groups and explore the tiny shops. Prior to the field trip, we practice appropriate reactions to anything unusual we might see, taste, or smell. The International District is a neighborhood. Pointing, talking loud, making faces or rude noises, just aren't acceptable. We are guests and we need to be polite and thoughtful. It's a great experience for these ten-year-olds, especially when they visit the herbal medicine shops, peer into the fish markets, cruise the vegetable stalls on the street, or enter the doors of Asian bakeries.

Once we arrive back in the classroom, we capture everything the students can remember in a list. Usually we end up with forty or fifty different things the students recall as interesting, important, or remarkable. Using the lottery box again, each child chooses one thing to record in our book. Using the quick-and-quiet format of picture and short paragraph, the process takes a little more than an hour. Having the kids title their topic as a question acts as a guide for their written responses. Shoulder-to-shoulder editing facilitates publishing. Students who are waiting their turn to edit with me work on drawing illustrations for their topic. We collect all the pages and bind them into a book. Sometimes we read the book out loud. Sometimes we set up a checkout system so that students can take it home. Sometimes we just leave it in the classroom for reading workshop.

The quick-and-quiet book can also become a textbook. One year we were really running behind and it looked like we were going to have to "do" pioneers in a week or not at all. So, I asked the students, "What's everything you ever wanted to know about pioneers?" We listed all the questions on the board, then we classified the questions by categories: hunting, wagon trains, homesteading, trails, and so on. Some of the questions grouped easily under larger topics, some remained highly specific. Back to the lottery box. Each child chose one question to answer. Using the quick-and-quiet format—picture and short paragraph—each child researched and found an answer to the question. In two days, all the questions were answered and the pages were complete. I ran copies of each child's work and we collated the pages into a book that became our textbook for the final two days of a pioneer preview. The kids loved it. Their writing was valued enough to become a textbook. Their research really needed to be accurate and authentic. Their drawings extended comprehension. It all mattered. It wasn't an onerous task dragging us all down by its sheer weight. Putting the children in charge of their learning was not only quick and quiet but effective (see pages 256–57 for detailed plans).

CREATING A WAX MUSEUM

As I think back, the year we started doing quick-and-quiet books must have been a year of the talkers. Quick-and-quiet books kept the students engaged for forty or fifty minutes in drawing and writing and thus kept talking at a minimum. About that same time, I devised the wax museum activity. While I would place it in the category of active learning now, I know my original motivation was more self-serving. I wanted some moments of quiet in my classroom.

The more my classroom uses integrated learning, the more verbal it becomes. I know that learners need to process information and ideas verbally. I also think learners need to have moments of quiet, to think and to reflect. They need to internalize knowledge and attitudes. So, another balancing act I practice these days is planning for quiet space and for considerate conversation. The discipline of quietness is as valuable as the jubilation of shared discovery.

The wax museum has grown enormously popular and my students look forward to it every year. We started it one Halloween, a holiday we celebrate in our school and one I really enjoy. However, over the years it had degenerated into scruffy costumes at best and crummy behavior at worst. It became a time to try out unacceptable behaviors. I was feeling more like a cop than a teacher and it wasn't much fun.

The wax museum began as a way to keep learning going, even on Halloween. I asked the kids to move from horror into history. We brainstormed a list of historical events. Then the children divided themselves into work groups, the only rule being that no one could be shut out and no one could work alone. Groups as large as eight and as small as two began working, choosing an historical scene to portray. We talked about our audience, which ranged from kindergartners through fifth graders. We talked about what could be kind of Halloweenish but not scary for the little kids, yet interesting enough for peers. Ideas came one on top of the other, and enthusiasm built at an exponential rate.

Students created backdrops and props out of butcher paper and cardboard. They collected clothing from home or borrowed from each other to complete their costumes. By Halloween morning each scene was set. Here's how it works.

Other classes in our school begin their Halloween observation with a visit to our classroom. We turn off all the lights and draw all the shades. Each scene is lit by a string of Christmas tree lights. The room takes on a pleasantly altered state, shadowy and very unschool-like. "Knock, knock, knock."

The children stop talking and check their positions in their tableaus. Each one is aware how much it means to stay in character—laughing, moving, taking the focus—will ruin the entire scene for everyone, spectator and actor alike. The door swings open and in troops a class. A hush falls over the visitors as they walk quietly around the room, viewing each scene, whispering behind their hands. The scenes are perfect—no one moves, no one blinks. I think some of the children even forget to breathe. In less than three minutes, that class is out the door. Everyone collapses! Chatter, giggles, and jiggles to work out the kinks from standing in one place so long and so still. "Knock, knock, knock." It's another class. Ready? "Welcome to the wax museum."

By three o'clock, every class in school has been by. My students are exhausted. All they want is a cup of cider, a doughnut, and permission to go home. Over their Halloween treats, they comment on what hard work it was, they recall individual students' reactions, and they exude a sense of pride in a job well done.

TARRY'S TEACHING TIPS: USING QARS TO GUIDE REPORT WRITING

QARs are a hierarchy of questions and their relationships to the kind of answer each question requires (see pages 154–56 for a complete description). The data questions asking "who" and "what" are relatively low level. For example, if a student were researching Eli Whitney, she might pose the following: "Who was he? What did he do to make history? What problems or challenges did he face?"

Explanation questions are higher-level questions and often begin with "why" or "how" Examples would include: "Why is what he did important? How are we affected by what this person did today?"

Evaluation questions are the highest level and require inferences on the part of the student. "If you had been Eli Whitney, what would you have changed, given you knew what we know today?"

I give my students 11"-by-17" copy paper on which they create a note-taking ladder, starting with the data questions and ending with one or two evaluation questions and at least one quote, preferably from a primary document. This ladder provides the skeleton for an informative report.

Meeting New Needs

As time goes by needs change. Case in point: The infusion of standardized testing into the school year has squeezed the instructional day almost dry. I really question the activities that I used to spend time on, like the wax museum, and drop them if they don't pay off in terms of student progress. However, I know this is no time to revert to the "olden days" of opening a text, reading a chapter, and answering canned questions. Instead, I need to teach smarter, identifying big ideas and I need to teach leaner, deliberately selecting those skills that will produce more capable and competent learners. Plus, I need to keep the learning environment invitational, motivational, and challenging.

To begin with, I changed the time of year to do the wax museum activity, moving it from Halloween to the end of first semester. By waiting until later in the year, the kids have more information and more experience with working in groups. They can reasonably be expected to succeed at using skills and knowledge at a higher level of competency. Now the wax museum becomes a scaffold between the Revolutionary War and the Civil War, providing glimpses of what happened to whom between 1791 and 1860. Looking at the skills that could be introduced or practiced, I chose reading nonfiction, organizing written research, using primary documents, and working collaboratively with others. The wax museum is streamlined; integrates specific reading and writing skills; and educates the class about significant moments, events, and people in a given period of history.

First, each child chooses a topic featuring an event that happened or a person who lived between the French and Indian War to the Civil War. To provide a "menu" for the kids to choose from, I have them scan their social studies text, looking for some person or event that piques their interest. Using the question/answer relationship strategies, the kids pose a minimum of six questions to help guide their research and write their reports. After presenting their reports to their classmates, the kids organize themselves into groups that "fit" based on chronology or event. Rather than making full backdrops, they focus their limited time on creating a tableau. This time, however, instead of remaining still like wax figures, the students come to life and summarize their reports from a first-person point of view in order to share their information.

Picture the audience sitting on the floor in the middle of the classroom, with the tableaus circling the outside edge. Lights out. Suddenly, a spotlight shines on the first tableau. Each character in the tableau speaks briefly, identifying who they are, why they are in the tableau and share their feelings. For instance, a tableau featuring Lewis and Clark might also include Sacajawea,

169

York (William Clark's slave), Charbonneau (Sacajawea's trapper husband), and President Thomas Jefferson. The scene might be when the boat they were traveling in almost overturned. It was Sacajawea who saved the stores on board.

Imagine as the spotlight shines on the group, still as wax figures, and then William Clark speaks, quoting a primary source document—his own diary: "*A verry Clear Cold morning a white frost & some fog on the river the Thermomtr Stood at 33 above o, wind from the S.W. we proceeded verry well until about 6 0 clock a Squawl of wind Struck our Sale broad Side and turned the perogue nearly over, and in this Situation the Perogue filed with water.* . . (Journal of William Clark, Brown Bear Defetede Creek, Montana; written on May 14, 1805, as quoted in Bruchac 2000, 79). When William's voice fades, each of the other characters speaks, adding a comment or an explanation to elucidate the event. Charbonneau panics. Sacajawea grabs the medicine kit, saving it from destruction. York and Jefferson each comment, in character, about the near tragedy. Then the spotlight is extinguished. Moments later, another tableau is spotlighted. Another moment in history is revealed. By the end of the presentation, guests have been treated to a visual and oral interpretation of history "in the round," satisfying to both guests and presenters.

REFLECTIONS

One of the nicest things about being a "seasoned" teacher is that I've lived long enough to collect and create a wide range of lesson strategies and student activities. I can remember when there were basically two kinds of activities in the classroom, workbooks and art projects. And neither one of them had anything to do with what else happened to be going on in the room. Those days are gone. Now I collect and create activities because they are age-appropriate, further understanding, apply a skill, stimulate thinking, or appeal to one of the intelligences. I don't use all the activities I mentioned in this chapter every year. I choose from these and others to provide a rich and varied learning environment, as well as to meet the needs of my kids.

I am careful to evaluate an activity or a strategy each time before I use it. Does it really fit this moment in time? Will it move us forward? Is it engaging? Will it be worth the time, energy, and resources needed? What is good for one class may not be particularly helpful to another. No two years are the same, yet each year is familiar and similar. Making choices, solving problems, creating new things, applying tested activities, and using successful strategies make teaching fun and learning active.

Time lines

Chapter Seven

MAKING TEACHING AND LEARNING CHALLENGING

SOCIAL STUDIES TEACHING AND LEARNING IS POWERFUL
WHEN IT IS CHALLENGING.

—NCSS's "Vision"

Two features make social studies a unique school subject. The first is the diversity of disciplines it comprises. Anthropology, archeology, economics, geography, history, law, philosophy, political science, psychology, religion, and sociology are integral social studies disciplines. The second unique feature is that it brings the controversial and ethical dimensions of a topic to students' attention. Students need to examine social policy and weigh their decisions in the light of it. It is this challenge to deal with public, as well as personal, dilemmas that promotes social understanding and civic efficacy (NCSS 1993, 214).

The instructional strategies we choose can promote seriousness of purpose and thoughtful inquiry or they can trivialize learning. I find that as my skill, understanding, and knowledge of the issues in social studies grow, the substance of the study in my classroom deepens. I no longer use single-sided activities, ones that expose students to only one point of view or one learning orientation. It is the multidimensional nature of social studies teaching and learning that makes it both exciting and interesting. Students work independently, but also in groups. Interacting with people as well as with ideas and issues is an important part of social studies. I believe the reason some teachers and students don't enjoy social studies is that they have only experienced it in one dimension—the open-the-book, read-the-chapter, answer-the-questions dimension.

THINKING CREATIVELY, CRITICALLY, PRODUCTIVELY

I knew something was missing in my early teaching. Then educational researchers began to identify and define higher-order thinking. It made sense. I began to monitor my teaching to see where I could eliminate "monothinking" and find opportunities to challenge all students intellectually. I was appalled when courses, packages, books, and curriculums began to advocate teaching higher-order thinking skills in isolation. I found myself in workshops that demonstrated how to move children through levels of thinking skills for the sake of the levels, not the content: What they were thinking about didn't seem important. Why not, I wondered, think about the content that fifth graders needed to know? Couldn't we incorporate higher-order thinking skills into social studies? So, armed with a new pedagogy, I examined my own teaching for ways to expand the learning spectrum in my classroom.

I discovered that teaching from multiple perspectives facilitates higher-order thinking. Studying an issue from different points of view raises questions that require thoughtful examination. Students can't simply retrieve an answer from their memory bank. They must shift focus and generate alternative solutions.

ENSURING EQUAL ACCESS

I also found I needed to look carefully at my teaching style to ensure all students were getting an equal opportunity to practice higher-order thinking skills. Teachers are basically kind, caring people. In our efforts not to embarrass a child, put him or her on the spot, we may unintentionally exclude that child from higher-level intellectual practice. For instance, in my teaching I noticed that I tended to call on the children I perceived as less capable (for whatever reason) less often when probing for higher-level thinking responses. I was ashamed and embarrassed. How could a child ever learn to think in more complex patterns if never given any opportunity to practice? If kids sense they don't have an equal opportunity to become valued members of the classroom community, it doesn't matter how challenging teaching and learning are.

Fortunately, there are actions we can take to foster positive perceptions. For example, if I let a longer period of time elapse between my question and my call for a response, the answer is better thought out. There is solid data showing that different ethnic groups have different "wait" times between hearing a question and offering a response. Shy children often need more time as well.

A friend of mine asks, "Do you want me to go on to someone else and come back to you later?" Her technique works with ESL students as well. Most researchers agree that we should allow at least five seconds between a question and the call for a response.

We can also make it a point to be aware of the number of times each child has an opportunity to respond during the day, what levels of questions she or he responds to, and the quality of that response. Is the student answering a question that requires her to connect ideas, to reason and evaluate? Is he retrieving a single right answer from a limited number of choices? What about prompts? Do we encourage every child with positive comments or only some? "Gena, I know you've got the answer on the tip of your tongue. I'll give you a little more time."

Acknowledging a response with a smile, a comment, or a pat on the shoulder validates that child's contribution. Do we distribute those acknowledgments equitably? If you received consistent, positive acknowledgment of your participation in class, wouldn't you find it rewarding? Wouldn't you like to continue that positive cycle of response, acknowledgment, response, acknowledgment?

Where the action happens in the classroom, and the teacher's position within it, influences student learning as well. Proximity to the teacher empowers learners. My classroom is an ever-changing kaleidoscope of desks. My students frequently rearrange their seating, and I'm almost always up and moving among them.

Other factors, such as whether and how we touch them and whether and how we reproof them, influence how students learn. If we want to promote challenging teaching and learning, we need to be aware of the effects of our interactions with our students.

WRITING IN ANOTHER'S SHOES

Looking at events and comprehending issues from a historical perspective is challenging for most intermediate-grade age students. To introduce this strategy, I start with a picture book, *Through My Eyes* by Ruby Bridges (1999). With that model in mind, the kids move to the biographies of their choice. Aaron chooses *The First Woman Doctor: The Story of Elizabeth Blackwell, M.D.* by Rachel Baker (1944), an insightful book integrating health and history that is still available through Scholastic's *Supplementary Materials* catalog. I ask the

Making Teaching and Learning Challenging

students keep a journal as if they are the main character, capturing each chapter in a entry that reflects what the subject knows, does, and feels (see page 251 in the Appendix, for a detailed plan). I suggest that explanation, supposition, and evaluation questions will make their journals more interesting and challenge the students to fool me, to make me think it is really the subject of the biography doing the writing (see Figure 7–1). Aaron, who's always been the master of few words, turns in the following:

MY JOURNAL BY ELIZABETH BLACKWELL THROUGH THE EYES OF AARON KARLEN

CHAPTER 1
I just found out that we are moving to America. Last night there was a fire in the sugar house. Everything was destroyed. Some men offered Dad a loan, but he turned it down and said, "I have decided to emigrate to America with my family." We began packing and waiting. The poor Irish immigrants who came each Spring had been struck by Cholera so when 4 days had passed and no new cases had been reported, we set off.

CHAPTER 2
Father died. I always spend time at the Stowe's home. Our new home is a lot smaller than our old home back in England. My sisters took me to a public debate at Town Hall. The issue was woman's rights. One man said "A woman's career was only in the kitchen." I did not like that. It was against my father's way of thinking. I got my first taste of what I want to grow up to be. I want to be a physician!

CHAPTER 3
I take the Packet to Philadelphia because it is the cheapest way. I get seasick along the way. I like Dr. Elder very much. I asked Dr. Jackson if I could be a student in his school. He said there never had been a female doctor before in the U.S.A. I was really, really discouraged when Dr. Jackson said he was unable to help me. Many schools had turned me down. I am very sad. On the twenty-seventh of October, a letter and document came. It said they would let me in!

Aaron's model is marvelous, so I want all the students to hear what a peer has created. We talk about the strength of his writing, the vocabulary he chooses, and how he stays in character. We discuss what we know about travel and attitudes toward women during this period in history. We look at what was going on in other parts of the world, what discoveries were being made, and what other issues were important to the day. Reading, and reflecting on

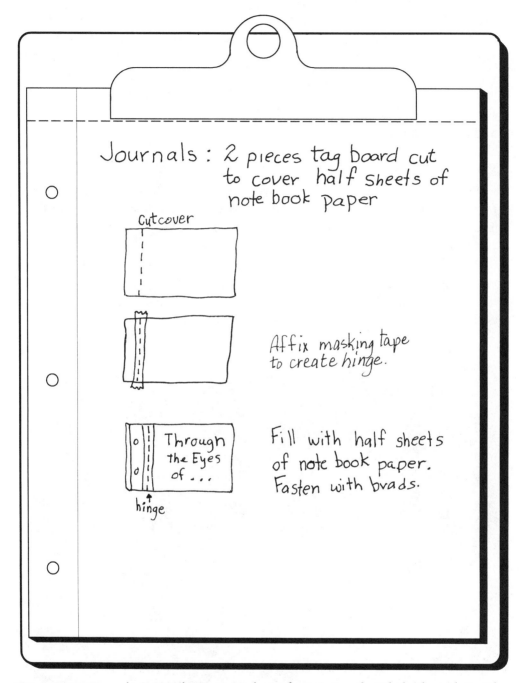

Figure 7–1: Journals © 2002 by Tarry Lindquist from *Seeing the Whole Through Social Studies, Second Edition*. Portsmouth, NH: Heinemann.

Making Teaching and Learning Challenging

that reading, is important in my classroom. Whether the students are entering their reactions in a personal response journal, discussing their reflections with peers in small groups, or assuming a character's perspective, the time taken is more than compensated for by the depth of learning that is fostered. (See Figure 7–1 for directions for making journals for this strategy.)

SETTING GOALS

New Year's is a great time to talk about resolutions. My students set personal goals using a Daruma, a Japanese folk doll that is a symbol of patience and perseverance (see page 237 in the Appendix for a detailed plan and model). The custom is to paint in one eye of the doll when you set your goal, then paint in the other eye when the goal is accomplished (see Figure 7–2).

Setting personal goals focuses responsibility for learning on the child. The kids determine what is important and valuable to them, and together we work to achieve these goals. Helping students achieve competence in something they feel is important reinforces the reality that children are the center of the classroom.

Figure 7–2: It must be early in the year: the Darumas have only one eye filled in.

LEARNING THROUGH THE LAW

Some teaching strategies promote critical thinking and civic understanding better than others. A number of law-related strategies offer challenging learning. Mock trials and mock hearings, debates, hypothetical situations, and case studies all appeal to the intellect of the intermediate-grade student. Law-related education tends to deal with substantive issues. It is from real life. It promotes thoughtful participation, frequently challenging students to think on their feet and present reasoned arguments before an audience.

Finding an Issue

Imagine this. We have released our salmon into a local stream. We have practiced thinking on many different levels using real content. The time is right to focus on an issue of concern in our region.

In the 1920s, a canal was cut from Lake Union in Seattle into Puget Sound. Locks were put in to facilitate boat traffic, accommodating businesses in Lake Union. The canal was cut where there had been a small river, a river by which steelhead and coho salmon traveled to and from their spawning beds, so "fish ladders" were constructed to accommodate them. Then in 1972, Congress passed the Marine Mammals Protection Act, forbidding the killing of any marine mammals. By 1987, sea lions were becoming a nuisance in many places up and down the Pacific Coast. One group of sea lions moved into the entrance of the locks, gobbling up the returning salmon like pigs at a banquet. State fisheries agents became increasingly concerned as the sea lions feasted on greater and greater numbers of salmon and the fish runs became smaller and smaller. Scientists therefore began experimenting with ways to divert or remove the sea lions.

One sea lion in particular, dubbed Herschel, caught the fancy of the reporters and their readers. Evening telecasts featured the big, brown-eyed mammal. Newspapers carried him on their front pages. Herschel and his buddies foiled many different schemes to rid the locks of the sea lions. Vile-tasting condiments, rubber-tipped arrows, and underwater noise did not deter them. Marine biologists even trucked Herschel and his buddies down to California. It took only fifteen days for the "boys" to make it back to the locks, hungrier than ever. It looked like federal law was going to protect one species, which was abundant, to the annihilation of another, which was becoming increasingly rare.

This story is an example of the kind of regional issue that can capture intermediate-grade students' intellectual attention. I decided to use this real-life scenario for a mock trial (Armancas-Fisher et al. 1991). My students had never staged a trial before, but this material seemed tailor-made; it involved current issues and two distinct, appealing players: the steelhead salmon and the sea lion. It was a real dilemma with no single solution. It would require research into state and federal laws, like the Marine Mammals Protection Act. Several concerned groups formed themselves into some surprising alliances. Native American groups, sports fishermen, and commercial fishermen sided with the State Department of Fisheries to force Herschel and his buddies out, dead or alive. Greenpeace, federal agents, and ecologically concerned citizens formed an opposition group that insisted the Marine Mammals Protection Act should not be revised or amended in any way. The trial simulation wrapped many of the separate threads we had been studying throughout the year into a single, cohesive pattern.

Preparing for the Trial

Mock trials are interesting intellectual exercises. Everyone, child or adult, is excited by courtroom drama. In the process of planning the defense or prosecution students encounter higher-level thinking skills at every turn. They must analyze the evidence, synthesize arguments, propose suppositions in the form of questions, and develop well-reasoned arguments. The students acting as jurors must come to a decision that is defensible. Additionally, the students learn how a trial really works, which is a far cry from most television trials. I invite lawyers, law students, or judges to my classroom to help the students develop their cases. I don't know that much about trials, but there are a lot of people who do and who are pleased to be asked to come into the classroom for an hour to work with students.

The students have to work cooperatively in groups during a mock trial. I've found it is important not to assign specific roles until the last minute; having teams work on prosecution and defense strategies, rather than immediately assigning three students to be prosecutors and three others to be defense attorneys, keeps the whole class more involved. Assigning two people to every witness role so that they can practice their testimony in pairs also increases interest and enhances preparation.

We begin by researching salmon-industry and endangered-species issues. Using the Lexus computer network, I select newspaper articles from the *Los Angeles Times*, the *Seattle Times*, and the *Washington Post*. Each article highlights a different point of view and reveals important information. The students read the articles in small groups and identify the facts that support the sea lion and the facts that support the steelhead (see Figure 7–3).

While developing their understanding of the issue, the students also become familiar with procedural justice, in other words, "due process." We recall our study of the Constitution and the Bill of Rights, other threads of justice and law that weave in and out of our year's work.

Next, the class investigates trial procedures. They identify the major steps in a trial and the parties to civil and criminal cases (see page 249 in the Appendix for a detailed breakdown of trial steps). At this point, a lawyer speaks to the class about the concept of "innocent until proven guilty beyond a reasonable doubt." Then, using stipulated facts and witness depositions, the students complete a time line of relevant events.

Now come the most challenging activities. First the students describe the main arguments in favor of each side. Then they identify the facts that support or weaken each major argument. Finally, they are ready to write an opening argument for each side.

Figure 7–3: Kevin researches data for his team's trial presentation.

Making Teaching and Learning Challenging

Armed with all this information, the students compose possible questions for direct examinations and cross-examinations. The witnesses rehearse their stories, being sure they stay within the facts of the sworn statements. The day before the trial, a lawyer friend comes in to preside over a rehearsal. The alternates play the roles and the others to watch and learn.

Presenting the Trial

On the day of the trial, the students dress up, looking as professional as ten-year-olds can. Some carry briefcases. The boys wear sports coats and ties. The girls pull their hair back and wear colored tights under their good dresses. Some parents attend, and we invite the other fifth-grade classes. A photographer shows up from the local paper. Herschel the sea lion is tried for the murder of Sam Steelhead at the Ballard Locks.

While the jury deliberates, the judge, a Washington State Supreme Court Justice, debriefs the attorneys and the witnesses, commenting on the strength of their cases, things they might have added, and how this mock trial differed from an actual one. She explains her rulings on objections and discusses the effectiveness of their strategies. Finally, the jury files in: guilty!

Considering Alternatives

We hold a final debriefing as a class. We analyze the weak and the strong points of each case as it was presented. Then we evaluate the trial from the standpoint of its success in achieving justice. Finally we ask, "Could we have accomplished this in a different way?"

I don't want children to leave this activity thinking that litigation is the only way or the best way to solve a problem. Certainly our yearlong commitment to mediation cannot be abandoned, either in the classroom or in the community. The children need to know arbitration is also an avenue for solving differences. While mock trials are very engaging, I use them sparingly. They tend to foster divisiveness, a win-lose mentality I work hard to move children away from.

We revisit the problem using mediation or arbitration that so the children experience different options and have an opportunity to verbalize what they feel, know, and do as they compare multiple ways we can use to solve problems.

CONTROVERSIAL ISSUES IN THE CLASSROOM

Teaching and learning is challenging in a classroom in which controversial issues are examined. How do we study these issues without letting our own

TARRY'S TEACHING TIPS: THE VERTICAL OPINION POLL

To provide students with opportunities to "try out" their opinions, I often use the vertical poll. This is an old social studies standby that I use to give students a format for beginning debate. Begin by stating an evaluation question like, "Do you think students and teachers should wear uniforms in public school?" I draw an imaginary line across our classroom. One end is designated "Yes, I agree" and the opposite end is designated "No, I don't agree." Students move to whichever end of the room indicates their opinion. Those who don't know can stand somewhere along the middle.

After the kids have chosen their position, I ask them to share their reasoning, alternating sides of the issue. When everyone has had an opportunity to speak, I give the kids a chance to change positions. Often, those who were ambivalent or reluctant to make a choice move to one side or the other. Sometimes kids who had strong opinions change sides. Sometimes popular or persuasive kids tilt the outcome. However, this is not a win or lose activity. This is practice in stating one's opinion and in verbalizing one's reasoning. It is also an exercise in listening and in marshaling arguments that might persuade others to one's point of view.

I often use the feature article of the weekly news magazine we take to pose the question. I do this after the kids and I have read and discussed the article so that they have some basis for their response other than their "gut." Civic issues, whether local or global are usually rich topics to draw from. Science topics from deforestation to global warming provide a wonderful blend of data and personal opinion. I do think it is important that this strategy emphasize the need for civility. Too often today's student thinks that to have a difference of opinion means to shout an opponent down; verbal battering is featured on talk shows daily. We need to model and practice civil discourse in our classrooms.

---

biases and values block independent, thoughtful critiques by students? Here are some steps that work for me:

- *Expose* students to sources of information that include diverse perspectives and offer conflicting opinions.
- *Teach* students how to present a point of view in a reasoned manner. Practice using language associated with reasonableness: from my point of view, one consideration, some people feel, my personal opinion is, based on evidence from.
- *Provide models* for examining content thoughtfully and with seriousness of purpose. I frequently invite lawyers and judges into my classroom and ask them to tell us how they go about thinking about an issue. I urge them to give us samples of their thinking, examples of the way they phrase their thoughts. At first the students mimic the

Making Teaching and Learning Challenging

models. Later, the habits of thoughtful speaking find their way into the children's speech.

♦ *Weigh* costs and benefits. We used to talk about pros and cons, but in our increasingly complex world, issues are seldom so clearly defined. Instead, most issues fall somewhere in between, depending on one's point of view. Solutions to most issues are multiple. The choice frequently depends on the perception of balance between the costs and the benefits.

♦ *Share* information on student decisions without creating a win-lose mentality. Conducting opinion polls, placing choices along a continuum, and writing editorials are all strategies that encourage students to make decisions in a reasoned, thoughtful manner rather than based on what a best friend thinks.

DEAR EDITOR

Writing editorials or letters to the editor is a worthwhile, challenging activity for intermediate-grade learners as a unit of study draws to a close. Letters to the editor can be mailed; editorials can be published in the classroom. Preparing opinions for print encourages careful as well as thoughtful writing.

Sometimes we publish a "What I Think" paper, collecting everyone's ideas into one culminating statement. Like letters to the editor, these papers identify the problem, look at alternative solutions, choose one, and give reasons for that choice.

Why pretend when there is a real audience out there? Real writing is what we want these students to do when they grow up, so let's start now. Real writing has an immediacy to it, and a real-world application shouldn't be missed. Mailing a child's letter, whether to the local newspaper, a children's magazine, or a television program, authenticates it. We collect a list of "People to Write To," placing names and addresses on a chart that hangs at the back of the room. Students then have wide choices for making their writing real.

The following letter was written by Matt at the conclusion of a study the class did on old-growth forests and the spotted owl controversy. The students researched different points of view and simulated a Senate hearing. Some students role-played legislators whose responsibility it was to make a decision regarding this intensely emotional local issue, while others represented various community groups with a vested interest in the outcome.

Lakeridge Elementary School
8215 SE 78th
Mercer Island, WA 98040

Editor

The Seattle Times
P. O. Box 70
Seattle, WA 98111

Dear Editor,

I am in the fifth grade and have been studying the spotted owl controversy. The owls should be protected as should the old growth forests. The logging industry has been too caught up in cutting down as many trees as possible in order to make a profit. Because of this, they have not done a good job replacing the trees. The logging industry is going to go out of business sooner or later if they keep clear-cutting. We should stop now and save many trees.

We should start by training some of the loggers for other jobs. The minimum number of loggers should be left, so we can cut the fewest trees needed to provide products such as paper, pencils, etc. The loggers should have to replace what they cut with a variety of different trees. Also, effort should be put into trying to replace wood with another substance whenever possible, so that fewer trees will have to be destroyed. In the future, we should ban clear-cutting completely. Only cutting little sections of the forest should be allowed. From my point of view, that would be the best way to do things.

Sincerely,

Matt

LEARNING THROUGH COMMUNITY SERVICE

Engaging in community service combines hands-on, heads-on, and hearts-on learning in an especially effective way. "Integrating service to the community intentionally with curricular content . . . has proven to be a more effective and long-lasting educational method than classroom instruction alone" (Armancas-Fisher et al. 1992, 2).

Community service provides challenging learning because students need to:

1. Identify a problem.
2. Choose a solution.
3. Devise a plan of action.

Making Teaching and Learning Challenging

4. Organize and carry out the plan.

5. Evaluate the results.

The types of projects intermediate-grade students can successfully carry out are many and varied: adopting and cleaning up a local stream, tutoring younger children, recycling school wastepaper, conducting a food drive as part of a study on hunger. Participating in community-service learning grounds learning in real-life connections and challenges.

TARRY'S TEACHING TIPS: USING SURVEYS IN THE SOCIAL STUDIES CLASSROOM

My students love creating surveys about social issues they are interested in, like "What people would actually be willing to do to save the rainforest." Peter, a fourth grader, posed this question and then followed this procedure, which was developed by John Swang of Mandeville Middle School in Mandeville, Louisiana. (For further information, contact him at *NSRCMMS@aol.com* to access not only this survey design format but an experimental design as well.)

First Peter stated his *purpose*—to find out what people would actually do to save the rainforest and his *hypothesis*—people are willing to do a lot to save the rainforests around the world.

Then he developed a *survey*, which he gave to twenty-five people at the local grocery store. (Most of my students survey their classmates or students in our elementary school.) Then he *analyzed* his data to see if he should accept or reject his hypothesis.

From his data, Peter learned that 25 people thought it was important to save the rainforest—22 out of 25 were willing to write their congressmen, 20 out of 25 said they would support a ban on exotic woods, only 9 out of 25 were willing to go to the rainforest to protect it. He learned that people were unwilling to leave their families and their jobs. He also learned that 19 out of 25 were willing to donate money to save the rainforest. Additionally, he discovered that those surveyed were willing to give an average of $25 per year.

Finally, in his *conclusion*, Peter accepted his hypothesis that people were willing to do a lot to save the rainforest. He *summarized* the four things people were willing to do: write their congressmen, ban exotic woods, donate money, and boycott products.

Peter wrote a one-page scientific abstract, following very tight guidelines to share his information. Organized into four sections, Peter wrote a Statement of Purpose and Hypothesis, Methodology, Analysis of Data, and a Summary and Conclusion.

HEARING FROM THE EXPERTS

Teaching and learning in the social studies lend themselves to bringing outside experts into the classroom. The expert may be a renowned practitioner in a particular field, a parent or a neighbor who knows about something special that fits into a current focus of study, or a community service agent who has a special point of view. While inviting the expert has long been a teacher function, in the child-centered classroom the students select the topic, contact the speaker, arrange the schedule, and follow up with a thank-you note.

Expertise can be developed within the classroom as well. Students can be challenged to obtain and share expertise in selected topics that will enrich and extend the knowledge of the whole class. In my classroom, this expertise is usually acquired through research and shared through oral presentation. Plenty of resources, plenty of time, and a clearly understood goal are essential; models or prototypes are helpful (see Figure 7–4).

Remember, though: Don't have twenty-eight experts give twenty-eight oral reports one right after the other. If your goal is to enlarge and enrich the class's understanding, awareness, and appreciation, back-to-back presentations by each member of the class guarantees defeat. Your rule of thumb: divide them up. Never plan more than four or five presentations a day. Start the morning off

Figure 7–4: Erica knows becoming a classroom expert takes resources, time, and work.

Making Teaching and Learning Challenging

with one session. Change focus and do something that involves the whole class or a different kind of skill. Have another session after morning recess. Take time prior to lunch for a third session. After lunch, work in a fourth session. Midafternoon, present a fifth. If needed, have a final session before school is dismissed.

Here are additional suggestions for keeping interest alive:

1. *Change the ambience.* Have a gallery opening, with refreshments catered by the presenters. Set up a scientific convention, or pattern the presentations on popular television formats (*Meet the Press, Crossfire, Oprah, People's Court*).
2. *Expect listeners to interact with student experts.* Sometimes one-third of my students are responsible for presenting, one-third are responsible for writing newspaper reviews of the presentations, and one-third act as a participatory audience. Each student in the audience is expected to ask at least one question during a question-and-answer session. The students rotate roles so that in three days each of the students has experienced all three kinds of interaction.
3. *Expect experts to use more than one style of informing the audience.* Charts, music, movement, and pictures are all part of well-rounded presentations. Expecting student experts to add these components to their oral presentations challenges them to be creative as well as accurate. Their information will be more memorable to the classroom audience because the multiple intelligences are tapped.
4. *Give students an opportunity to practice.* Split the class up into several small support groups of four or five students. Ask them to listen to and to critique one another's presentations. Any information the students hear more than once has a greater likelihood of being re-membered later.
5. *Collect and publish the products of the presentations.* Charts, graphs, keywords, steps in a process, or pictures can be captured for review-ing and reliving. Classroom newspapers, videos, booklets, bulletin boards, or displays are some ways we like to publish.

EMBRACING TECHNOLOGY

Increasingly sophisticated instructional tools and data resources are available for use in our classrooms. I find it challenging to keep up with and integrate the latest technology. Electronic mail, computerized databases and software programs, laser disks, hypermedia, and scanners have the potential to profoundly influence my teaching and my students' learning. My students have discovered that video reports are challenging to conceive and carry out. They find that incorporating visual images can make their message more powerful than when conveyed through words alone.

Although some studies have been done to investigate the best application of these innovations, we'll need to experiment ourselves, weighing costs and benefits. Moving the application into higher-level thinking, not creating a room full of data jockeys is the trick. Simply using a modem to talk to a student somewhere else in the world does not make a superior social studies program. It is what the students talk about that matters. Playing "Oregon Trail" does not make a technologically savvy social studies program. Probing the reasoning behind real rather than random choices creates critical thinking. Hypercard stacks that simply present low-level facts are probably not worth the time they take to create. Pulling isolated facts from a computer encyclopedia does not create facile writers who communicate with integrity and passion. Multimedia presentations in elementary schools often sacrifice depth for glitz.

We need to be careful that technology tools aren't functioning as technology tricks, distracting students from a deeper comprehension of content. Of course, in the act of acquiring skills in technology, first steps will be shallow in terms of content manipulation. Helping students to move beyond surface skills to use technology effectively and managing multiple resources are roles for teachers to continue to explore (NCSS 1993, 222).

Certainly, combining technology standards with social studies content reaps rich rewards. Whether the student is practicing word processing skills when doing forced revisions of letters to Morning Girl and Star Boy, creating a spreadsheet to track responses to a school survey on bullying, or searching the Web to find out what kind of clothing people wore in the fifteenth century, placing content at the center of technology reduces the risk of the computer becoming a workbook in a new form. While computer skills are critical to today's citizen, we need to remember that our students should be exposed to all kinds of learning tools, of which computers are one. Balance, once again.

WRITING A SCIENCE CONNECTION

Technology and subject-matter content demonstrated through literacy skills can work in tandem as the culminating activity to our study of space. The kids had just finished individual research projects to answer questions they had about different aspects of space. They had studied Mars thoroughly, including taking an all-day field trip to the local air museum. While there they role-played scientists going to Mars to run a research station. Each student was assigned a role that was vital to the mission. They had to work cooperatively, respond to emergencies, and carry out protocols to ensure the safe docking of their spaceship. To round out our whole space study, I read *The Green Book* by Jill Paton Walsh (1982) to the kids. A thin paperback, taking about five twenty-minute sessions to read aloud, it is about the last spaceship to leave Earth, which is so polluted life could no longer be sustained. The families in the spaceship hope to establish a new colony in space. The natural integration of science and social studies is apparent: the science of learning about a new planet and the social studies of setting up a new society. When I finished reading the book, I could tell the kids were poised to write their own "green books." They had a depth of knowledge and experience to draw from, they had a model that intrigued them, and they were ready for a challenge.

After discussion, we decided their books would have at least five chapters. The organization of the chapters could be: 1. Leaving Earth, 2. Living in the Spaceship, 3. Sighting the New Planet and Landing, 4. Establishing a New Colony, and 5. Ten Years Later. We also decided that we would take no more than five weeks to write our books and the work would all be done on the computers at school, including drafting, revising, editing, and polishing. I also slid in some of our technology standards, including being able to import art into a document, using the draw program, choosing different fonts, and knowing how to use the word count and page numbering tools. The kids would demonstrate their ability to use these tools by accompanying each chapter with a graphic they imported or a drawing they made. They would show they could use different fonts in their chapter titles and elsewhere in the body of their work. They would number the pages when the book was complete and do a total word count. I also added an art part by requiring the students to create a watercolor cover for their book, including title and author. Paradise Island Press would be the publisher!

The kids worked eagerly. While word processing assisted some students drafting directly on the computer, other's lack of typing skills hindered their storytelling. Structuring the chapters prior to writing helped the whole class get started. Following the model of *The Green Book*, most of the kids wrote in first person, using a journal format. I was worried that we'd end up with hackneyed space aliens, once-removed from Saturday cartoons. It didn't happen, mostly because they were writing at the end of a unit about space. They had a great reservoir of knowledge to draw from, and they did! In addition to writing a story with a beginning, a middle, and an end, this assignment was a perfect vehicle to work on sequencing as well as describing and collecting details. The finished product was a joy.

From my point of view, the most rewarding outcome was that most of the kids made the problem of their story the establishing of a new colony, not fighting space aliens. Best of all, the kids loved their stories. They read them to themselves, they read them aloud to the class, to a peer, and to a kindergarten buddy. At the end of the work, I overheard several kids remarking how fun the writing was and how they might be authors or scientists or space pioneers some day!

REFLECTIONS

Challenging teaching and learning come in many forms. They are communicated by how we teach as well as what we teach. They are fostered through a variety of experiences that tap into different kinds of knowing and doing. One of our roles as teachers is to make sure students' thinking is stimulated and challenged through the multidimensional qualities of social studies. As Caine and Caine (1997) remind us, complex learning is enhanced by challenge. The brain/mind will make maximum connections when in an environment that encourages taking risks (106). We must also communicate to our students the value of careful work, thoughtful comments, and critical thinking. Our reactions to student thinking are a way to communicate these values. By not accepting a student's answer at face value but probing for the reasoning behind the answer, we set a higher standard for thinking. Challenging student assumptions sensitively, in a trusted relationship, encourages intellectual growth and development. In the intermediate grades, we can habitually require students to explain their answers, asking them to use content as the basis for their reasoning. "Just because" no longer is an acceptable response.

It has been my experience that what learning students consider challenging they also view as worthwhile. Simulations, real-world connections, and projects involving the multiple intelligences challenge students and teachers to solve problems creatively and to share their solutions. Challenging learning and teaching combine the hands, the head, and the heart so that doing and knowing matters, so that learning makes a difference.

Friday Files

Chapter Eight

ASSESSING STUDENT ACHIEVEMENT

I PROMISE YOU EVERY DAY YOUR CHILDREN WILL LEARN
SOMETHING. SOME DAYS THEY'LL BRING IT HOME IN
THEIR HANDS. SOME DAYS THEY'LL BRING IT HOME IN
THEIR HEADS. AND SOME DAYS THEY'LL BRING IT HOME
IN THEIR HEARTS.

—Valerie Welk

Three times a year I am expected to grade my students. It's not my favorite thing to do. In a classroom where integrated learning is taking place, the traditional notion of a teacher "giving grades" has little relevance. Fortunately, a new language is developing in the profession, a language of assessment that has little to do with grades. Now we assess student progress based on established criteria or developmental continua. These structures assist us in communicating to parents how their kids are doing. But the notion of the "almighty A," the "basic B," and the "acceptable C" dies hard. The teacher "giving grades" is an American stereotype firmly engraved in the minds of parents and public alike. Most elementary teachers are required by their employers to grade student progress anywhere from two to eight times a year. These grades are based on, most often, evidence of each child's performance on assigned tasks as well as less observable traits such as behavior, effort, and cooperation.

I frequently question the purpose of the whole process of grading when I am staring at the first of twenty-eight report cards to be filled out. However, I am always pleasantly surprised at what I learn about my teaching when I focus on where all the children are at a particular point in time. Going through the process of assessing student progress does help me spot weak areas in my teaching. It helps me identify concepts and skills that need further practice. It reminds me of the developmental level of my students. It nudges me to acknowledge the good, the wonderful, the competent, and the creative things my students do. And, though it sounds odd, by analyzing what each child has done, I gain wisdom and insight into the learning attained and the social and emotional growth attained.

I don't use grades daily in my classroom: It's a waste of time. If I graded every single piece of work we produce, we'd do much less. The students would have less practice and less-varied experiences. They would become dependent on me to tell them the value of their work. I want my students to be able to value their own work, to be able to identify personal bests, and to look at both the process and the product with a critical eye, storing away what they will do next time to improve both. I do, however, collect scores daily in math, record percentages in spelling, and occasionally note reading and writing benchmarks. I don't do this to grade the students; I do it to assist me in planning. Do I need to reteach a math concept or provide more practice in spelling? Do my kids need another minilesson on questioning styles or additional attempts at identifying the sequence of a story?

The application and synthesis of knowledge and attitudes is an ongoing, ever-improving sort of activity. Why should we grade each little step in students' widening sphere of accomplishment? Learning something new is like throwing a pebble in a pond. A first small circle of understanding appears when the pebble hits the water. Successive practice expands learning and broadens the circles of knowledge. I don't think we need to grade every ripple. Why not, instead, provide more practice for multiple kinds of intelligences and different learning styles? Why not study a topic more deeply, eschewing the shallow coverage that garnering grades often promotes? I do, however, use rubrics often. Some of these I use to inform the students of how I view their work. Some of the rubrics are used by the kids to assess their own work or the work of a peer. The best rubrics are those that the students help create, before the assignment or activity is begun.

I find that many students look at a grade as an end product; they don't interpret it as "becoming" or "growing" or "developing." Neither do many of their parents. They read it as, "This is IT!" Frequently the grade becomes the attitude—"I got a C in geography, but that's okay because I don't like it much anyway." In addition, when that child grows up to be a parent, teachers hear, "Oh, I wasn't good in geography either. That's why Johnny doesn't do well."

Rubrics are very helpful in weaning parents and students away from the almighty grade.

As I have moved deeper into integrated learning, I have discovered traditional grading simply doesn't communicate the process of learning I value. A's, B's, and C's or 1's, 2's, and 3's have little to do with monitoring or mentoring the daily effectiveness and quality of student participation in lessons and activities. After teaching a split fourth- and fifth-grade class for a couple of years and having half the class as fourth graders one year and fifth graders the next, I've also discovered that one school year is not really enough time to determine what a child has learned or what I have taught. I noticed, for instance, that skills the fourth graders were not able to produce consistently in June were fully mastered when they walked in the door in September to begin fifth grade. Something good must have happened over the summer! Maybe it's because understanding is a process. It doesn't always happen when a lesson is taught. Sometimes it occurs hours, weeks, even months later.

I wish we could look at learning from kindergarten through fifth or sixth grade as one continuum instead of trying to parse it up into finite bits for evaluation. Learning is truly cumulative at this age. Learning is like weaving—sometimes the same threads are used in the same pattern, sometimes the same threads are used in a new pattern. Sometimes new threads are used, combining with the familiar threads to deepen an existing pattern or to create a new one. One day, from the myriad of threads, a beautiful holistic pattern emerges. Knowing emerges at different times for different children. Each pattern is individual and unique. Each worthy and valuable. Perhaps that's what we should really be evaluating (see Figure 8–1).

HIGH-STAKES TESTING

If integrated learning has an enemy, it's high-stakes testing. As I travel around the country working with teachers, I hear more and more comments indicating that they feel like they are being held prisoner by their own classroom. Gone is their autonomy because, for many, the test has become the curriculum. Many teachers feel like helpless victims. They know one test does not tell us much about a child's accomplishments or potential. Yet they feel forced to move away from holistic teaching and learning to the memorization of factoids, kibbles, and bits, attempting to cover as much of the course materials as possible, thus preparing students for the volume of information included on the tests. In their

Figure 8–1: Julie designs a brochure
to show what she knows.

efforts to meet the requirements placed on them, many teachers feel threatened. What do we know about a brain that feels threatened?—it withdraws,
becomes less creative, less inclusive, less able to problem solve. Survival becomes the overriding concept in the classroom. Survival drives daily decisions,
interactions, and outcomes. The ramification is that teachers choose methods
that are often ineffective, repetitive, boring, and teacher-centered. Gone are
the projects, the presentations, and the performances. In fact, in some schools,
art, music, and even recess are sacrificed on the "alter" of testing. More dis-
turbing to me is the number of teachers who don't teach what isn't tested. Most
often this is social studies and science.

Prior to the advent of high-stakes testing, I said that assessment should be
a part of the journey, not the destination. Sadly, in many classrooms across this
country, testing is not only the destination, it's the reason for taking the trip! I
feel the emphasis on a single test at a given moment in time is tearing apart
the fabric of classrooms' intellectual and emotional cohesiveness. I continue to

be disturbed by the notion that such a single test can reveal everything we need to know about a student, a teacher, a school. I like what Jay McTighe, education consultant and co-creator of the Understanding by Design program, is quoted as saying in the ASCD's May 2001 *Education Update:* "Good assessment should be thought of as a photo album rather than a snapshot. We should use different pictures and different lenses to get at different aspects of learning over time" (8).

Grant Wiggins, president of Learning by Design, encourages teachers to move away from bad teaching, such as repetitive worksheets, loss of student autonomy, single sources of information, and so on, to do well on tests. He insists that we need to teach better, not worse, to achieve high test scores (Wiggins and McTighe 1998). I want to encourage teachers to believe in their ability to make good decisions for kids. I want to give teachers the courage to shut their doors and teach in ways that honor and invite the whole child into a community of lifelong learners and to structure school days that focus on depth and meaning.

Teaching for the Test

In 1999, Robin Fogarty of Skylight Professional Development published a booklet titled *How to Raise Test Scores.* In her opening, she encourages teachers to teach *for* the test, not *to* the test (6). In other words, teach the skills and generalizations kids need no matter what content they are being tested on. If the kids develop these problem-solving strategies, they will be more successful. If there are certain organizational structures in place, the kids will do better. What are these surefire winners? No secrets. Just good teaching and learning.

1. Organize the class into small, cooperative groups. I've found that four kids in a group is plenty. Three and two often work better.
2. Teach test-taking strategies explicitly. Because most tests end up being reading tests, teach students to look for keywords, read all of the instructions before beginning to work, and underline the important parts. Look for overarching statements, find categories, use outlines and webs. Make it fun, not frantic. Weave the practices within the content being studied.
3. Activate prelearning strategies. This means give kids practice in true/false tests, multiple choice, and essay-style questions. Demonstrate techniques and invite the kids to make up the questions for you to answer or to "Stump the Experts," when classmates take on the challenge from their peers.

4. Use graphic organizers when you present information. Make concept maps, flow charts, and cause-and-effect columns a natural extension of your teaching style. Expect your students to use similar devices when they are manipulating information. Although Fogarty doesn't mention kinesthetic organizers, I believe that folding and constructing organizers, such as the little book, storyboards, or the step book, provide children concrete devices for manipulating information and supports for students' success.

5. Teach with mnemonic devices and visual clues. Whether using a sentence to remember how to spell a word like "geography" (*George Engle's old grandfather rode a pig home yesterday*); devising acronyms to remember a list like the Great Lakes (HOMES: Huron, Ontario, Michigan, Erie, and Superior), or encouraging students to use color, exaggeration, or action to remember a vocabulary word, a metaphor, or a place, these all-purpose strategies boost learners' success.

6. Capitalize on student interest by allowing freedom of choice. I don't think this means that a student can constantly choose whatever he or she wants to do, but I do think it means that within each assignment and activity, students are not forced to respond to the teacher's single option. Rather, out of a list of topics, a selection of books, or a menu of writing styles, kids may choose what interests them. Out of a collection of strategies, students may select the ones that engage their attention. Out of a series of due dates for a project, students may arrange the order in which they'll meet those deadlines. And occasionally, the door is wide open for student choice, such as in portfolio presentations.

7. Foster reflection. We know students learn best when they get a chance to digest and think back on what they have experienced and learned. We recognize that students learn best when they are not threatened, but relaxed and alert. In addition, we have confirmed that when kids learn in a context of authentic, interactive experiences, something very good and powerful occurs. This something is integrated learning.

ASSESSMENT FOR MULTIPLE INTELLIGENCES

Teaching and Learning Through Multiple Intelligences differentiates between assessing the intelligences directly and how to assess *through* the intelligences (Campbell et al. 1992, 199–200). The more I think about it, the more I find assessment needs to be "multiplied" into diverse forms so that children have several options for demonstrating what they know, can do, or feel.

The notion of multiple ways to assess reforms the traditional idea of grading. As I experiment with assessment in my classroom, I find each year that it becomes more individual, more child-centered. The Campbells and Dickinson suggest "menus" as a way to infuse variety into classroom assessment (203–205). Drawing from their lists, I've fashioned a menu for the social studies–integrated classroom that draws from multiple intelligences. These options could be used as a goal for all the students to sample during a school year:

- **Linguistic**,
   Use storytelling to explain_____
   Write journal entries on_____
   Write a letter to_____

  Logical/Mathematical,
   Create a time line of_____
   Make a strategy game that includes_____
   Select and use technology to_____

  Kinesthetic,
   Build or construct a_____
   Role-play or simulate_____
   Design a model for_____

  Visual/Spatial,
   Chart, map, cluster, graph_____
   Use a memory system to learn_____
   Design a poster, bulletin board, mural of_____

  Musical,
   Write song lyrics for_____
   Collect and present songs about_____
   Write a new ending to a song or musical composition so that it explains_____

  Interpersonal,
   Identify and assume a role to_____
   Use a conflict-management strategy to_____
   Help resolve a local or global problem by_____

  Intrapersonal,
   Set a goal to accomplish_____

TARRY'S TEACHING TIPS: THREE THINGS PARENTS CAN DO TO IMPROVE STUDENT SUCCESS IN SCHOOL

Here's a process I've found to be very successful in my classroom. In the fall, usually around Thanksgiving, our school district does elementary conferences. The first step in getting parents to join me in improving their kids' success in school kicks in. At Curriculum Night earlier in the year, I have taught my students' parents and/or guardians three things they can do to increase their children's success in school.

First, have daily, positive conversations about school. This means that when the child comes home, Mom may ask, "So, what did you learn today that will last a lifetime?" Or, "What did you do to help someone else? Or, "Tell me three things you learned today that you thought were important." No more, "What did you do today?" followed by, "Nothing."

Second, model learning. Too often, kids don't see their parents learning something new. They don't seem parents using skills learned in school, like reading, writing a letter, or making a budget. It's not that parents don't do these things, it's just that they often do them when kids aren't around. Kids often do pick up negative examples, however. Picture the dad who locks himself out of the house. He has to get in quickly to retrieve something he needs at work. Time is running short. Does he calmly go about solving his problem or does he curse, kick the door, blame others in the family, and then leave in a huff? These are life lessons for children. They are models of how to deal with problems. Do we see that behavior mimicked in school? You bet!

Third, communicate expectations. Usually parents have something that bugs them about our schools in general, their kids in particular. It often deals with low-level skill mastery, like spelling words correctly, using legible handwriting, or getting 100s on daily math papers. Sometimes a parent will say he wants his child to love reading, have friends, or go beyond minimum requirements in assignments. Whether a specific target or a generalized feeling, we need to know, and the student needs to know, what mom, dad, or a guardian expects.

Thanks to Gary Phillips for sharing this advice. I share this information with parents at Curriculum Night every year. And every year positive growth results. It's almost magical.

Describe how you feel about_____
Write a journal entry about_____

Naturalist,
Teach why_____(*leaves turn color in the fall*)_____to a younger student
Identify symmetry in_____
Collect songs about_____(*the weather*)

This kind of assessment is exciting for both teachers and students because the students own the whole process from beginning to end and it's natural, not forced. No one has to fit a single mold. No one has to demonstrate knowing, doing, and feeling in a single "right" way.

TEST THE TEACHER

I don't use traditional tests a lot, but when I do, it is mainly to give students practice in taking tests. I happen to believe that the test tests the teacher. Did I teach what I thought I was teaching? How well? To how many? What do I need to do differently next time? Do I need to find another way to provide practice? What do the students know, what can they do, and how do they feel? What will they remember ten years from now?

It's my job to use instructional strategies that elicit and support the objective of the specific assignment and the overall goals of the year. Because my overall goal is "to help young people develop the ability to make informed and reasoned decisions for the public good as citizens of a culturally diverse, democratic society in an interdependent world" (NCSS 1993, 213), I need to have a large repertoire of activities from which to draw.

OLD SKILLS, NEW APPLICATIONS

Sometimes I think we try too hard to invent new strategies when old familiar strategies are not only comfortable, but still useful. For example, many students, like many of us, need to do something more than once to do it well. That's one reason I use letter writing as a part of assessment all year. I've found using a familiar format, like a friendly letter, encourages intellectual risk-taking over time. If the child is always concentrating on the format of an activity rather than the content, that activity does little to further academic application or creative thinking. By repeating a format, many students relax and reveal their knowledge, skills, and attitudes. Balance, of course, is needed to ensure no activity is overworked.

NEW SKILLS, OLD APPLICATIONS

When introducing a new skill to my students, I've often found it helps if we practice the new skill in an old context. For example, when moving from reading time lines to creating them from research, setting up the same familiar format and having the students "fill in" the missing information as we discuss the process helps every child practice before applying the new skill independently. Working in pairs or small groups often supports new learning. The notion of "trying on" new skills several times before assessment seems obvious, but sometimes in our hurry-up days, the rehearsal gets lost, the scaffold or support is missing. Students are often required to jump from introduction to mastery.

Students need to practice. They need to practice again and again over time to maintain and develop concepts and skills introduced early in the learning sequence. This practice need not be exactly the same. Options for extensions and enrichment should be available to keep interest keen. Integrated learning gives students time to find appropriate and meaningful ways of integrating information and solving problems across the curriculum.

ALTERNATIVE ASSESSMENT

Alternative assessment is defined as all the ways a student can demonstrate what he or she knows, feels, or can do by any means other than a traditional multiple-choice standardized achievement test (Worthen 1993, 445). I almost always use alternative forms of assessment. Just as many teachers were beginning to move to more holistic assessment, fear of failure in high-stakes testing caused them to fall back on traditional formats. My own observation tells me that kids who do experience integrated learning do as well or better on standardized tests as kids who spend a year prepping for state-mandated exams.

Just like the process of integrated learning, alternative assessment should feature the student at the center. I believe part of our responsibility as intermediate-grade teachers is to help students become accurate self-assessors and authentic peer assessors. This is a learning process, the same as reading or writing are. It takes modeling, discussion, practice, and reflection.

Student-Created Criteria
I save copies of student work from previous years. These models don't have to be the best or the worst. They are the ones kids never get around to taking home or specifically ask me to keep to share "next year." Introducing an activity by holding up a student model I ask, "What is effective about this particular model?" The students discuss what they find effective. I probe, "What could have been done to make it more effective?" and we chat about improvements. I review the points raised, usually writing them on the overhead. When the students begin their own work on the activity, the overhead is left on so

that they have the "criteria" to refer to easily. Inviting students to identify and specify criteria in advance promotes higher-quality products.

It is quite easy to take the student criteria and change them into a rubric with a range of points given for each description, category, or quality. Often, the students help determine the "worth" of each description. By the time the students have completed the project, they are very capable of arriving at an authentic assessment of their work. More important, they perceive assessment as an ever-widening circle of competence, rather than a dead-end grade.

Student-created criteria predict what the children hope to accomplish and with what degree of mastery, creativity, and/or cooperation. By setting up the criteria prior to the practice, students have a guide to success in terms they comprehend because they fashioned the measurements.

Interim Assessment

Remember when Aaron wrote as if he were Elizabeth Blackwell? Before the students began writing their entries, we talked about criteria. What would make our journal entries not just acceptable, but terrific? The students decided the entries had to be believable, accurate, and complete. In this way they predicted, if you will, what success would look like.

After the class had read three chapters and made three subsequent journal entries as Elizabeth, I asked them to exchange journals with a study buddy, a trusted partner chosen by them. The study buddies read the entries against these criteria:

1. Believable? Why or why not?
2. Accurate? Why or why not?
3. Complete? Does it do the job?
4. What is your overall impression?

Sarah, a fifth grader, wrote this assessment to her fourth-grade partner:

> Aaron,
> While I was reading your delightful entries, I had a smile on my face. The cause of this was your writing. Yes, your writing was so exciting. I could feel your disappointment or your happiness all in your lively sentences.
> You got your info. from the book but you wrote the ideas down in a way as if you were Elizabeth looking back at the day's achievements.

> I also like the way you opened and closed your entries. The opening was like you wanted to read on and the closing was like you had just finished an exciting adventurous book.
>
> I could go on and on (as I've already started to do) but I will just say, Elizabeth Blackwell is a fabulous writer when she is written through the eyes of Aaron!

In all honesty, it wasn't so long ago that if I had read Aaron's finished journal along with twenty-seven others, my assessment comment probably would have been "Good job!" Assessment while an activity is in progress informs the participants. It gives students an opportunity to monitor and adjust, either through their own eyes, the eyes of the teacher, or the eyes of peers.

Peer assessing is powerful. Of course, all children don't respond as Sarah did. So, I asked Sarah's and Aaron's permission to share her assessment. I read it to the class, asking "What is effective about this assessment?" and then we listed the positive attributes. We talked about how it would feel to receive such an assessment. I asked Aaron to describe how he felt when he got it, what he learned from it, and what he planned to do for the next journal entry.

Postpublication Assessment

Assessment can also take place postpublication. I happen to like having the students use publication as an extension of the assignment. An extension activity often reveals quality—is the journal truly believable, accurate, and complete, for example.

When the children finished *The First Woman Doctor: The Story of Elizabeth Blackwell, M.D.*, an example of this occurred. We discussed magazine interviews: "Have you ever read one?" Several had. They shared their observations about the form and content of a magazine interview. We discussed the kinds of questions used in interviews and concluded that open-ended ones are more conducive to interesting responses.

We spent time brainstorming the kinds of questions we might ask Elizabeth Blackwell if we could interview her for a magazine article. I wrote the questions on the overhead, collecting about fifteen, then gave the assignment: "Using only your journals, pretend you are a reporter for a magazine and you have the opportunity to interview Elizabeth Blackwell, the first woman doctor. Choose questions from the overhead or make up other ones of your own and interview Elizabeth. Write both the questions for the reporter and the answers for Elizabeth. Remember the 'voice' writing trait." I asked the students how many questions they thought would "do the job," and they came to a consensus that seven questions and responses would be enough. Here's Aaron's interview:

ELIZABETH BLACKWELL WAS THE FIRST WOMAN DOCTOR

Aaron: WHAT WAS THE BIGGEST SURPRISE FOR YOU IN YOUR EARLY YEARS?

Eliz: My biggest surprise that I had in my early ages was when my father told my family and I that we were moving to the states [America].

Aaron: WHAT WAS YOUR BIGGEST ACCOMPLISHMENT IN YOUR LIFE?

Eliz: My biggest accomplishment in my life was opening my hospital.

Aaron: WHY DID YOU NEVER MARRY?

Eliz: I never married because men were unfair to women. I didn't want to be ruled by another human being.

Aaron: WERE YOU EVER ABOUT TO QUIT BEING A PHYSICIAN ANY TIME IN YOUR LIFE? WHY OR WHY NOT?

Eliz: Sometimes I wanted to quit because of the rough times of riots and injuries.

Aaron: WHY DID YOU DECIDE TO ADOPT A CHILD?

Eliz: I decided to adopt a child because the child would fill in the missing part in my life. Since I adopted a child I wasn't lonely any more. I had someone to keep me company.

Aaron: WHERE DID YOU BECOME A DOCTOR (OR LEARN TO BE ONE?)

Eliz: I learned to be a doctor at La Maternite, a French hospital. I was a nurse there.

Aaron: WHERE DID YOU PRACTICE?

Eliz: I practiced in the poor neighborhoods where the people there needed me the most.

Aaron: WHAT WERE SOME OF THE TOUGHEST TIMES YOU WENT THROUGH IN YOUR TIME BEING A DOCTOR?

Eliz: Some of the toughest times that I went through as a doctor were when there were riots and things like that.

Aaron: WHAT DID YOU WANT TO BE AS A CHILD AS A GROWN
         UP?

Eliz: I wanted to be a surgeon, but my dreams were totally
         shattered when I squirted some vaccine in my eye at La
         Maternite.

Once again, the students handed their work over to their study buddies for peer assessment. Once again the students assessed whether the work was believable, accurate, and complete, and then summarized their overall impression. Sarah's response to Aaron follows:

Dear Aaron,

It was great how you did [America] in the first answer. That is really what they do for interviews.

This really sounds like an interview with Elizabeth Blackwell. While I was reading it I could see Elizabeth and the journalist talking. This is just how Elizabeth would answer.

You did an excellent job of telling very important facts in an unique way. Maybe next time you might tell a little more. Your writing is superb. You used great words.

Your interview is very well done. It tells the things it needs to tell and leaves out the unimportant things. You need good judgment for this and you sure have it!

Your length is perfect! You did extra work—you have 9 questions! You corrected 99% of your spelling mistakes.

Your sentences are complete along with your entire interview.

If I was grading it I'd give it an A!

I ask my students to do assessment activities all through the year. The procedure just described can easily be a self-assessment instead. However, it can't be a one-shot deal. Children need to learn how to assess their work, they need to learn to identify quality, and they need practice in doing both.

Parents as a Part of the Process
I like to make parents my partners in assessment. Rubrics go home early in an assignment and parents may choose to read and mark the final draft according to the rubric. When they do, I gain a deeper understanding of their values and their perceptions about their children's capabilities and successes. Parent input becomes part of the matrix when the students and I conference about their work. I read the rough draft in detail, because I learn more about

TARRY'S TEACHING TIPS:
MAKING PARENT CONFERENCES MATTER

For that first fall conference, I ask parents and guardians to come with at least one expectation. It needs to be something I can help the child accomplish in school. I can't do much for a child who still wets the bed or fights with his sister. But I can help that child bring papers back to school or provide opportunities for him to work successfully with others. As I meet with each student's parent or guardian, I write down on a note card what expectation has been communicated to me. To make sure I understand what they value, I often ask, "And what would this expectation look like or sound like if your child achieved it?"

The following two weeks after conferences, I meet with each child individually and ask, "What do you think your folks think is important for you this year?" Usually the children just smile and shrug their shoulders. Sometimes they make a guess, like "Get good grades in spelling?" So I read to them what their parents have communicated to me. Then I ask, "And how do you think we can work on that expectation the rest of the year?" Another shoulder shrug. "Well, who do you know in class that . . . gets good grades in spelling, loves to read, gets along with others, uses nice handwriting, etc., etc.?"

Over the years, I've learned that when a student identifies another student with the desired behavior, then it doesn't take much prompting for that student to begin listing specific actions that embody the desired behavior. "How do you know Taylor loves to read?" "Oh, you've noticed that she always carries a book with her? And the books she chooses aren't always big thick ones? Sometimes she chooses skinny books? And she sometimes chooses to read rather than play at recess? And she likes to talk about the books she's reading? And you've even seen her sneak reading during class sometimes?" I continue, "Let's make a list of all the things you've noticed Taylor doing that shows she loves reading. Then you can star the one you want to start with. Wouldn't it be great if you ended this year loving to read?"

The first week back after New Year's often finds us using the goal-setting Daruma. As each student lists one or two goals for the trimester, I notice that many of them personalize their parents' expectations. Instead of "My mom wants me to love reading," Herb writes, "I want to like reading better." As the second trimester closes, I ask the kids to write a letter to their parents, telling them what they have done to achieve their parental/guardian goal as well as their own. Interestingly, this process seems to stimulate a halo effect that tickles both student and parent perceptions, creating a positive aura for improvement. Don't ask me why, but it seems to work.

what I need to teach from a rough draft. I don't invite parent input on the rough draft because many times parent expectations exceed the child's developmental and skill level.

Inviting parent assessment also gives me an opportunity to teach parents about praise and positive comments. I encourage them to balance compliments to criticism two for one. Giving a compliment, then a suggestion for improvement, followed by another compliment is often called a "compliment sandwich."

Criticisms sandwiched between compliments work just as effectively for children as for adults. Opening the assessment process to parents increases support for classroom activities.

Self-Assessment

Self-assessment in my classroom is ongoing. Students are constantly asked to reflect on what they have learned, or what they can do, or how they feel. Self-assessment is a good way to culminate an educational field trip; if the child finds the trip worthwhile, the parents realize its value as well, and I know it was worth the time and expense.

I especially like to use self-assessment as a form of immediate feedback when the students are presenting. As an example, let's take an activity in which the students read a biography and then prepare a three-minute oral presentation

---

HOW IT WORKED FOR ME—MARJ, 39 YEARS OF EXPERIENCE

Stats and Facts: Eighth grade, teams of 85 kids divided into four classes; heterogeneous grouping including special needs; urban population; 37 different languages spoken at home; one-third of kids qualify for free lunch; 88 percent of high school graduates pursue further education

When I read about biography billboards I thought they were a terrific idea, but not for those of us concerned about noses too big, lips too thin, and, heaven forbid, zits. I needed to channel that enthusiasm around early adolescence.

Our legislature had just given us the present of another century in our eighth-grade curriculum, ninety more years, 1790–1880, to be tested in the high-stakes exam in May. After much anguish and complaining, we decided to divide the decades into themes: arts and daily life/technology, slavery and abolition, the changing map, and biography, which we call Movers and Shakers. After reading Joy Hakim's *Freedom for All?* and wallowing in the wealth of material during this period, eighth graders chose a person and began a project that had three parts: research, bio poster (see Figures 8–2 and 8–3), and Movers and Shakers Day.

The wonderful day came when research crystallized into bio posters (see page 260 in the Appendix for bio poster description and assessment rubric). Thoreau was on a drum, a different drummer. Sacajawea was on a canoe. Melville was on a great white whale and Twain was on a riverboat with the author himself in the wheelhouse. Dorothea Dix was in a jail cell; Narcissa Whitman was in a prairie schooner; Audubon was superimposed on a fabulous watercolor of a duck, and Louisa May Alcott was an open book, complete with ribbon bookmark. They presented their posters. My favorite moment was when one special needs boy who had never felt proud of his work sidled up and asked if he could redo his poster for the next day, luckily a Monday. Of course he could and did, and it was smashing. The digital photo of his Frederick Douglass *Liberator* poster became the cover of eighth-grade portfolio.

Assessing Student Achievement

Figure 8–2: Biography billboards come to life: Daniel as James Madison.

Figure 8–3: Justin as Sojourner Truth.

as if they were the person. They are to use the present tense and at least one appropriate prop. Before the students even select the books they'll read, we develop an assessment sheet for this activity.

After classroom discussion, I suggest they take it home and hang it in an appropriate place when they practice. Then, after the students make their presentations to the class, they mark an assessment sheet, and so do I. We compare our opinions and discuss the differences. Almost always, the students are more critical of themselves than I am.

One year we decided to do oral biographies but wanted a new twist. Pretending to be the famous person is fun but we wanted something more. This time, after reading the biographies, we created storyboards about the subject. The panels of the storyboard were highly structured:

BIOGRAPHY STORYBOARDS

Panel 1—Title.

Panel 2—Main character.

Panel 3—Setting as child or young person.

Panel 4—Situation before becoming famous.

Panel 5—Problems he or she had to overcome.

Panel 6—Greatest accomplishment(s).

Panel 7—Death or what is currently happening in life today.

Panel 8—A six- to ten-sentence paragraph of your feelings about this person. Do you admire him or her? Why or why not? Would this person have been a good friend? Are you inspired because of this person's life? Why or why not?

Then, using tagboard and markers, the students created Biography Billboards to enhance oral presentations of the information collected on the storyboard. Creating authentic clothing for the people the students chose to study posed a bit of a problem. I didn't want the kids to put Vasco da Gama or Joan of Arc in modern dress (see Figures 8–4 and 8–5). Putting their person of choice in historically accurate garb is a kind of primary document, isn't it? We found a

Figure 8–4: Jeslyn as Juliette Gordon Low.

Figure 8–5: Jon as Davy Crocket.

HOW IT WORKED FOR ME—JENNY, THREE YEARS OF EXPERIENCE

Stats and Facts: sixth to eighth grades, 30 students, inclusion classroom, team teaching, blue-collar community

I was offering drama for the first time in our school this past year for sixth to eighth graders. I love it but my ambition was also full of nervousness, "Will this work? How will the kids react?" One of the beginning lessons is identifying the who, what, where, why, when, and how behind the characters we portray. Since the only budget for the program came from my pocket, I was thrilled to use Tarry's biography billboards as an aid in costuming. However, with the "too-cool" attitudes of some middle schoolers, I wasn't sure if this strategy would be sort of young for the drama class. Wrong! Right up to the very last class we had together, these super kids were still wearing their "boards" and bringing made-up characters into daily class conversations. My proudest moment? Travis, shy, sweet, and confident as a shrinking violet, burst into the drama room on June 6, wearing his superhero, "Plunger Man," billboard complete with a plunger tied to his head and superhero tools made out of toilet paper rolls. Using the billboards helped my checkbook stay closed and gave my kids the confidence to fly—especially Travis!

website that helped us greatly. Go to *www.bonus.com* and type in "costumes." This is a kid-friendly site and the resource is amazing, a 150+-year-old German magazine section featuring dress from ancient times to the mid-1900s in an easy-to-download format. The students presented their storyboards orally and then responded to questions from the audience. It was fun and required them to use their heads, hands, and hearts in order to complete it.

Projects of Excellence

Teachers need to select activities carefully, not draw them at random from a grab bag. The activities we choose must provide the appropriate practice and the measured extensions needed to nudge children along academically and emotionally. I do, however, think we need to culminate and measure learning periodically, establishing benchmarks that reflect how knowledge and skills practiced in the past have been applied to new content.

For example, my students have been writing letters, drawing diagrams, writing newspaper articles, identifying different techniques of persuasion, and designing effective posters. Now, as a benchmark, I assign a project of excellence centered on the topic "inventions."

1. Choose an invention you think has had a significant impact on the world. Research it on note cards. Be sure you have all the facts re-

corded: who, what, where, when, why, and how so that you can share its history.

2. Draw a diagram of your invention, using colors and labels effectively.

3. Prepare a magazine ad to "sell" your invention. Use one of the techniques of persuasion we studied in health.

4. Write a letter to a friend as if you are the inventor the day you got your invention to work. Reveal what you did, what you know, and how you feel.

5. Write a newspaper article as if you are a reporter who has just interviewed the inventor or has just seen the invention working and are breaking the story.

6. Arrange the numbers 2 through 5 on a piece of 24"-by-36" posterboard so that it can be displayed on the bulletin board.

7. Present your invention at a scientific convention. Use a demonstration to introduce your invention to the group and be prepared to answer questions. Be sure to convince us of its positive impact on the world.

So many pieces of learning are collected in this project! Hands-on, heads-on, hearts-on activities take precedence. The students have to create a product, present information orally, and share values with their peers. The project also requires high-level thinking: analysis, synthesis, evaluation (see Figure 8–6). We'll find out if the research skills we've been practicing all year are mastered. Individual students will be challenged to organize and meet several deadlines in a timely fashion. They'll use problem-solving skills and practice wisely using time. The whole project will be done in class. I learn much more about individual students and their ability to problem-solve by watching how it happens than I do from simply having the final product in hand.

This is a final project, assigned in June. It not only is a review of the important skills we practiced throughout the year, but it also encourages the students to do their best work. I ask them, "If the only thing your next year's teacher would know about you would be this project, what would it say about you as a manager, a problem solver, a scholar, and a caring human being?" Hence the title, Project of Excellence.

Group Portfolios

As the second trimester draws to a close, my students are busily preparing for our first group portfolio presentation. All through the trimester, we have saved the products of our learning. The collection includes evidence of reading,

Assessing Student Achievement

Figure 8–6:   Emily and Susan proudly share their projects.

writing, art, music, dance, public speaking, group work, science, social studies, math, spelling, physical education, field trips, library, study skills, and problem solving. Keeping used copy paper boxes in the back of the room, plus assigning cubbies to each student, we've saved nearly everything we've done for ninety school days. From this collection, each student will select their best evidence of learning in eight venues: math, science, social studies, reading, writing, problem solving, working in a group, and creativity. Making the choices are hard because each product is evidence of more than one targeted venue in our classroom. So what Joan chooses as evidence of learning in science, Jim chooses as evidence of learning in social studies. Jerry selects it to prove he's learning to solve problems and Jessie finds it a perfect fit for writing. And they are all right! In the integrated learning classroom, it is not only probable that the kids will have duplicate products across the curriculum, it is expected.

Putting six or seven kids together on a team is easy. I just do it by what day after school their parents or guardians can come. Each student has had time to reflect on their product and how it relates to their chosen venue "I am going to share my evidence of problem-solving. My problem was I had to research an endangered species, pose four questions, find the answers, and present my findings in an interesting and attractive way." Each student has written notes about (1) how the product was created—"First, I had to find information about endangered species"; (2) what was learned—"From this activity I learned that we can save elephants from extinction through the cooperation of governments, wildlife organizations, education and money. I also learned that I need to start the research on a project like this sooner"; and (3) what emotional connection was made—"I feel like I did a really good job on this report. I answered the four questions I had come up with and I learned a lot more. I had fun reading about different elephants but I felt bad about the way some of them are treated. I think my organization in the little book format shows that I can put stuff together in a good way. I like my pictures." (See page 277 in the Appendix for a model.)

Imagine six of your students, sitting at a long table with the products stacked in front of them. Picture twelve or so parents or guardians sitting in front of them, ready to listen. The first child rises, welcomes the audience, and introduces himself and his parents. Then the other children, in turn, introduce themselves and their parents. The first child rises again, and says something like this:

> "We have been learning a lot this trimester and this afternoon we will show you evidence of our learning. We are going to start with reading. This double-entry journal writing is my evidence of learning in reading. I read *Morning Girl* by Michael Dorris. While I was reading *Morning Girl* I learned about figurative language. In my double-entry journal, you can see examples of metaphors and similes. Here's one, "Star Boy was a rock." Now I know Star Boy wasn't really a rock, he just acted like a rock, still and quiet . . . so still and quiet no one noticed him, not the people or the birds or the bugs. And that's what we mean by figurative language. It makes you use your brain more when you read. You get to make your own pictures in your mind. I like it.

Then the second child shares his evidence of learning in reading. He might use a product from a science or math class such as an ABC of Geometry book he created to demonstrate that he can read and apply definitions. He might use his Independent Reading Log as evidence of reading in more than one genre.

Thus, each of the six children presents their evidence in reading. Then they present evidence in writing, social studies, and so on. The process takes about an hour and it has become one of the most powerful hours of the year. Parents often worry about where their child ranks in a classroom because they have little opportunity to see where their kid "fits." The group portfolio lays unfounded fears at rest. Because the kids have practiced giving the whole presentation during class time and have seen their classmates practice, each child is successful. (These in-class practice sessions also serve as powerful models for the other students. Fine-tuning the presentations through observation and discussion ensures a positive experience for each student.) The parents truly see the gifts in their children and in their children's peers.

A huge bonus of this kind of assessment is that the parents finally get a concrete example of integrated learning. What one child chooses as evidence in reading another child chooses for problem solving, creativity, or social studies. The parent finally comprehends how this classroom is different from the one they attended as a child and why the child's daily attendance is so critical to success. They leave with a greater appreciation for the lack of competition that exists among the kids and for the positive attributes of cooperation that are fostered. They head for home, after cookies and lemonade to celebrate the students' achievements, feeling proud and with a greater sense of what is happening in the classroom and why it happens the way it does. Parental support just blossoms after a group portfolio session. It's almost magical. Considering it "costs" five hours after school, one hour each night for a week because I usually have about thirty kids in my room, it's time well spent.

Individual Portfolios

At the close of the school year, my kids often assess themselves and the year through an individual portfolio. Ruth Haynsworth of North Kingstown, Rhode Island, shared many of these ideas with me several years ago. I have found her Scavenger Hunt strategies to be very successful. Thanks, Ruth.

The key to meaningful portfolios is choice. Students need to be able to choose from a wide array of samples, examples, and products to prove evidence of learning. This evidence illustrates my students' exploration, examination, and expertise through the multiple intelligences and across the curriculum. Whether choosing a book the student made to demonstrate mastery of alliteration, a poster created as part of a presentation on why life might be possible on Mars, or including a videotape showing the student interviewing a grandparent for a writing/social studies project, the individual portfolio is exactly that, individual. (See page 272 for examples of a parent communication letter and the setup for portfolio assessment.)

Students who have had group portfolio experience are confident when approaching this assignment. Those for whom portfolio assessment is new need coaching and modeling. Some years my students do the whole portfolio in class. Some years they accomplish the task at home, often with parent input. Either way, the final product elicits responses from the kids themselves like, "I didn't know I knew so much." "I really feel proud of my accomplishments. I worked hard and it shows." "I never knew I could do so many things in one year. I know I am ready for sixth grade."

What Do You Know, What Did You Do, How Do You Feel?

Finally, assessment rests with the student. Voluntarily, Erica put together a Summary of a Wonderful Year and gave it to me on the last day of school. She included a time line of her favorite activities and a letter recounting what she valued. ("I have come to realize how many cultures and diversity our world has, yet everyone shares the same general qualities of the human race.") She added a critique of the year and closed with a poem about the bittersweet experience of saying good-bye. Daniel, on the other hand, left me a brief word processed note (see Figure 8–7):

Figure 8–7: "I think I'm really ready for 6th grade."

Assessing Student Achievement

Dear Mrs. Lindquist,

I would like to thank you for a great year. I think I have become a more thoughtful reader and writer. I really liked all the projects we've done: the rainforest, the desert, the Herschel trial, and lastly, the invention project. It's been a lot of fun. I think I'm ready for 6th grade.

REFLECTIONS

I've noticed a subtle shift in the relationship between my students and me, especially those students I've had for two years. They gradually move away from seeing me as the authority. They become self-assessors who are increasingly more autonomous, holistic learners. Kids who came up to me every three minutes the first week of school, just to check if they were doing okay, no longer need my approval. They sail confidently on their own, smiling at their own competence.

Assessment should be one part of the journey in the intermediate-grade classroom, not the destination. If you believe as I do that our students are always "becoming," never "done," then grading them in the traditional sense seems out of place and out of context. To be powerful, assessment should mirror our teaching and learning. It should be integrative, meaningful, value-based, challenging, and active. However, in this period of transition, we need to make the best accommodation we can between the old ways and the new.

Assessment needs to be authentic. All forms of assessment practiced in the classroom should be rooted in reality and refined within the community. That community might be one of learners inside the school building, in the neighborhood, or in a global arena. Knowing, doing, and feeling should be connected to the real world—with things that matter. We need to share a vision with our students of the wholeness of learning, infuse them with hopes and dreams, encourage them to look for connections, provide them with skills and strategies, and engage them in experiences and expertise that will last a lifetime. And they might, just possibly, change the world!

APPENDIX
A Teacher's Notebook

Some of the strategies in this Teacher's Notebook have been previously published in a slightly different form in resource handbooks that accompany Tarry's seminars: *Strengthening Your Fifth-Grade Program Using Outstanding Whole Language and Integrated Instruction Techniques*, © Tarry Lindquist, 1991, 1992, 1993; *Practical Strategies for Creating an Outstanding Fifth-Grade Program*, © Tarry Lindquist, 1995, 1996, 1997, 1998–99, 2000, 2002; and *Current Best Strategies to Strengthen Students' Reading and Writing Skills (Grades 3–6)*, © Tarry Lindquist, 2000, 2002, (all published by Bureau of Education and Research, Bellevue, Washington). Some strategies have also been previously published in *Ways That Work: Linking Literacy and Social Studies*, © Malcolm and Tarry Lindquist, 1995, 1996, 1997, 1999, 2000, 2001 (published by Heinemann Workshops).

DAILY SCHEDULE

Block: Integrated learning consisting of social studies, science, and/or health linked to language arts and art.

	Monday	Tuesday	Wednesday	Thursday	Friday	
9:00 9:10	Teacher/Student Contact Time	Teacher/Student Contact Time	Teacher/Student Contact Time	Teacher/Student Contact Time	Teacher/Student Contact Time	9:00 9:10
9:20 9:30 9:40 9:50 10:00 10:10 10:20	Math	Math	Math	Math	Math	9:20 9:30 9:40 9:50 10:00 10:10 10:20
10:30 10:40 10:50	Block	Block	Block	PE	Block	10:30 10:40 10:50
11:00 11:10	Recess	Recess	Recess	Recess	Recess	11:00 11:10
11:20	SSR	SSR	SSR	SSR	SSR	11:20 11:30 11:40 11:50
11:30 11:40 11:50	Music	Block	Block	Block	Block	
12:00 12:10 12:20	Library		Music			12:00 12:10 12:20 12:30 12:40 12:50
12:30 12:40 12:50	Block		Block			
1:00 1:10 1:20 1:30	LUNCH AND RECESS					1:00 1:10 1:20 1:30
1:40 1:50 2:00 2:10 2:20 2:30	Reading	Reading	Reading	Reading	Reading	1:40 1:50 2:00 2:10 2:20 2:30
					PE	
2:40 2:50	Recess	Recess	Recess	Recess	Recess	2:40 2:50
3:00 3:10 3:20 3:30	Block	Block	Block	Block	Block	3:00 3:10 3:20 3:30

WHO BINGO

Who can swim?	Who can speak another leanguage?	Who loves math?	Who read ten books this summer?	Who had relatives come visit?
Who went to an island?	Who went to camp?	Who went to Europe?	Who went to Asia?	Who made a new friend?
Who helped someone?	Who tried something new?	Your name here	Who knows what Yom Kippur is?	Who knows a good joke?
Who played on a team?	Who took lessons?	Who likes to eat humbow?	Who can name one important news item?	Who has attended a pow-wow?
Who can spell our principal's name?	Who knows how many days are left in fifth grade?	Who can use a computer?	Who had a job this summer?	Who loves to write?

ME

Name: _____

Birthday: _____

Favorite Sport: _____

Favorite TV Program: _____

Favorite Foods: _____

Favorite Beverage: _____

Favorite Colors: _____

Favorite Subject: _____

Favorite Book: _____

Future Occupation: _____

Favorite Place to Visit: _____

_____

Something I'm Proud I've Done: _____

_____

ABC VOCABULARY CHART*

MATERIALS

Large drawing paper
Colored markers

PROCEDURE

1. Demonstrate to the students how to fold a large piece of drawing paper into 32 squares.
2. After they have folded their own paper, have them outline each box with a ruler and black marker and then put one letter of the alphabet in the same corner of each square (the extra squares can be used for a title and author identification).
3. Have the students identify elements of a topic or country they are studying, a novel they are reading, or a field trip they've taken using the ABCs as organizers. For example, if the topic is rainforests: A—Australia, Africa, Asia, Central and South America, Amazon, the anaconda; B—Brazil, Belize, butterflies, banana; C—chocolate, Colobus monkey, cashew nuts, Tropics of Cancer and Capricorn; and so on. They may write it "fancy," illustrate it, or use vocabulary words in context sentences. Encourage creativity.
4. Display in the classroom, while it is a work in progress. Encourage students to go "walkabout" and look at their peers' work. This encourages sharing rather than competing, sets models for those kids having trouble, and stimulates those slow starters.

VARIATION: ABC BOOKS

ABC books are another way to culminate study. We do coloring books for the planet, zoo books with our kindergarten buddies after a field trip, and Chinese books after a unit of study on China. Choose a standard format, use a stencil set for the letters, and encourage the students to write a sentence about their picture.

* *This strategy came to me from Marte Peet, Lockwood Elementary, Bothell, Washington.*

VARIATION: VOCABULARY CATCHER

Make a two-page step book, then fold in fourths. Cut on each fold line up to the top sheet of paper. Students should end up with twelve tabs. As students read, encourage them to write vocabulary words that intrigue or puzzle them on a tab. Write the definition above the word. Draw a picture if desired.

Literacy Connection
This kinesthetic organizer gives students practice in selecting vocabulary in context with the study of a particular topic or concept—for example, westward expansion, rainforests, space. Student comprehension is demonstrated as words are explained, often through using the words in context. Student attention to the index of reference books occurs as they compile their alphabet. The exercise provides students with practice in skimming for information and fosters analysis as the students decide which words fit the criterion and which ones don't.

EXPLORERS DATA DISK

A PARTIAL LIST OF EXPLORERS

Christopher Columbus	Marco Polo	Vasco de Gama
John Cabot	Balboa	Ibn Battula
Ponce de León	Cartier	Pytheas
de Soto	Drake	James Cook
Onate	Hudson	Champlain
Coronado	Cortes	Alexander the Great
Dias	Magellan	Eric the Red
Pizarro	Verrazano	Leif Ericson
Vespucci	Frobisher	Sebastian Cabot
Cabeza de Vaca	Orellana	Cabral

PROCEDURE

1. Place all students' names in a hat and draw them out one at a time. First person drawn gets to choose an explorer. Continue until every student has chosen a different explorer.

2. Use *The World Book Encyclopedia*, any other standard reference set, electronic encyclopedias, or individual books about explorers to create your list and then have students find the following information:

   Years born and died
   Early life
   Nationality
   Major exploration
   Importance of exploration
   Interesting information

3. Using references ranging from the encyclopedia to books about the individual explorers, have each student draw and/or write in the information on a data disk divided into six sections. I use the largest piece of paper our copy machine takes (11″-by-17″), draw a circle and divide it into six sections, and run one copy for every student. I'm interested in getting the kids into researching the explorers. If you want to create an interesting math problem, show the kids a disk that is divided into six

parts and challenge them to create their own. I only let my students write "bits of data" on the data disk—no complete sentences. This reduces plagiarism and scaffolds nicely into note-taking later.

4. Use a brad to attach a smaller circle, with their explorer's name on it in fancy writing, to the center of the disk.

5. Ask the students to line up according to their explorers' year of death, earliest to latest. Thereby they will create a living time line.

6. Ask each student to introduce his or her explorer to the class using information from the disk.

7. Hang the disks in chronological order on the classroom wall. Refer to the disks when studying about events in history—for example, the War of 1812 or the Alamo. Explore what impact the early explorations did have on later-day history.

Literacy Connection

This strategy works well at the beginning of the year or with novice researchers. The limited space reduces copying from the book, the limited categories make it possible for every student to succeed. (I tell my students that they may not find all the information requested. Life is like that, isn't it? It doesn't always fall into six tidy categories.) The data disk works as an effective scaffold to later, more sophisticated and student-centered research.

VARIATION: THE REVEAL DISK

For several years my colleague and friend was a young woman named Paula Christoulis. She took the data disk and personalized it with her own engaging flair.

1. Cut two data disks, the same size. Cutting them together at the same time ensures two disks that are exactly alike.

2. On the bottom disk, follow the directions for the data disk. On the top disk, cut out one-sixth of this disk (one pie-shaped segment). Put the explorer's name on this disk and graphically illustrate events, symbols, and outcomes resulting from the explorer's ventures on the remainder of the disk. The graphics, structured carefully, can reveal much about the students' comprehension of their explorers (e.g., "Create a symbol for the outcome of Columbus' meeting with the Taino people").

3. Use a brad to attach the top disk to the bottom one. Turn the bottom disk to "reveal" the information collected.

VARIATION: BUDDY DISK AKA VERY IMPORTANT IDEA DISK

To expedite partner reading, try using a data disk you have divided into segments that equal the number of chapters in the book the partners will be reading. Select partners by reading interest and reading speed. Don't pair the slowest reader with the faster, unless you like chaos! Give each pair one data disk. Instruct each pair to read the same chapter individually. When done, the partners should discuss the chapter, agreeing on the most important part. For that chapter, they should write down that part on the corresponding segment of the disk. Then they should read the next chapter, and so on. Easy to monitor, the teacher passes by, looking at the data disk. If the partners are "right on," the teacher leaves them alone, or gives a compliment. For those who are not hitting the mark, the teacher can work with them independently, coaching so that they are able to identify important points.

Literacy Connection
Simply moving information from one source to another is challenging for many third and fourth graders. Finding specific information from a written source requires students to use skimming and scanning reading skills. Interpreting the written word and summarizing material are skills that need practice, and that demonstrate student reading comprehension.

BOOKS OF KNOWLEDGE

MATERIALS

Half sheets of drawing paper
Smaller rectangles of lined paper
Black fine felt-tip pens
Colored pencils or markers (optional)

PROCEDURE

1. To culminate or review a unit of study, tell your students they are going to write and illustrate a Book of Knowledge—a series of drawings and descriptions of the things they've learned. For example, a student creating a Book of Knowledge about Northwest Coastal people might choose to draw a totem pole, an oceangoing canoe, salmon being smoked, a longhouse, and/or a Chilkat blanket as representative of his or her study of this culture.
2. First, students do a drawing, then write a description on lined paper and glue it on the drawings (one item per page). I require my students to determine if the information they are sharing is important to know or simply interesting.
3. Set a certain number that will be acceptable. (I find fifteen or twenty items very revealing in terms of student comprehension.)
4. Students should create a cover. Some students like to write a dedication. Some teachers require a table of contents. Others have students create an index. Some teachers combine this activity with an ABC theme. It's a very flexible activity and extremely useful.

Literacy Connection

This strategy gives students practice in beginning research skills and note-taking as they determine what is interesting or important. Students also must craft their own statements, not copy from a source. Using the structure of a book (i.e., the index, table of contents, and glossary) stimulates students in finding a wide range of information. Requiring students to draw as well as write about their selections ignites both sides of the brain, tapping multiple intelligences.

Categorizing the material adds higher-level thinking practice. This Book of Knowledge also lends itself to comparison and contrast focuses.

VARIATION: LEDGERBOOKS (SEE PAGE 100 FOR DESCRIPTION)

Sample Rubric for Ledgerbook

Procedure: Check best response for each section
Content: Interesting, informative, demonstrates thoughtful word choice
Conventions: Complete sentences, appropriate punctuation, correct spelling

1. The Early Years
   Content:
   __ Doesn't meet criteria
   __ Doesn't meet criteria
   __ Could have more information
   __ Thoughtful word choice evident
   __ Outstanding
   Conventions:
   __ Did you proofread?
   __ Could have edited better
   __ Very few errors
   __ Excellent editing

2. Family
   Content:
   __ Doesn't meet criteria
   __ Could have more information
   __ Varied sentences evident
   __ Outstanding
   Conventions:
   __ Did you proofread?
   __ Could have been edited better
   __ Very few errors
   __ Excellent editing

3. Elementary years
   Content:
   __ Doesn't meet criteria
   __ Could have more information
   __ Transitions evident
   __ Outstanding

Conventions:

___ Did you proofread?

___ Could have been edited better

___ Very few errors

___ Excellent editing

EARLY AMERICAN TRADES

MATERIALS

Copeland, Peter F., *Early American Trades Coloring Book*
Stockham, Peter, *Little Book of Early American Crafts and Trades*
(Both can be ordered from Dover Publications, East 2nd Street,
Minneola, NY 11501.)

PROCEDURE

1. Show the coloring and crafts books to the students as you discuss jobs
   in colonial America and the concept of indentured servitude.
2. Give each student a large piece of paper or tagboard (18″-by-24″ works
   well). Tell them they are to pick a trade or craft from colonial times:
   a. The name of the trade (e.g., cutler)
   b. The tools of the trade
   c. An illustration of the "trade in action"
   d. An ad (from a master in colonial America to entice someone in
      Europe to come over and work as an indentured servant for him)
   e. A letter (from an indentured servant to a friend or relative back in
      Europe describing what he or she does at work, how he or she
      feels about America, what he or she plans for the future
3. Display the poster in the classroom. Share during a class period.

Literacy Connection

Illustrating student visualizations of colonial times provides a graphic demonstration of student comprehension of the period. Writing letters "home" provides evidence of inferential thinking and comprehension. Descriptive and narrative paragraphs are frequently employed by students as they complete this strategy.

CEREAL BOX CONSTRUCTION OF COLONIAL HOUSES

MATERIALS

Lots of empty cereal boxes   Scissors
Tempera paint   Masking tape

PROCEDURE

1. Collect cereal boxes a week or two before introducing the project. Store the boxes by taking out any liner material and flattening the boxes by opening a seam. These boxes are easily cut with school scissors and can be shaped as desired with masking tape. By turning the boxes inside out, your students will discover a surface that takes tempera painting very well. Doug Selwyn (Lindquist and Selwyn 2000) taught me about using cereal boxes for construction when we wrote the book, *Social Studies at the Center*.

2. With the whole class, brainstorm the kinds of climate and natural resources that would be common to colonists living in each of three regions: New England, the middle colonies and the southern colonies. Would these factors influence the kind of houses people would build? Talk about the houses we live in—do they reflect prevailing weather conditions and/or local resources? How do houses differ from generation to generation? Go to the library or use the Internet to find pictures of dwellings during the colonial period. Give the kids time to share the illustrations they find and their generalizations about their findings.

3. Ask the kids to choose a region and to design a house for it. Make sure the house fits within the colonial period (1620–1775). With the class, determine group work requirements, if any; a work schedule; and clean-up routines. I like to put a large tarp on the floor for the kids to sit on while they paint. I also put an assorted materials table at the side of the room so that the kids can search for just the perfect garnish for their houses. I usually put an all-call out to the children's families in my room, asking for donations. The diversity and quantity

of stuff that comes in is often overwhelming. I keep it all in big see-through plastic sacks to make finding the perfect bit and clean-up easier.

Funny, most of the kids will start out working alone and then end up working with two or three others. They often fabricate a whole scene—a plantation with outbuildings, slave quarters, and the big house or a New England village. I use lapboards (made of Masonite, cut about 24"-by-36") in my classroom all the time. Whether doing a drawing project, working math problems with a buddy on the floor, or placing a house on the lapboard, the boards facilitate movement and storage for my students.

4. When finished, some kids like to write journals from their houses' point of view. To provide a kinesthetic organizer for the journal, we use the little book strategy on page 235 but make it bigger. They may also want to create paper doll people to live in the houses. When my students do paper dolls, I provide a pattern for a boy and a girl. These are quite plain, full-body renditions that the kids can dress in historically accurate clothing. Materials and notions are frequently used to dress the dolls appropriately. The full body pattern does help those kids who are reluctant to draw. I don't require the kids to use the patterns, but provide them as prompts for those who want to use them. Both of these extensions are valuable and provide more entry points for kids to demonstrate their knowledge of the colonial period.

A wonderful book to focus the students' thinking about climate, resources, the colonial period, and houses is *William's House* by Ginger Howard (2001).

Literacy Connection
The little bigger book, Journal of a House, as described on page 114, gives students practice in writing descriptive and narrative paragraphs. Word choice, sentence fluency, and voice are writing traits that are frequently the focus of this strategy.

QUILTS

MATERIALS

Drawing paper cut into eight-inch squares
Colored markers, pencils, or crayons

PROCEDURE

1. Have your students read one or more quilt stories. Discuss how a quilt combines from many fabrics and colors into a new pattern and useful product, just like the United States combines many cultures into a productive society.

2. Divide your class into groups representing immigrant nationalities you've studied (e.g., Hispanic Americans, Asian Americans, African Americans, European Americans). I include Native Americans not as immigrants, but as First Americans.

3. Give each group six or eight squares of drawing paper and large felt markers in three different colors. Tell them to depict their cultures' contributions to our society, one contribution per square. They need to decide what they want to depict and who will draw it.

4. When the drawings are finished, ask each group to arrange their "quilt squares" attractively on a piece of tagboard or construction paper. As each group finishes, join it with others until a large "blanket" is formed, pieced together "by the common threads of justice, democracy, and equity." Discuss how the whole quilt is more pleasing and more useful than the individual squares alone, but that the individual squares provide interest and strength. Write or sing songs about America's heritage.

5. For a fabulous individual follow-up, on paper divided into four-inch squares, have the students create their own individual quilts. Sometimes my students enjoy creating different designs. Other times, we have brainstormed all the activities we have done during the year. During the last week of school, each creates a memory quilt, drawing pictures or symbols of the things they liked best. It's a graphic reflection of the year! Laminating the finished product brings out the colors

and protects the hard work it has taken to produce a personal quilt. (See cover for an example of the student-created quilt described here.)

Literacy Connection

Ask students to reflect on their quilt:

- Describe what they did (descriptive paragraph)
- Tell what they learned or know as a result of their work (narrative paragraph)
- Explain how they feel about the process and the product (expository paragraph)

STORYBOARDS

MATERIALS

12″-by-18″ white construction paper for each student
Marking pens or colored pencils

PROCEDURE

1. Have the students read a novel.
2. Ask them to fold the construction paper into eight equal rectangles.
3. Use a straightedge to outline each rectangle with a black felt-tip marker.
4. Set up the criteria for each box:
   1st—Title, rewritten by (student name)
   2nd—Main character
   3rd—Setting (time and place)
   4th—Situation or conditions before problem
   5th—Antagonist/problem
   6th—Conflict
   7th—Resolution
   8th—Denouement or "The End," wrapping up the loose ends
5. Encourage students to use colored markers. Insist that students use some text and some drawing in most boxes.
6. Have a reading seminar in class. Each student reads another student's work then exchanges with someone else until everyone has had an opportunity to read several students' storyboards. Asking readers to write a one-line positive comment, makes the sharing even richer: "I really liked your pictures." "I think you found the real problem in this story." "Your description makes me want to read the book."

ALTERNATIVE CRITERIA FOR STORYBOARDS

FICTION

1. Title, retold by (student name)
2. Main character

3. Problem

4–6. Attempted solutions

7. Climax

8. Resolution

NONFICTION

1. Title, researched by (student name)

2. and 3. Data questions student had

4. and 5. Explanation questions student had and answers found

6. and 7. Evaluation questions student had and answers found

8. Recommendation or purpose

VARIATION: FLIP BOOK (SEE PAGE 142 FOR DIRECTIONS.)

VARIATION: LIFT DOOR POSTER (SEE PAGE 125 FOR DIRECTIONS)

Literacy Connection

Storyboards provide so much reading and writing practice! First of all, the finished product definitely demonstrates student comprehension as students are called on to summarize, retell, or analyze the story. In a sense, the student is making a visual and textual outline of the story using the storyboard format.

STORYBOARDS WITH A ZOOM LENS

MATERIALS

9"-by-12" pieces of white construction paper or tagboard
Colored markers or pencils

PROCEDURE

1. Follow the storyboard procedure.
2. Tell the students to pretend they have a zoom lens and that they are going to focus on the feelings of the main character in the story. On one piece of paper, they are going to draw the main character during the most critical or eventful part of the story and cut the character out. The character should be at least seven inches tall.
3. On a second piece of paper, they should draw the background appropriate for the part of the story they are featuring; then using an accordion fold, they are to make the main character's figure "pop up" from the page.
4. Have them cut out a "thought" bubble and in it write a first-person account of how the main character is feeling at this time. For example, Amelia Earhart, on a deserted island in the Pacific, might be thinking: "I hope someone finds me soon. I feel so alone. I wonder if there is anyway to get off this island? I know I can figure a way out. I've solved bigger problems than this in my life." Have the students glue the bubble on the background scene and share the storyboard with the class.

Literacy Connection

Inferential thinking is demonstrated through the zoom lens variation of the storyboard. The student must first comprehend the story and then infer how the main character is feeling. The affective domain is tapped through this strategy, demonstrating higher-order thinking.

LITTLE BOOKS

MATERIALS

Rectangular white drawing paper
Scissors
Marking pens and/or colored pencils

PROCEDURE

1. Students read a novel or nonfiction book.
2. Ask them to fold a little book and put the following information* on the pages to demonstrate their comprehension.
   Page 1—Title and author
   Page 2—Main character and a quote
   Page 3—Another character with five descriptive words
   Page 4—A picture with a quote
   Page 5—Summary
   Page 6—Pictorial map
   Page 7—Two problems and how they were solved

ALTERNATIVE PROCEDURES

1. Have your students create little books to debrief a field trip—What I did, What I learned, What I felt.
2. Have your students use the little book format for Believe-It-or-Not Books of Facts about science or social studies topics.
3. Use the little book to practice figurative language, such as the Little Book of Alliteration, the Little Book of Transitions, or the Little Book of Metaphors and Similes.
4. Make a Little Book of Measurement to keep notes about standard or metric measures.

* These categories were suggested by Oralee Kramer, Chinook Middle School, Bellevue, Washington.

5. Use a minibook (8″-by-11″) as a notebook for field trips, or use as a book report, focusing on the six elements of fiction.

6. Create little bigger picture books of fiction or nonfiction, using 18″-by-24″ for these.

Literacy Connection

The little book format lends itself to the demonstration of comprehension and reading response. Additionally, students can practice all kinds of writing, demonstrate their ability to create questions and find their answers, retell stories, summarize information, make conclusions, support decisions with details, and apply criteria to critiques. This kinesthetic organizer easily replaces the traditional book report, extends the study of important topics, and records needed data. It is truly a gift to teachers and students alike!

DARUMA

In Japan, one good-luck symbol is a Daruma-san (dar-rooma sahn). *Daruma* is a nickname for a Buddhist priest from India named Bodhidharma. *San* is a title of respect. Wearing a red robe, he sat with his legs and arms crossed, thinking about serious problems. Some say he meditated for nine years; he sat so still, he lost the use of his legs and arms.

To people in Japan, Daruma-san stands for the spirit of courage and determination. He is symbolized by a folk-art doll, constructed so that no matter how he is tipped, he bobs back upright. There is a saying that goes with Daruma-san:

SEVEN TIMES YOU MAY FALL

BUT

EIGHT TIMES

YOU RISE UP AGAIN

A Daruma-san may be given to you if you are starting something new. Often in Japan, one is given to the owner of a new business. Daruma-san invites personal goal-setting: the custom is to paint in one eye when you set your goal, and paint in the other eye when it's accomplished. In Japan, there are male and female Darumas, painted in many different ways.

PROCEDURE

1. Give each student a copy of the Daruma-san drawing (enlarge the drawing shown on the next page).
2. Ask students to color their Daruma-san brightly, leaving the eyes blank, and then cut it out.
3. Have them set a goal and write it on the back of the Daruma-san cutout. (I ask my students to choose one related to school that we can work on together.)
4. Have students color in one eye.

5. Display the Daruma-sans in the classroom. Encourage the students to color in the other eye when they reach their goal.

Literacy Connection
Goal-setting is important to student success. Some teachers might ask students to include a literacy goal as part of this strategy. Working on clear sentence construction and following appropriate conventions (mechanics) are part of completing this strategy correctly.

POEMS FOR TWO VOICES*

MATERIALS

Fleischmann, Paul, *Joyful Noise: Poems for Two Voices*

PROCEDURE

1. Copy samples from this book and distribute them.
2. Ask for volunteers to read the samples aloud. Discuss the form.
3. Working in pairs, ask the students to write similar poems of their own and to share them orally.

Note

This strategy is a wonderful way to present two perspectives or opposing points of view. Students can write them individually or in pairs, but either way, the poem is a dialogue for two opposing points of view that is best when read aloud by two people.

The structure is quite simple. Each voice speaks individually and then the two voices speak together, commenting on something about which they agree or about which they agree to disagree. It is best to arrange the lines in three columns with the speeches moving down the page in the sequence in which they will be read aloud. I have my students fold a piece of notebook paper in half lengthwise. The midpoint is where both voices together are written.

VOICE ONE	BOTH VOICES TOGETHER	VOICE TWO
"_____"	"_____"	
	"_____"	"_____"

The actual length is up to the author(s), but there needs to be enough written so that the ideas are explored in depth. It is also important to remember that the two sides do not have to agree by the end of the poem. They may simply agree that they cannot agree on the issue.

This strategy invites integration through content and skills. Whether exploring social studies, such as having students write about the Revolutionary War or

* *This strategy came to me from Marj Montgomery, Day Junior High, Newton, Massachusetts.*

Civil War from different points of view, looking at more than one side of Constitutional amendments, or debating political issues such as arms treaties and social security; or science-centered concerns, such as deforestation, global warming or AIDS epidemics, the poems-for-two-voices structure is a powerful culminating strategy.

Literacy Connection

Higher-level thinking skills are called into action in poems for two voices. Students must make conclusions about an issue. Then, in tandem, each composes poetry in cooperation with another person, demonstrating their comprehension of two sides of an issue or from diverse points of view. This demonstration also shows their ability with word choice, ideas, and organization of writing. To demonstrate fluency through oral reading, encourage the pairs to rehearse reading their poetry several times before sharing with the whole class.

INTERIOR MONOLOGUES*

BACKGROUND

Interior monologues provide students with an opportunity to explore a topic in depth. This strategy is also a way for students to make a topic more personal. Interior monologues are an exciting "stretch" for students. You will be building for success in this activity and probably will want to repeat it several times over the course of a year.

PROCEDURE

1. Tell the students that today they are going to be philosophers, people who think seriously about issues and topics that matter.
2. Ask the students if they ever have conversations inside their heads, if they ever think about both sides of a conversation. Mention that many people do this, and it is often very helpful. We can plan, ramble on, or revise without anyone but us ever knowing! This process is called an "interior monologue." There are two formats for interior monologues:
   a. As yourself or a character, pretend you are talking to someone else. We introduce ourselves and then proceed to tell the other person some of our innermost thoughts. We can ramble on and explain in some detail because the person to whom the narration is addressed will never actually hear the thoughts.
   b. We write down our thoughts about the topic or issue an interior monologue. It is the depth of thought that counts. In fact, it is similar to poetry. This is a good way to get students to take a personal stand on an issue in a story or current event.
3. Give the students an opportunity to write their own interior monologues on a given subject.

Literacy Connection
The interior monologue strategy combines writing with reading when the students take on the character from a novel. The process helps clarify compre-

* *This strategy came to me from Marj Montgomery, Day Junior High, Newton, Massachusetts.*

hension by revealing inferences made by the students. Because this strategy provides a synthesis of knowledge and values, it is most effective when used toward the end of a unit of study. When students have had multiple opportunities to explore an issue or an event through both fiction and nonfiction resources and when they can choose any character they wish, whether historical or invented, powerful writing occurs.

CIVIL WAR PERSPECTIVE NEWSPAPER

MATERIALS

Regular classroom supplies

Manila envelopes or file folders

Access to a copy machine that accommodates reductions, *or* a computer program for producing newspapers in the classroom

Newspaper (optional)

PROCEDURE

1. Label manila envelopes or file folders, one for each perspective. Provide a prototype for each group (see graphic).
2. Group students by perspective: Southern white, Northern white, free African American, Westward Ho!
3. Tell the students that, as a culminating activity, they are going to jointly create a newspaper to share what they have learned about the Civil War era. Each group needs to choose an editor for their material. Discuss the qualities of an editor (can spell, writes well, works well with others, is organized and responsible). Ask each group to identify their editor.
4. Brainstorm sections of a newspaper. (You might want to bring in a real newspaper to act as a prompt.) Common sections of newspapers include editorials, news articles, special features, regional news, religion, sports, horoscope, deaths, comics, classifieds, crossword puzzles, business, Dear Abby, music, and advertising.
5. Tell the students that each group is responsible for creating a page that reflects that group's perspective or point of view. Each student must contribute an article for the paper that is acceptable to the editor and handed in by the deadline. Show the students how to "size" their article by putting lined paper over their assigned section and drawing the shape. Recommend that they write the articles in pencil first, then go over in black fine felt-tip pen after editing.

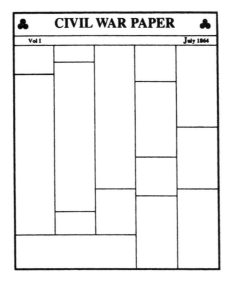

6. Set a reasonable deadline (two or three class periods is adequate). Meet with the editors to help them keep on track.
7. Take at least one reading period to share the newspaper and evaluate it as a class.

VARIATION: NEWSPAPER IN A DAY

Cut classroom notebook paper in half lengthwise. This half sheet becomes a "column." Instruct students to title, byline, and dateline the beginning of each article; print the article in pencil; proofread with the editor or teacher; go over the article in black fine felt-tip pen after corrections and turn it in. All other kinds of material (cartoons, graphs, surveys, etc.) should be one or two columns wide, depending on nature of the material, and should be done in black fine felt-tip pen.

Using the reducing feature of a copy machine (I usually use 64 percent) reduce all the articles by the same percentage. Take the reduced columns and "paste" these into newspaper-like format on the largest size paper the copy machine can reproduce. Draw in lines between columns. Copy each page and collate into a newspaper. Don't forget the masthead on the front page (see Figure 3–3 on page 81 for sample).

Literacy Connection
Students practice writing the parts of a newspaper story: headline, byline, lead, quote, body, and ending. Using prewriting strategies, they select a subject and

collect details. In their draft, they write the lead or first paragraph and continue with the main part of the story. When they revise, they improve their writing by making sure that they have included all the important facts and details in the story. Finally, editing and proofreading take place with the student editor and the final copy is added to the group's newspaper. This format is excellent for communicating with parents. Whether the topic of the newspaper is social studies content, a special field trip, or a summary of skills learned in math the past month, this strategy provides a place for every single student in your room (see Figure 5–4 on page 143 for sample).

ONE-PAGE PLAYS

MATERIALS

Lined notebook paper

PROCEDURE

1. Tell the students they are going to have one period to write a one-page play. The rules are:

   THREE CHARACTERS

   NO LONGER THAN:

      BOTH SIDES OF ONE PIECE OF PAPER, BY HAND

      IN BLACK FINE FELT-TIP PEN, LEGIBLY; OR

      ON COMPUTER, ONE SIDE, SIZE 12 OR LARGER FONT

   THERE MUST BE A PROBLEM AND A SOLUTION FEATURING

   . . . (An amendment from the Bill of Rights, a newly landed immigrant, a salmon trying to survive, a pioneer family moving West, a student faced with a decision about drugs/alcohol, etc.)

2. Discuss the construction of a script. I tell my students that they must start a new line every time a different character speaks, that they don't have to use quotation marks, and to bracket stage directions. The challenge is to tell the story through conversation, so I don't let my students use narrators.

3. After the plays have been written and turned in, make three photocopies of each play.

4. Randomly pass out the students' scripts, stopping when everyone in the class has a part. Instruct the students to read the play they've been given silently, then begin rehearsing a reader's theater presentation with the others in their play. This should take between ten and fifteen minutes. (I do not let authors act in their own plays.)

5. One group at a time, call the students up to present their play. When all the plays in that round have been presented, start another round. Keep repeating the process until all the plays have been presented.

6. Ask the playwrights to write a critique of their own play, stating:
   What they liked.
   What they'd change.
7. Hand back the plays and encourage the playwrights to revise their scripts. I find giving one to two class periods the best way to encourage revision.
8. Copy the revised scripts, give to the same actors and re-present them.
9. Discuss the value of revision.
10. Decide whether to polish for production or to stop here.

Literacy Connection

This is a great way to give struggling readers an opportunity to practice fluency. Kids know that actors rehearse many, many times. Even though they don't like to reread books or articles, they will practice a play over and over. Use these one-page plays as reader's theater. Give the kids several opportunities to practice, both in their small group and for an audience. Multiple practice will help shape more fluent readers.

THE STEPS IN A CRIMINAL TRIAL

1. *Opening of the court.* The court clerk announces that the court is ready to begin. He or she also introduces the judge.
2. *Swearing in the jury.* The court clerk or the judge asks the jurors to take their seats. He or she then asks them to swear that they will act fairly in listening to the case.
3. *Introduction of counsel.* The judge asks the counsels to introduce themselves.
4. *Opening statement by the prosecuting attorney.* This lawyer begins by telling the jury the important information about the case. This includes the parties in the case and the facts that led to the lawsuit. The prosecuting attorney presents the prosecutor's side of the case to the jury.
5. *Opening statement by the defense attorney.* This lawyer begins by stating his or her name and the defendant's name, then tells the jury that he or she will try to prove that the prosecutor does not have a valid case. The defense attorney then presents the defendant's side of the case to the jury.
6. *Prosecution's direct examination of witnesses.* The prosecuting attorney calls the witnesses for the prosecutor one at a time to the front of the room. The court clerk asks each witness to swear to tell the truth. The attorney then asks questions of the witness. The questions are based on the facts the witness has to offer. The defense has an opportunity to cross-examine.*
7. *Defense's direct examination of witnesses.* The defense then calls its witnesses. The clerk swears in each witness and the defense counsel questions them. The prosecutor has an opportunity to cross-examine.
8. *Judge's instruction to the jury.* The judge explains to the jury what the principles of law are in this case. He or she asks the jury to make a fair decision.
9. *Closing arguments.* Each attorney sums up the main points from the evidence that help his or her client's case and argues why his or her side should win. The prosecutor is the first to present the arguments, followed by defense counsel, with the prosecutor getting a second, and last, chance to convince the jury.

---

* *Cross-examination of witnesses.* During cross-examination, an attorney tries to get the other side's witness to admit something that will help his or her client, or tries to show that a witness is not dependable.

10. *Verdict.* The jury talks about and makes a decision in the case. In a real trial, the jury leaves the courtroom to reach a verdict. In a mock trial, the jury can talk about the case and come to a decision in front of the rest of the class or leave the room to hold their deliberations in private. A majority vote of the jurors will decide the verdict. (In a real criminal case, all jurors must agree on guilt or innocence. If they fail to reach agreement, it is a "hung jury").

Literacy Connection

A mock trial gives many opportunities for students to demonstrate acquisition of literacy skills. From reading and researching the issue to developing an opening statement, from examination of witness to closing argument, mock trials provide students the opportunity to label, list, match, recall, select, state, describe, explain, paraphrase, interpret, summarize, organize, use, categorize, differentiate, find patterns, infer, outline, compose, create, formulate, hypothesize, write, conclude, judge, support with details, and apply criteria—most of the skills we want a literate student to be able to demonstrate.

JOURNALS

MATERIALS

Paper appropriate for journal writing
Binding materials (optional)
Samples or journals (optional)

PROCEDURE

1. Share samples of journals with the students if you choose.
2. Tell the students they are going to read a novel and keep a journal as if they were the main character. Set the number of entries and minimum length expected. Decide if you will accept drawings. It helps focus the students if you require a "think," a "feel," and a "do," in each entry. Tell the students whether they must bind their journal. (You may decide to make this a class art project.)
3. Give some class time each day for journal writing.
4. Set up an assessment by peers. Have the students trade journals and select two or three entries, then answer the following questions; provide examples from the journals to back up their comments.
   a. Are the entries believable?
   b. Are the entries accurate?
   c. Are the entries complete?
5. Provide an opportunity for the author to respond to this peer assessment.

Literacy Connection

Student writers have an opportunity to develop their voice as writers in this strategy. Summarizing, interpreting, and synthesizing also are called on as students demonstrate their comprehension skills through this higher-level thinking strategy.

STORY LADDERS

MATERIALS

12"-by-18" white construction paper for every student
4.5"-by-12" panels of white construction paper for each student
Marking pens or colored pencils

PROCEDURE

1. Ask the students to fold construction paper into four equal rectangular panels.
2. Have them use a straightedge and a black felt-tip marker to draw a line between each panel, on the fold.
3. Instruct the students to retell a story through pictures and words in the four descending panels (i.e., "Identify the four most important parts of the story").
4. On the back, ask the students to identify the title, author, publishing date, and number of pages.

Extension Activity

5. Give the students a single panel of 4.5"-by-12" paper and ask them to create a different ending to the story, add it to the story ladder with cellophane tape at the left side of the last panel, folding it back so it doesn't show, or hinge it like a door.
6. Ask each student to display the story ladders with their new ending hidden, then "walk" the class down the ladder, revealing the new ending.
7. Discuss whether any of the new endings change the power or impact of the story.

VARIATION: STORY SCREEN

Turn the story ladder on its side. Refold it like an accordion and stand it up like a Chinese screen. I like my students to choose the four most important parts of the story to display on the screens. My kids like to cut and color the top of the segments to symbolize something within the story.

Literacy Connection

Listing the six elements of fiction (storyboard) makes students practice analyzing or taking apart a story. The story ladder and story screen ask them to synthesize this process as students identify the four most important parts of the story. Here the students put the story back together.

LETTERS

MATERIALS

Writing materials: Some teachers prefer to have their students create or personalize the stationery they use. Others suggest that the students make the stationery match the time period of the story—for example, quill pen and tea-stained paper to simulate the letters written on parchment in colonial days or a clever computer-designed letterhead to fit today's business world.

PROCEDURE

1. Any time during the reading of a novel or when completed, ask the students, as characters in the novel, to write:
   to a pen pal explaining the situation
   to a lawyer seeking advice
   to a relative
   to someone not in the story about another character
   to another character in the story, sharing feeling
   to the editor of the local paper
   to a government official
2. Ask the students to "buddy up" and read their letters aloud to each other.

VARIATION: SEQUENTIAL LETTERS

Later in the year, try assigning three or four sequential letters to be written as the students progress through a book. These letters should reveal increasingly more comprehension as the novel unfolds and more inferences as the student identifies with the characters. Here's an example using *Freedom Train: The Story of Harriet Tubman* (Sterling 1954).

1. Write your first letter *about* Harriet. Pretend you are a character in the story so far and write about what Harriet does, what she knows, and how she feels. Create stationery that fits the time in which Harriet lived. (My students decided that they should use their very best cursive writing for this letter, replicating how 1850s folks would communicate.)

2. Write your second letter after you have read half of the novel. This letter should be *from* Harriet to another character in the book. Once again, through your writing, show what Harriet has done, what she has learned, and how she feels. Create stationery that reflects Harriet's heritage. (My kids researched patterns in African art, like kinte cloth, and copied them for their stationery. Additionally, after much discussion about how Harriet couldn't read or write, they decided that if she could, she would use manuscript.)

3. Your last letter should be *to* Harriet, from you, today. Pretend you can write to her. Use the word processor and tell her about life now. Tell her what you learned from reading her story, speculate about what she might like to see and what she might find troubling. Create stationery with your computer program. (We made envelopes for each of the letters. The kids enjoyed creating stamps and postmarks while practicing addressing envelopes correctly. Creating a cover and back out of the tagboard, we sandwiched the letters between, and using plastic coils, we bound the whole activity into a book. It reminded me of the *Jolly Postman* format.)

Literacy Connection

In addition to demonstrating reading comprehension, this strategy stretches young writers as they make inferences from different points of view, express themselves using different voices, sequence events, retell, summarize, and identify what is important from another's point of view. Students also practice the formats of different kinds of letters and ways to address envelopes.

QUICK AND QUIET BOOKS
AKA WRITE YOUR OWN TEXTS

MATERIALS

Regular lined notebook paper
4″-by-7″ plain paper rectangles

PROCEDURE

1. At the beginning of a unit, ask the students to list all the questions that they have about the topic. Write the questions on the board or on the overhead.

2. After generating enough questions so that there is at least one question for each student, read and evaluate the questions. Are there any repeats? Could some be combined? Is anything important left out?

3. Hold a drawing. After each student has selected a question, give time for the research. This research may be done in the field, obtained from invited guests, or found in books and magazines.

4. When you're ready, give the students a plain rectangle of paper and a piece of notebook paper. (You may decide to wait until the unit is finished. On the other hand, you may decide to have the students answer the questions and make a book of the answers as the primary source for the unit.) Tell them to place the top of the rectangle of paper on the top line of the notebook paper and lightly draw a line around its edges.

5. Tell them to write their questions in their nicest handwriting on the notebook paper directly under the rectangle. On the rest of the page, they should write a paragraph, answering their questions, first, in pencil, then after proofreading, in fine-tip black felt pen.

6. Tell the students to draw pictures to illustrate each of their questions and answers on the blank rectangle and glue it on the notebook paper.

7. Copy each page for every student. Bind into a book and use it for class study of the topic. This is a particularly effective way to affirm students' research writing. When the "text" is a book they have created, writing is validated as a worthwhile endeavor.

Literacy Connection

Using nonfiction and/or textbook information to practice retelling or summarizing is key to the success of this assignment. Being able to form appropriate questions from textbook headings demonstrates a higher level of comprehension. In addition to providing students practice for studying the text's information (I teach students my variation of the SQ3R method: *S*can the material for *S*chema (prior knowledge). Form *Q*uestions. *R*ead. *R*eform questions, w*R*ite, and *R*emember.) The quick and quiet book also fosters mental imaging as students illustrate the information they have read.

SPELLING ACTIVITIES THAT INVOLVE AND EXAMINE

HOW MUCH IS IT WORTH?

Decide on a value for each letter of the alphabet (e.g., a = 1 cent, b = 2 cents, c = 3 cents, d = 4 cents, e = 5 cents, and so on, up to 26 cents. Add the value of each letter in the word. If the sum 100 cents, then the word is worth $1.00. "Riddle," for example, is worth 52 cents. "Zoology" is worth $1.15.*

- Challenge students to find the words that are worth exactly one dollar.

- Find the total "worth" of the spelling list.

- Change the values (e.g., all vowels are worth a nickel, consonants equal 6 cents—a good way to practice those pesky hard-to-learn times tables).

- Have kids find out who has the most expensive list, . . . the least expensive.

- Slide over to codes and have the kids create symbolic codes, other letter codes, word codes—anything that requires them to really look at (analyze) their spelling words.

CATEGORIES

Demonstrate some categories that could be used to "sort" words, such as those that demonstrate one of the four basic spelling questions:

When do you double the final consonant?
When do you change the "y" to "i"?
When do you drop the final "e"?
When do you use "s" or "es"?

* Note: Adapted from Burns, Marilyn. 1995. *The $1.00 Word Riddle Book, Revised.* White Plains, NY: Math Solutions.

Other categories could include:

| Words with long vowel sounds | Words with silent "e" | Words that are related |
| Words that have two syllables | Words that rhyme | Homophones |

One way to introduce a new spelling list is to have the students categorize the words based on one or more of the preceding. After the kids have had some experience categorizing words, encourage them to create their own categories and agree on how many categories they must create. For example, I might say, "Try to create four categories for your spelling words." Then, later I might increase the difficulty by specifying that no word can fit more than one category.

Literacy Connection

Finding engaging ways to get students to look at the way words work in our language and assisting them as they construct personal understanding is one way spelling works in my classroom. I want kids to leave my classroom knowing not only that words matter, but that some rules and organizational structures govern our language.

BIOGRAPHY POSTERS*

You are to create an attractive poster that represents your individual. Follow these directions carefully, please.

1. Cut your poster into a shape that relates to your person. An example of this would be George Washington's poster cut into the shape of a horse, Betsy Ross' cut to the shape of a flag and so on.
2. Place a picture of your person on the poster and *be sure to* include his or her full name. Copy or draw these pictures from books or encyclopedias or import from the Internet or a CD-ROM.
3. Place four other pictures which help to describe or identify your person, on your poster. Examples might include his or her home, an important person in his or her life, an action picture.
4. From your resources, locate three quotations that describe the CHARACTER of your person. Look for quotes about what they stood for, believed in, or fought to achieve.
5. Using the first-person point of view, complete the following five open-ended sentences:
   a. I am most proud of the following three accomplishments in my life . . .
   b. When I look back on my life, I am saddened by . . .
   c. When people remember me, I want them to say . . .
   d. If I could have changed anything in my life, it would have been . . .
   e. The person who influenced me the most in my life is . . . because she (he) taught me . . .
6. Place the title and the author of the book on your project. Don't forget your own name!

This activity can easily be turned into a personal biography by tweaking the directions just a tiny bit. For example, students might cut the shape of a skateboard, a cello, or a basketball and glue on a picture of themselves. They, too, could place four more pictures relating information about themselves. They could find quotes that describe their own character and complete the sentence stems pretty much as provided. Obviously, no author or book is required but

* Thanks to Marj Montgomery and her colleagues from Newton, Massachusetts, for sharing this integrated strategy.

they might use standard reference formats to identify the books or sources for their quotations.

Literacy Connection

A dramatic way to demonstrate comprehension of biographies. A wonderful way to share knowledge with peers. This strategy works on organization, word choice, voice (point of view), and mechanics (quotes).

Name:	Grade:			1 2 3 4
Scoring Rubic for a Bio Poster				
	1 Outstanding, memorable	2 Well done	3 Adequate	4 Some problems, omissions, or inaccuracies
The shape of the poster relates to the person.				
Poster is neatly cut out.				
Includes picture of subject.				
All pictures are neatly glued down—no tape.				
Each of the pictures is well chosen and representative of the person's life.				
Includes three important quotations.				
Everything that should be is written in full sentences.				
Answers the five open-ended questions.				
Subjects and verbs agree.				
The answers are all in one tense only.				
The five questions use the first person (I, me, my, mine).				
All words are spelled correctly.				
All writing is very neat or word processed.				
Includes the title (underlined or italics if word processed) author, publisher, and copyright date.				
Overall appearance.				

THE STATES PROJECT OF EXCELLENCE

MATERIALS

1 large paper for a travel poster
1 regular plain paper for an outline map
1 small cardboard for a postcard

PROCEDURE

1. Write a research report using the enclosed forms for your three main topics. Add a suitable introduction and conclusion or summary.
2. Make a postcard showcasing your state. Describe it on the back in a pretend note to me.
3. Draw a physical, political, or pictorial map of your state. Indicate the landforms and water (lakes, rivers, oceans) that are important. Locate the capital.
4. Identify one Native American nation that lives in your chosen state. Write one paragraph about their culture, draw a picture, or construct a diorama of their traditional homes, transportation, and dress.
5. Create a travel poster about your chosen state, showing something wonderful that would make tourists want to visit.
6. Write a business letter to the Department of Tourism requesting information about your state. (Look in an almanac or call the public library for the address.) Or get on the Internet and try these addresses for further information: *www.yahoo.com*, or Global Network's Travel Center, *www.gnn.com/gnn/meta/travel/re/countris/html* for region, county, state, or city. You can also get the same listing from *www.city.net/site*.
7. Prepare a one-minute oral presentation as if you were the governor of your state.

HAVE FUN!

GENERAL DATA ORGANIZER

YOUR NAME _____

CAPITAL:	STATE GOVERNMENT:
AREA IN QUARE MILES:	NUMBER OF REPRESENTATIVES:
	NUMBER OF STATE SENATORS:

ELEVATION:
  HIGHEST:
  LOWEST:
	CHIEF PRODUCTS:

POPULATION:	STATE ABBREVIATIONS:
STATE TREE:	STATE BIRD:
STATE FLOWER:	STATE SONG:
STATE MOTTO:	

LAND REGIONS:	CLIMATE:
	  HIGHEST TEMPERATURE:
	  LOWEST TEMPERATURE:
	  RAINFALL (PRECIPITATION):

CULTURAL DATA ORGANIZER

YOUR NAME _____

PEOPLE:	SCHOOLS:
PLACES TO VISIT:	HISTORY:
FAMOUS PEOPLE:	IMPORTANT DATES:

ECONOMIC DATA ORGANIZER

YOUR NAME _____

NATURAL RESOURCES:	MANUFACTURING:
AGRICULTURE:	MINING AND OTHER INDUSTRIES:
TRANSPORTATION:	COMMUNICATION AND TECHNOLOGY:

STATES PROJECT OF EXCELLENCE EVALUATION

(50) _____ RESEARCH REPORT:
                                    Interesting introduction
                                    General data
                                    Cultural data
                                    Economic data
                                    Conclusion or summary

(10) _____ POSTER AND POSTCARD:
                                    Colorful
                                    Creative
                                    Informational
                                    Carefully done

(10) _____ BUSINESS LETTER:
                                    Correct format
                                    Neatly done

(10) _____ NATIVE AMERICAN INFORMATION:
                                    Shelter
                                    Dress
                                    Transportation

(10) _____ MAP:
                                    Accurate
                                    Carefully done

(10) _____ ORAL PRESENTATION:
                                    Effective voice
                                    Eye contact
                                    Convincing message

(100) [   ] TOTAL

Comments:

THE PEACEFUL CLASSROOM UNIT

OBJECTIVES

By the end of this unit the students will:

1. Contribute to the classroom community positively.
2. Acquire a greater understanding of and appreciation for "peace."
3. Gain skills in solving problems peacefully.
4. Develop a sense of ownership and responsibility for the classroom.

PROCEDURE

Lesson One

Materials: scratch paper, butcher paper and marker, picture books about peace

1. On a piece of scratch paper, ask the students to jot down two or three ways they could make the classroom a terrible place to learn, a place where no one would ever feel good, an environment students would want to avoid—for example, "Everybody talk whenever they want," "Never listen to anybody," "Take whatever you want from anyone," or "Make faces at people and call them names." (I exclude violence. Students are safe in this classroom. I will protect them, no matter what.)
2. Go around the class, asking the students to share one of their ideas, being careful not to repeat what someone has already shared. Make a list of each child's suggestion on a large piece of butcher paper. Enjoy the silly, the absurd, and the oh-so-true, such as "Never do your work," "Get into other people's desks," "Call people bad names," and "Don't listen."
3. When every child has had an opportunity to share, stop. Reread each suggestion and probe for the reason why the way listed would hurt rather than help students learn.
4. Read any picture stories you have about peace, learning, support, and friendship.
5. Leave the butcher paper list up where the children can see it. Tell the students they will be referring to it again.

Lesson Two:

Materials: three sheets of copy paper per student, markers, crayons, or colored pencils

1. Ask the students if they know what their "mind's eye" is. Continue to probe until you are sure the students understand that the *mind's eye* is a visualization of an idea or mental imagery. Ask the students to visualize "peace." Some may wish to close their eyes, others may simply choose to relax. Playing soft, safe, unfamiliar music often helps students with visualizations or mental imagery.
2. After a few moments, ask the children to share what peace looks like. Accept all descriptions without qualification.
3. Ask the children, "What does peace sound like?" Elicit answers from many children.
4. Ask the children, "How does peace smell or taste?" Continue collecting many opinions.
5. Ask the children, "How does peace feel?"
6. Ask the students to demonstrate peace with just their fingers, then their hands, then their arms or upper bodies. Invite children who are comfortable doing so to demonstrate how peace would move using their whole bodies.
7. Pass out three sheets of copy paper to every child. Show the students how to place the paper so that they have about a one-inch overlap on each paper. Check to make sure all the children have their paper laid out properly. Demonstrate how to fold the paper so that they end up with a six-page booklet (see sketch on page 52).
8. Tell the students that this is their Personal Peace Book. The first page is the title, and then they should label each flap with one of the five senses starting with the stem "Peace (feels) like . . ." Repeat the stem with tastes like, smells like, sounds like, and looks like. Students should also draw a picture of that "peaceful" sense on the page. Give ample time for the students to work on this assignment. Encourage sharing and enjoying. Play peaceful music while the children work or read them more stories about peace.

Lesson Three

Materials: none

1. Have a "peaceful share circle." Say to the students: "Hand your booklet to someone." Or, "Take a booklet from someone." "Read and enjoy

Appendix

the book. When you are done, hold the book up. Exchange it with someone else who is holding up a book. Read and enjoy several books in this peaceful way." Provide ample time for peaceful, silent reading of peer work.

2. Open a discussion after sharing by asking, "What did you learn about peace from your friends?" (Collect the booklets.)

3. Redirect the students' attention to the negative (Wreck the Room*) list generated earlier. Ask, "What was our objective when we created this list?" (To make sure no one learned or liked school.) "What do you think our objective could be?" (To make sure everyone learns and likes school.) "How could we do that?"

4. Rewrite the negative list to positives as the children dictate—for example, "Talk when it's your turn," "Listen to each other," "Take things only with permission," "Only make nice faces at people," or "Tell people good things like 'nice try' and 'good sport.'" Throw away the negative list because that kind of behavior certainly wouldn't happen in this classroom!

Lesson Four

Materials: Large piece of railroad board or tagboard, marker

1. Hang the tagboard on the board or lay it on the floor and ask the students to sit on the floor around it. Ask the students which they would prefer for the rest of the year, a peaceful classroom or an unpeaceful one. Suggest to them that sometimes rules or common agreements help keep peace. Ask if anyone can think of an example. Discuss.

2. Write a heading on the tagboard, "In our peaceful classroom . . . " Ask the students for suggestions. Pare down the list to a manageable few. This is a list of agreements one of my classes suggested:
    1. We raise our hands.
    2. We are respectful of others.
    3. We listen and pay attention.
    4. We have a positive attitude.
    5. We like people for themselves.
    6. We are calm (quiet) ourselves.
    7. We eat only at lunch and snack.

* Note: As the year progresses and a child forgets and "wrecks the room," just remind the child by whispering, "Oops, be careful. You're wrecking the room."

3. Ask all the children to read the list of agreements aloud. We say it every morning the first few weeks of school. Also, our first trip to the computer lab checks typing skills by assigning the kids the replication of our Peaceful Classroom Rules, using fonts, centering, and accurate typing.

4. Pass back the Peace booklets. On the back of the last page, ask each child to write a personal goal he or she will strive to accomplish to ensure a peaceful classroom. Hang the peace booklets on a bulletin board and then store them for the portfolio.

PORTFOLIOS

LETTER TO PARENTS

Dear Parent(s),

A portfolio is more than just a container full of stuff. "It's a systematic and organized collection of evidence used by the teacher and the student (and parents) to monitor growth of the student's knowledge, skills, attitudes in specific subject areas."

Today your child is bringing home a very important folder. Inside are products and papers from work we have done all year. Now it is time for your child, with your support, to select pieces for his or her Fifth-Grade Portfolio.

Please read the accompanying paperwork. You will see that your child needs to have a chunk of time carved out of your busy schedules to accomplish the requirements for the Fifth-Grade Portfolio. Please note that the portfolio is due on Thursday, June 13.

I hope that you will be able to sit with your child and help him or her select items to complete the Portfolio Scavenger Hunt. The discussion between you and your child, reflecting over the year's work, is an important part of the process. Your opinion and your time is valued by your child, Lakeridge, and me. As you are still the most important influence in your child's life, this conversation about learning can set a positive path for your child's success at the middle school next year.

While your child needs to fill out the Student Reflection sheets independently, discussing with you the attributes prior to writing would be highly beneficial. You might use the following questions to help guide your child's selection and reflection:

1. Why did you choose this piece?
2. What did you learn?
3. What are your strengths?
4. How do you feel about yourself as a problem solver? Can you solve problems in more than one way? Is it valuable to have multiple ways to solve problems? Why or why not?

5. How do you feel about yourself as a reader and a writer? Has this assessment changed since September?
6. What are some goals you have set for yourself?

Thank you for your continued support.
Sincerely yours,

Tarry Lindquist

*************************************** cut here ***************************************

I have read the Portfolio Scavenger Hunt and accompanying directions. I understand that this critical assignment is due on Thursday, June 13. I will see to it that my child has time set aside to accomplish this important task.

Signed: _____

PORTFOLIO SCAVENGER HUNT*

Of the fifteen possible pieces listed below, you must choose at least ten. You may do more. You must identify evidence of the starred (*) items. You will need to select examples of your work that represent the following:

*1. Evidence that shows a sample of you learning new information.
2. Evidence that shows a sample of an error you made because you did not follow directions.
3. Evidence that shows your ability to retell or summarize a longer story.
4. Evidence that demonstrates your ability to apply a specific writing skill.
5. Evidence that demonstrates your ability to organize and manage information.
6. Evidence that shows a sample of your creativity.
*7. Evidence that demonstrates a new math skill you learned.
8. Evidence that demonstrates your understanding of the basic story elements.
9. Evidence that demonstrates your ability to present a point of view.
*10. Evidence that demonstrates your ability to solve a problem, explaining the strategy you used to solve this problem.
*11. Evidence that demonstrates your ability to cooperate with others, explaining what you contributed to the group.
12. Evidence that demonstrates how you can use drawing to learn new information.
*13. Evidence that demonstrates your ability to do research.
14. Evidence that demonstrates your exploration of your own multiple intelligences.
*15. Evidence that demonstrates your ability to organize information and share it with others.

* *Many thanks to Ruth Haynsworth of North Kingstown, Rhode Island, for sharing her ideas about portfolios.*

274

THINKING STEPS AS YOU ORGANIZE YOUR PORTFOLIO

IDENTIFY

1. As you look through your folder, remember to focus on the example from the Scavenger Hunt for which you are looking.
2. You may find more than one piece of evidence that meets the criteria on the Scavenger Hunt.
3. Choose the best representation of each example on the Scavenger Hunt. You cannot use the same example or paper more than once. (This means you will identify at least ten individual pieces of your work this year.)

REFLECT

4. Think about your piece and write a Student Reflection that is appropriate for the evidence you have chosen. Include in your reflection the following:
    a. What you did.
    b. What you learned.
    c. What you'd change if you did it again (things you'd add, things you'd delete), or how you might apply this process or product in your learning next year.
    d. How you feel about this piece.
5. Staple the Student Reflection to the front of the piece of evidence and number it to correspond with the Scavenger Hunt.

ORGANIZE

6. Create a Table of Contents using the Scavenger Hunt as your guide.
7. Arrange the pieces of evidence in the order they appear in the Table of Contents.
8. Store in the folder or any organizer of your choice. Bring to school on Thursday, June 13.

FINAL THOUGHTS

9. Write at least a paragraph about what you learned about yourself as a student by putting together this portfolio. Tell what you like about yourself as a student and a learner. Tell about what you would like to improve on in sixth grade. End your thoughts by setting at least three goals for yourself as a student: one for this summer, one for the first two weeks of middle school, and one for your sixth-grade year. (Parents are invited to add their thoughts here about the portfolio process and to comment on the evidence of your learning this year.)

10. Place this thoughtful paragraph in front of your Table of Contents.

STUDENT REFLECTION— PORTFOLIOS

NAME:

EXAMPLE NUMBER AND SCAVENGER HUNT STATEMENT:

WHY THIS PIECE FITS THE REQUIREMENT FROM THE SCAVENGER HUNT:

A. What I did

B. What I learned

C. What I'd change if I did it again (what I'd add, what I'd delete) or how I might use this process or product next year.

D. How I feel about this piece (is it a personal best?).

REFERENCES

Allington, Richard L. 2001. *What Really Matters for Struggling Readers: Designing Research-Based Programs*. New York: Longman.

Armancas-Fisher, Margaret, Julia Ann Gold, and Tarry Lindquist. 1991. *Teaching the Bill of Rights: A Guide for Upper Elementary and Middle School Teachers*. Tacoma, WA: University of Puget Sound Institute for Citizen Education in the Law.

Armancas-Fisher, Margaret, Julia Ann Gold, and Kate McPherson. 1992. *Community Service Learning Guide to Law-Related Education*. Tacoma, WA: University of Puget Sound Institute for Citizen Education in the Law.

Association for Supervison and Curriculum Development. 2001. "Trying Too Hard? How Accountability and Testing Are Affecting Constructivist Teaching." *Education Update*, 43 (3): 8.

Baker, Rachel. 1944. *The First Woman Doctor: The Story of Elizabeth Blackwell, M.D.* New York: Scholastic.

Bellanca, James and Robin Fogarty. 1991. *Blueprints for Thinking in the Cooperative Classroom*. Arlington Heights, IL: IRI/Skylight Training and Publishing.

Bloom, Benjamin S. 1956. *Taxonomy of Educational Objectives: The Classification of Educational Goals—Handbook 1: Cognitive Domain*. New York: McKay.

Bragaw, Don. 1986. "From the Corner of the Eye." Speech given at Washington State Council for the Social Studies Statewide Inservice Day, Seattle: October.

Bridges, Ruby. 1999. *Through My Eyes*. New York: Scholastic.

Bruchac, Joseph. 2000. *Sacajawea*. New York: Silver Whistle.

Brumbeau, Jeff. 1999. *The Quiltmaker's Gift*. New York: Pfeifer-Hamilton.

Burns, Marilyn. 1996. The *$1.00 Word Riddle Book, Revised*. White Plains, NY: Math Solutions.

Caine, Renate Nummela, and Geoffrey Caine. 1994. *Making Connections: Teaching and the Human Brain*. Menlo Park, CA: Innovative Learning.

———. 1997. *Education on the Edge of Possibility*. Alexandria, VA: Association for Supervision and Curriculum Development.

Campbell, Linda. 1989. "Multiplying Intelligences in Teaching and Learning." Workshop given at Mercer Island Public Schools, Mercer Island, WA: February.

Campbell, Linda, Bruce Campbell, and Dee Dickinson. 1992. *Teaching and Learning Through Multiple Intelligences*. Stanwood, WA: New Horizons for Learning.

Copeland, Peter F. 1980. *Early American Trades Coloring Book*. Minneola, NY: Dover.

Culham, Ruth. 1998. *Picture Books: An Annotated Bibliography with Activities for Teaching Writing*. Fifth Edition. Portland, OR: Northwest Regional Educational Laboratory.

Dingle, Derek T. 1998. *First in the Field: Baseball Hero Jackie Robinson*. New York: Hyperion Books for Children.

Dorris, Michael. 1992. *Morning Girl*. New York: Hyperion Books for Children.

Fleischman, Paul. 1988. *Joyful Noise: Poems for Two Voices*. New York: Harper & Row.

Fogarty, Robin. 1997. *Brain Compatible Classrooms*. Arlington Heights, IL: Skylight Training and Publishing.

———. 1999. *How to Raise Test Scores*. Arlington Heights, IL: Skylight Professional Development.

Forbes, Esther. 1943. *Johnny Tremain*. Boston: Houghton Mifflin.

Fox, Mem. 1993. *Radical Reflections: Passionate Opinions on Teaching, Learning, and Living* San Diego: Harcourt Brace.

Fritz, Jean. 1983. *The Double Life of Pocahontas*. New York: The Trumpet Club.

Gardner, Howard. 1985. *Frames of Mind*. New York: Basic.

———. 1999. *The Disciplined Mind: What All Students Should Understand*. New York: Simon & Schuster.

Golenbach, Peter. 1990. *Teammates*. San Diego: Harcourt Brace Jovanovich.

Grutman, Jewel H., and Gay Matthaei. 1994. *The Ledgerbook of Thomas Blue Eagle*. Charlottesville, VA: Thomasson-Grant.

Haddix, Margaret Peterson. 1995. *Running Out of Time*. New York: Simon & Schuster.

———. 1998. *Among the Hidden*. New York: Simon & Schuster.

———. 2001. *Among the Imposters*. New York: Simon & Schuster.

Hagerty, Patricia J. 1992. "Readers' Workshop: Real Reading." Workshop given at Regis Whole Language Institute, Denver: July.

Hall, Susan. 1994 revised. *Using Picture Storybooks to Teach Literary Devices: Recommended Books for Children and Young Adults*. Phoenix: Oryx Press.

Harvey, Stephanie. 1998. *Nonfiction Matters: Reading, Writing, and Research in Grades 3–8*. York, ME: Stenhouse.

Hermes, Patricia. 2000. *Our Strange New Land: Elizabeth's Diary*. New York: Scholastic.

———. 2001. *The Starving Time: Elizabeth's Diary, Part Two—Jamestown, Virginia, 1609*. New York: Scholastic.

Hoose, Phillip. 2001. *We Were There, Too! Young People in U.S. History*. New York: Farrar, Straus, and Giroux.

Hopkinson, Deborah. 1995. *Sweet Clara and the Freedom Quilt*. New York: Random House.

Howard, Ginger. 2001. *William's House*. New York: Millbrook Press.

International Reading Association. 2000. *Standards for the English Language Arts*. Newark, DE: International Reading Association.

Irvine, Joan. 1999 (rev). *How to Make Super Pop-Ups*. New York: Morrow Junior.

Jackson, Jesse. 1988. "Common Ground and Common Sense." Speech at Democratic National Convention: July.

Jacobs, Francine. 1992. *The Tainos: The People Who Welcomed Columbus*. New York: Putman Publishing Group.

Javna, John. 1990. *Fifty Simple Things Kids Can Do to Save the Earth*. New York: Scholastic.

Jensen, Eric. 1998. *Teaching with the Brain in Mind*. Alexandria, VA: Association for Supervision and Curriculum Development.

Keene, Ellin Oliver, and Susan Zimmerman. 1997. *Mosaic of Thought: Teaching Comprehension in a Reader's Workshop*. Portsmouth, NH: Heinemann.

Kemper, Dave, Ruth Nathan, and Patrick Sebranek. 1995. *Writers Express: A Handbook for Young Writers, Thinkers, and Learners*. Wilmington, MA: Write Source/Houghton Mifflin.

Kovalik, Susan, with Karen Olsen. 1993. *Integrated Thematic Instruction: The Model, Second Edition*. Village of Oak Creek, AZ: Books for Educators.

Krey, DeAn M. 1998. *Children's Literature in Social Studies: Teaching to the Standards*. Washington DC: National Council for the Social Studies.

Kusugak, Michael Arvaarluk. 1999 (reprint). *Baseball Bats for Christmas*. Toronto: Annick Press.

Levy, Elizabeth. 1987. *—If You Were There When They Signed the Constitution*. New York: Scholastic.

Lindquist, Tarry. 1997. *Ways That Work: Putting Social Studies into Practice*. Portsmouth, NH: Heinemann.

———. 2001 (rev). *Practical Strategies for Creating an Outstanding Fifth-Grade Program: A Resource Handbook*. Bellevue, WA: Bureau of Education and Research.

———. 2002 (rev). *Current Best Strategies to Strengthen Students' Reading and Writing in the Content Areas (Grades 3–6): A Resource Handbook*. Bellevue, WA: Bureau of Education and Research.

Lindquist, Tarry, and Douglas Selwyn. 2000. *Social Studies at the Center: Integrating Kids, Content, and Literacy.* Portsmouth, NH: Heinemann.

Lord, Bette Bao. 1984. *In the Year of the Boar and Jackie Robinson.* New York Harper & Row.

Lynch, Priscilla. 1992. Keynote Address. Regis University Literacy Institute, Denver: July.

Martin, Jacqueline Briggs. 2001. *The Lamp, the Ice, and the Boat Called Fish.* Boston: Houghton Mifflin.

Marzano, Robert J., Debra J. Pickering, and Jane E. Pollock. 2001. *Classroom Instruction that Works: Research-based Strategies for Increasing Student Achievement.* Alexandria, VA: Association of Supervision and Curriculum Development.

Masoff, Joy. 2000. *Colonial Times: 1600–1700.* New York: Scholastic.

McGovern, Ann. 1964. *—If You Lived in Colonial Times.* New York: Scholastic.

Mercer Island Public Schools. 1988. *Guidelines for Fifth-Grade Social Studies.* Mercer Island, WA: Mercer Island Public Schools.

Mochizuki, Ken. 1993. *Baseball Saved Us.* New York: Lee & Low.

Morris, William, et al. 1982. *The American Heritage Dictionary,* Second Edition. Boston: Houghton Mufflin.

National Council for the Social Studies (NCSS). 1990. *The Essentials Statement.* Washington, DC: NCSS.

———. 1993. "A Vision of Powerful Teaching and Learning in the Social Studies: Building Social Understanding and Civic Efficacy." *Social Education* 57 (September): 213–23.

———. 1994. *Expectations of Excellence: Curriculum Standards for Social Studies.* Washington, DC: NCSS.

O'Dell, Scott. 1980. *Sarah Bishop.* New York: Scholastic.

Opitz, Michael F., and Timothy V. Rasinski. 1998. *Good-bye Round Robin: Twenty-five Effective Reading Strategies.* Portsmouth, NH: Heinemann.

Paul, Ann Whitford. 1991. *Eight Hands Round: A Patchwork Alphabet.* New York: HarperCollins.

Penner, Lucille Recht. 1998. *The Liberty Tree: The Beginnings of the American Revolution.* New York: Random House.

Philbrick, Rodman. 2000. *The Last Book in the Universe.* New York: The Blue Sky Press.

Potts, Jody. 2000. *Adventure Tales of America: An Illustrated History of the United States: 1492-1877, Volume 1.* Dallas: Signal Media Corporation.

Raphael, Taffy. E. 1982. "Improving Question-Answering Performance Through Instruction." *Reading Education Report* (March): 32.

Raphael, Taffy E., Laura S. Pardo, Kathy Highfield, and Susan I. McMahon. 1997. *Book Club: A Literature-Based Curriculum.* Littleton, MA: Small Planet Communications.

Rappaport, Doreen. 2001. *Martin's Big Words: The Life of Dr. Martin Luther King, Jr.* New York: Hyperion Books for Children.

Roop, Peter, and Connie Roop. 2000. *Christopher Columbus.* New York: Scholastic.

Scholes, Katherine. 1989. *Peace Begins with You.* San Francisco: Sierra Book Club.

Shoemaker, Betty Jean Eklund. 1991. "Education 2000 Integrated Curriculum." *Phi Delta Kappa* 73 (June): 793–97.

Slapin, Beverly, and Doris Seale. 1992. *Through Indian Eyes: The Native Experience in Books for Children.* Philadelphia: New Society Publishers.

Spencer, Philip. 1955. *Day of Glory: The Guns at Lexington and Concord.* New York: Scholastic.

Sperry, Armstrong. 1940. *Call It Courage.* New York: Scholastic.

Spizzirri, Linda. 1989. *An Educational Coloring Book of Eskimos.* Rapid City, SD: Spizzirri Publishing.

Sprenger, Marilee. 1999. *Learning and Memory: The Brain in Action.* Alexandria, VA: Association for Supervision and Curriculum Development.

Staub, Frank. 1999. *Children of the Tlingit.* Minneapolis: Carolrhoda/Lerner.

Stefoff, Rebecca. 2001. *Revolutionary War.* New York: Benchmark Books.

Sterling, Dorothy. 1954. *The Story of Harriet Tubman: Freedom Train.* New York: Scholastic.

Tookoome, Simon, with Sheldon Oberman. 2000. *The Shaman's Nephew: A Life in the Far North.* New York: Stoddart Kids.

Uchida, Yoshiko. l971. *Journey to Topaz.* Berkeley, CA: Creative Arts.

Vaugelade, Anais. 2001. *The War.* Minneapolis: Carolrhoda/Lerner.

Viola, Herman J. 1998. *Warrior Artists: Historic Cheyenne and Kiowa Indian Ledger Art.* Washington, DC: National Geographic Society.

Walsh, Jill Patton. 1982. *The Green Book.* New York: Farrar, Straus, and Giroux.

Wiggins, Grant, and Jay McTighe. 1998. *Understanding by Design.* Alexandria, VA: Association for Supervision and Curriculum Development.

Worthen, Blaine R. 1993. "Critical Issues That Will Determine the Future of Alternative Assessment." *Phi Delta Kappan* 74 (February): 444–54.

Yep, Laurence. 1975. *Dragonwings.* New York: Harper & Row.

Yolan, Jane. 1992. *Encounter.* San Diego: Harcourt Brace Jovanovich.

Young, Ed. 1992. *Seven Blind Mice.* New York: Philomel.

Zarnowski, Myra. 1998. "Coming Out from Under the Spell of Stories: Critiquing Historical Narratives." *The New Advocate* (Fall): 345–57.

Zemelman, Steven, Harvey Daniels, and Arthur Hyde. 1998. *Best Practices: New Standards for Teaching and Learning in America's Schools,* Second Edition. Portsmouth, NH: Heinemann.

Credit lines continued from page iv

Chapter 2: Susan Kovalik, *Integrated Thematic Instruction: The Model*, 1993, Books for Educators.

Chapter 3: National Council for the Social Studies, Martharose Laffey, Executive Director. *The Essentials Statement*, 1980.

Chapter 4: Mem Fox, *Radical Reflections: Passionate Opinions on Teaching, Learning, and Living*, 1993, Harcourt Brace & Company.

Chapter 8: Linda Campbell, Bruce Campbell, and Dee Dickinson, *Teaching and Learning Through the Multiple Intelligences*, 1992, New Horizons for Learning, Stanwood, WA.

Thank you to Judith Slepyan of Mercer Island for giving permission to use her wonderfully revealing photographs of children learning in my classroom.

Thank you to the teachers who contributed to this edition by taking time to write about their extensions and enrichments of some of the stategies in this book:

Marte Peet	Jessica McCollum
Marie Toburen	Jenny Pitsos-Lindstrom
Lynn Hulkow	Marjorie A. Montgomery